CHRISTINA ROSSETTI

Books by the same author

CHARLOTTE MARY YONGE
MRS GLADSTONE
JOHN KEBLE
QUEEN ALEXANDRA
SHAFTESBURY
RELUCTANT PIONEER

Christina Rossetti by her brother Dante Gabriel

Georgina Battiscombe

Christina Rossetti

A DIVIDED LIFE

HOLT, RINEHART AND WINSTON
NEW YORK

Library of Congress Cataloging in Publication Data
Battiscombe, Georgina.
Christina Rossetti, a divided life.
Bibliography: p.
Includes index.
1. Rossetti, Christina Georgina, 1830–1894—Biography.
2. Poets, English—19th century—Biography.   I. Title.
PR5238.B32   1981   821'.8 (B)   81-47451   AACR2
ISBN: 0-03-059612-2

First American Edition

Printed in the United States of America
1 3 5 7 9 10 8 6 4 2

To Lawrence and Aurea
with gratitude

Contents

	Foreword	9
1	The Child Christina	13
2	Change and Crisis	28
3	First Love and the Pre-Raphaelite Brotherhood	44
4	Enter William Bell Scott and Elizabeth Siddal	58
5	Charles Cayley	76
6	*Goblin Market*	94
7	'My lot is cast'	114
8	A Critical Illness	132
9	The Tragedy of Dante Gabriel	146
10	A Time for Grief	159
11	Devoted Daughter	178
12	'Sleeping at last'	196
	Notes and References	209
	Select Bibliography	220
	Index	223

Illustrations

Christina Rossetti by Dante Gabriel Rossetti
(*Ashmolean Museum*)   *Frontispiece*

Facing page

Christina and Dante Gabriel Rossetti. Max Beerbohm cartoon   18

Christina as a girl aged seventeen *(by courtesy of Mrs O'Conor)*   19

The Girlhood of Mary Virgin by Dante Gabriel Rossetti
(Tate Gallery)   48

William Bell Scott *(National Galleries of Scotland photo: Annan)*   49

Dante Gabriel Rossetti by Christina *(by courtesy of Mrs Dennis)*   66

William Michael Rossetti by Christina *(University of British
Columbia)*   66

Dante Gabriel Rossetti by Holman Hunt *(Birmingham Museums
and Art Gallery)*   67

Christina and her mother. Photograph by Lewis Carroll
(by courtesy of Mrs Dennis)   88

Sketches from the Zoo. Pencil drawing by Christina Rossetti
(by courtesy of Mrs O'Conor)   89

Golden Head by Golden Head, illustration from *Goblin Market*   124

You should have wept her yesterday, illustration from *The
Prince's Progress*   124

Drawing by Alice Boyd for *Sing-Song* by Christina Rossetti
(Dick Institute)   125

Drawing by Arthur Hughes for *Sing-Song* by Christina Rossetti   125

Maria Rossetti as an Anglican nun by Lucy Madox Brown
(by courtesy of Mrs Dennis)   154

Lucy Madox Rossetti and her daughter by Ford Madox Brown
(by courtesy of Mrs O'Conor)   155

Foreword

I am greatly indebted to two books, both of them essential to any study of the Rossetti family and Christina in particular. The first is William Michael Rossetti's *Some Reminiscences*, the second the biography of Christina by Mrs Lona Mosk Packer published by the Cambridge University Press in 1963. (Unfortunately Mrs Packer convinced herself that Christina was in love with William Bell Scott, and in trying to prove this theory true, turned a work of careful scholarship into a piece of special pleading.)

The bulk of the manuscript material previously belonging to the Rossetti family is now in the possession of the University of British Columbia; and my thanks are due to the authorities of that University for permission to use these papers. I am very grateful to Professor William E. Fredeman for helping me to gain access to this material and for his kindness in bringing over to me the many photostats which I needed. I would wish to thank all those who have allowed me to use letters and manuscripts and especially the authorities at Princeton and Yale University Libraries, the British Library, Newcastle University Library, the Libraries of the Ashmolean Museum, Oxford, and the Fitzwilliam Museum, Cambridge, and the Bodleian Library, where I am especially grateful to Mr D. S. Porter for much help and kindness.

I have found two unpublished theses particularly helpful, one on William Bell Scott by Vera Walker (University of Durham), the other on Christina Rossetti's unpublished poems by Gwynneth Hatton (St Hilda's College, Oxford), and I am most grateful to Mrs Smith (Vera Walker) and Mrs Hatton for lending me copies of these theses and allowing me to quote from them.

Among the many people to whom my thanks are due I would like especially to mention Lady Mander (Rosalie Glynn Grylls), Mrs Virginia

Surtees, Dame Annis Gillie, Dr George Harwood, Mrs Margaret Hill, Mr Michael Bishop (Kilmarnock Museum), Mr John Bell (Oxford University Press), Mr John Christian, and Mr A. R. Dufty (Kelmscott Manor). I am very grateful to Mr Raleigh Trevelyan for help with the Wallington Papers and more especially for his kindness in reading through my typescript and giving me valuable advice and criticism.

Finally, I owe a special debt of gratitude to three members of the Rossetti family, Mrs Lucy O'Conor, Mrs Imogen Dennis, and Mr Harold Rossetti. They have borne patiently with my many enquiries, and have shown me unstinted kindness and hospitality. Without their generous co-operation this book could not have been written.

CHRISTINA ROSSETTI

The Child Christina

'I think she is the best poet alive'—so the literary critic Walter Raleigh wrote in 1892. Later authorities have echoed his judgement, calling Christina Rossetti the finest woman poet of the nineteenth century. 'Fragments of her verse have been floating in the air,' the novelist Ford Madox Ford wrote in 1904; 'almost every person at all lettered has carried about with him some little piece.'[1] Today one at least of her poems is familiar to lettered and unlettered alike; fragments of her verse float in the air every Christmas. Thousands of people who have never heard of Dante Gabriel Rossetti or the Pre-Raphaelite Movement know and love Gustav Holst's setting of 'In the bleak mid-winter', which has become one of the most popular of English carols.

Apart from this carol and the half-dozen pieces to be found in almost every anthology Christina Rossetti's poetry is not calculated to make a strong appeal to the general public; it is at once too subtle and too sad. Yet this sadness gives it the quality of universality; 'she became the poet of the suffering' says Ford '—and suffering is a thing of all the ages.'[2]

Of suffering both physical and mental Christina Rossetti knew a very great deal. All her life was a battle against bad health and illness, some-times in painful and trying form; she was twice crossed in love; she saw her elder sister die of cancer and watched the tragic decay and death of the brother to whom she was devoted. But the sadness characteristic of her poetry has causes deeper than these external troubles. Outwardly, Christina Rossetti's life was an uneventful one; inwardly, it was a con-tinual conflict. A conflict between the two sides of our nature is the common experience of every human being. For Christina, however, the struggle was an unusually painful one, partly because being peculiarly gifted she was also peculiarly sensitive, partly because in her two cultural streams met and mingled without becoming a unity. Maybe truth, beauty, goodness, call it what you will, is not in itself an absolute but proceeds from the tension between two opposites. If this is so, the tension between two nationalities, two cultures, two ways of thought, meeting in one gifted personality can be very fruitful of results, though it will inevitably be the cause of much stress and suffering to the person concerned. From this tension genius can be born.

Although all four Rossetti children were born and brought up in London where three of them were to live and die, by blood they were more than half Italian. Their father, Gabriele Rossetti, was a native of Vasto in what was then the Kingdom of Naples. A clever, gifted boy born of working-class parents, he attracted the attention of a local nobleman who paid for his education at the University of Naples. After leaving the university he worked first as an operatic librettist, then as curator of marbles and bronzes at Naples Museum, meanwhile making a considerable name for himself as a writer of patriotic verse. A supporter of the Bonapartist regime, he was friendly with Joseph Bonaparte and also with Murat, who in 1808 succeeded Joseph as King of Naples, but after the fall of Napoleon and the return of the reactionary Bourbon King Ferdinand he found himself in danger of arrest because of his Liberal views. In 1821 he succeeded in escaping to Malta on board a British man-of-war, and after spending two years in Malta he made his way to London where he was to live the rest of his life in exile from his native land.

In England Gabriele met and married Frances Polidori, a girl of half-Italian blood, daughter of Gaetano Polidori, a political exile like himself. Yet even here, between the two Italian strains in Christina's ancestry, there were differences of class and country which could give rise to tension. Gabriele came from one of the most backward regions of southern Italy; his father had been a blacksmith; his mother could neither read nor write. The Polidoris were a professional family from Tuscany, well-born and well-connected (a Polidori *palazzo* is still to be seen in Orvieto). They moved in literary circles; some of them were themselves authors in a small way. In his youth Frances's father had been secretary to the poet Alfieri; her brother John was Byron's travelling physician and author of *The Vampire*, a romance frequently attributed to Byron himself. Frances was a clever young woman who admitted to 'a passion for intellect'. Had she been less intellectual and perhaps more prudent she might have made a better marriage for herself. When she was working as governess in the family of Sir Patrick Macgregor her good looks and witty tongue—she was sometimes described as 'a quiz'—caught the attention of her employer's brother. But intellect called to intellect, Italian blood to Italian blood; she refused the well-born, well-to-do Colonel Macgregor and married Gabriele Rossetti, a penniless exile eighteen years her senior.

Though she chose an Italian for husband, both by temperament and education Frances took after the English rather than the Italian side of her ancestry. Her mother, Anna Maria Pierce, came from a typically English professional background, soldiers, sailors, schoolmasters, lawyers and the like. Gaetano was a Roman Catholic, Anna Maria a member of the Church of England holding slightly Evangelical views; when they married it was agreed that the sons should be brought up as Catholics, the daughters as Protestants. This precedent was not followed when Anna Maria's daughter married Gabriele Rossetti. Though he always remained a nominal Catholic, Gabriele was in fact an agnostic, veering at the end of his life towards an undogmatic form of Christianity. He had no wish to see his sons educated as papists; all four children were therefore brought up by their mother as members of the Church of England.

Frances Rossetti was a handsome woman with regular features and an expression which called to mind the serenity of a Raphael Madonna. There was nothing Italian about her, however, except her appearance. While Gabriele was either in the depths of depression or afire with what his son William called 'the passionate fervour of the South Italian' Frances was imperturbed and imperturbable. She was a deeply affectionate person who felt no inhibition about showing her love, but she did so in a calm controlled manner which could embarrass nobody. Courageous, resourceful, and full of common sense—'what gift or grace can quite supply the lack of common sense?'[3] her daughter Christina was to query incredulously—she was the anchor upon which the whole family depended. She asked nothing for herself but was wholly devoted to the care of her husband and children.

In spite of these differences of age, class, religion and temperament the Rossetti marriage was a happy one. Religion was the subject upon which husband and wife were most apt to differ, and religion was to Frances, as to her daughters after her, a matter of supreme importance. But even here they could agree to differ amicably. 'Now and then two who have differed—and two who differ cannot both hold the entire truth—have loved on faithfully, believing and hoping the best of each other . . .'⁴ Christina may or may not have had her parents in mind when she wrote those words but, consciously or not, she was describing very exactly their mutual relationship. A cross or angry word seldom passed between them; their children never heard them quarrel.

Reared in this atmosphere of love and tolerance the four children grew up to form a singularly affectionate and united group though, as children will, they scrapped and argued happily enough among themselves. In age they were very close together, only a year separating each one from the next. The eldest, Maria, born in 1827, was a plain child, round-faced and black-eyed, showing a great resemblance to her peasant grandmother. She was the most intellectual of the children and also the most industrious, but unfortunately she was neither amusing nor attractive. She was, however, much beloved by the brilliant brother who came next in the family—'In my boyhood' he was to tell William Sharp, 'I loved Maria more than anyone in the world.'⁵ Christened Gabriel Charles Dante, he was known usually as Gabriel to his family, Dante Gabriel to outsiders. Remarkably good-looking, with a mane of hair which in childhood was nearly blond but later darkened, as a small boy he was already someone out of the ordinary, a dominant spirit. Even in childhood Dante Gabriel possessed that power of attraction which marks the born leader, but unfortunately he lacked that other quality essential to leadership, a sense of responsibility. This was to fall to the share of the third child, William Michael, a dutiful boy who never thought to compete with his brother; in fact of them all only the youngest, Christina Georgina, born on December 5th 1830, showed any sign of rivalling Dante Gabriel in brilliance.

Dante Gabriel and Christina were known as 'the storms', Maria and William as 'the calms'. 'Skittish', 'wilful', 'fractious', 'given to tantrums' —so the family described Christina, a curiously passionate child possessed of a temper which quickly flared out of control. On one occasion, when scolded for some fault, she seized a pair of scissors and ripped open her own arm. (In later life she was to teach herself to keep her hot temper well under control; describing her in middle age Watts-Dunton writes, 'A certain irritability of temper which was, perhaps, natural to her, had . . . been overcome, or at least greatly chastened . . .')[6] Though she was remarkably loving, intelligent and conscientious, in childhood she was the one of the four who presented her parents with the most problems. She was also the prettiest, the wittiest, and possibly the warmest-hearted.

'Very pretty, people considered her in those days,' her brother William was to write many years later. The only extant portrait of Christina as a child shows an engaging rather than a conventionally pretty little girl. Her straight brown hair is parted in the middle and drawn back on either side of a high forehead. The face is a perfect oval, the most remarkable feature being the enormous eyes, 'those bright, bright eyes' her father so much admired. It is the face of a child who looks at the world and the people in it with affection and interest, but also with a certain detachment, thinking her own thoughts and making her own judgements.

The Italian exiles who flocked to enjoy the Rossettis' simple hospitality naturally made much of this attractive child, all too clearly preferring her to her plain elder sister. Naturally Maria was jealous. She knew herself to be more deserving and more studious than Christina, who had no particular liking for books or lessons. Why should the clever elder sister be passed over just because the younger one had a witty tongue and a pretty face? Maria's jealousy was one of the few discordant notes disturbing the harmony of that loving family circle. Christina, however, did not appear to be unduly troubled; she went her own way, sure that everyone was her friend and that the world revolved round her small, determined self.

She was not however a spoilt child. Both parents scrupulously avoided making favourites, while lack of means prevented any more concrete form of spoiling. The salary earned by Gabriele Rossetti as Professor of Italian at King's College was so small as to oblige him to supplement it by taking private pupils; even in a good year his total income seldom rose as high as £300. The children were all born and brought up in Charlotte Street (now Hallam Street) near Portland Place, the family moving in 1836 from Number Thirty-eight to the slightly larger Number

Fifty. In their day the neighbourhood was a drab and not very respectable one; the front windows of Number Fifty looked out on to a cab-rank and a noisy public-house. The Rossettis lived in a very simple manner, having no desire whatsoever to 'keep up with the Joneses'. Frances Rossetti employed only one servant, and, breaking away from the almost universal practice of the English middle and upper classes, she had neither nanny nor nursery for her children but looked after them entirely herself. The children lived in the family sitting-room and spent most of their time with their parents, joining in their occupations and amusements and sharing their meals which often consisted of cheap Italian *pasta* instead of expensive English meat dishes. Of an evening the four little things would be all over the place, playing games and rolling about on the floor while their father sat at his desk working at some abstruse scholarly thesis.

The Rossetti children had few or no friends of their own age. They had some contact with the family of Cipriani Potter, Principal of the Royal Academy of Music, and with one or two other Anglo-Italian families, but with none of these boys and girls were they at all intimate. They were, however, encouraged to mix freely with their parents' friends. Though they were too poor to entertain in any formal manner the Rossettis were not inhospitable; any Italian exile was welcomed to their home whether he were a celebrity such as the violinist Paganini or a vagrant macaroni man. These visitors would be given a cup of tea or coffee and a slice of bread and butter, and entertained with much lively and learned conversation in their native tongue. The children would listen with all their ears, thrilled by exciting tales of escapes and conspiracies and unconsciously acquiring a very fair knowledge of current political and philosophical issues. Language was no hindrance for though they spoke English among themselves and with their mother from babyhood they had always spoken Italian with their father. At written Italian they were less practised; at the age of twelve Christina sends her father a charming Italian letter in which she accounts for her many mistakes by explaining that this is only the second letter she has ever written in that language. But although the children moved so freely in grown-up society they were never allowed to become noisy or assertive or to forget their good manners. Frances Rossetti was a gentle disciplinarian but a disciplinarian

'Well, Christina, your heart may be like a singing bird, but why do you dress like a pew-opener?' Dante Gabriel to Christina, Max Beerbohm cartoon

Christina as a girl aged seventeen; Dante Gabriel's first oil painting

none the less. In *The Rossetti Family* R. D. Waller gives a perceptive description of the family circle:

> . . . it is strange to think that while the company in Charlotte Street was probably among the most interesting and most bizarre in London, the family that lived there must surely have been among the most efficiently regulated and disciplined. Company and discipline alike helped to make the children a group apart in the literary disposition of the century.[7]

This discipline extended to matters of dress. Frances Rossetti brought up her daughters to dress scrupulously neatly but to pay no further attention to their appearance; their clothes were not merely unfashionable but often positively ugly. Years later Max Beerbohm was to draw a cartoon showing Dante Gabriel remonstrating with his sister: 'Well, Christina, your heart may be like a singing bird, but why do you dress like a pew-opener?'

Where money for necessities was short little or nothing could be spared for amusement. Circus-going was a very rare treat. Sometimes the children were taken to a scientific exhibition or a picture gallery, and once to a waxwork show where Christina was seized with shyness at the sight of so many famous figures. The well-known singer Lablache occasionally presented the family with tickets for 'the Italian Opera near Charing Cross'; in this way they heard the famous Madame Grisi and saw Rachel acting Chimène in *Le Cid*. The British Museum was to be a later discovery, a special delight of their teens.

For outdoor amusement there were expeditions to Primrose Hill, then bordering on open fields, and more frequent walks in Regent's Park where they could visit the recently opened Zoological Gardens. Among their favourite animals were armadillos, sloths, and 'a singing antelope' who belied his name by refusing to utter a single note. Christina was once quite badly bitten by a savage peccary. Birds were always to give her particular pleasure. On these visits to the Zoo she would grieve to see them shut up in cages and plan to lament their captivity in 'plaintive verse' which, however, she never seems to have written. One night she had a strange dream. She dreamt that she was walking in Regent's Park and saw a golden-yellow cloud rise from the trees and soar away over the roofs of the neighbouring houses. In her dream she knew that this cloud consisted of all the canaries in London, who had escaped for one brief night and met together in the Park, only to be obliged when dawn came to return to their cages.

Favourite indoor amusements included chess and various card games. The boys constructed a toy theatre and cut illustrations out of Skelton's *Theatrical Characters*, painting them in the brightest colours possible. All attempts at producing a play, however, ended in failure, none of the children being sufficiently adept with their fingers to be able to manipulate these paper puppets.

Gabriele had an appreciation of music and a fine singing voice; but none of his children inherited his musical gifts. At a very early age Dante Gabriel announced that he meant to become an artist. An astonished milkman once discovered the six-year-old boy crouching in a passage drawing a spirited likeness of the family rocking-horse—'Fancy a baby making a picture!' Christina showed a little of the same artistic aptitude but no real interest, preferring books to pictures. Unlike her brothers and sister, however, she was not a voracious reader; she would read a few favourite books over and over again but she would refuse to make an effort to master anything which she imagined might be either difficult or uninteresting.

Before she had learnt to write Christina started to make up her own verses and stories. Children delight in the sound of long words without troubling their heads over the meaning; Christina's first poem began thus:

> Cecilia never went to school
> Without her gladiator.

A little later she wrote, or rather, dictated, the beginning of a story called 'The Dervise' (is this a mis-spelling of 'dervish'?) in the manner of the bowdlerised version of *The Arabian Nights* which was her favourite reading. In 1840, when Christina had reached the mature age of nine, the four children agreed that they would each write a story. Dante Gabriel drew a title-page for the projected book of stories, but only his own contribution, 'Roderick and Rosalba, a Tale of the Round Table', was ever completed. Christina wrote the beginning of a story of the Crusades entitled 'Retribution', a choice of subject which reflected her current enthusiasm for the novels of Sir Walter Scott. About this date she also discovered Keats and, more surprisingly, developed a passionate liking for the poetic drama of the eighteenth-century Italian writer, Metastasio.

Her favourite reading, however, was not on this high intellectual level. Though Frances Rossetti tried hard to persuade her children to read such moral stories as *Sandford and Merton* and *The Fairchild Family* they would have none of these improving tales but turned instead to the type of book which Jane Austen made mock of in *Northanger Abbey*—'Are they all horrid? Are you quite sure they are all horrid?' When Christina grew too old for fairy stories or for her beloved *Arabian Nights* she took to reading the blood-curdling romances of Mrs Radcliffe, 'Monk' Lewis, and Maturin. A craze for the horrific seized all four children; they devoured every book of this kind that came their way.

One author the Rossetti children could not and would not read though in later life they were all to become his devotees. 'Dante Alighieri was a sort of banshee in the Charlotte Street house;' wrote William, 'his shriek audible even to familiarity, but the message of it not scrutinized.'[8] Gabriele was obsessed with Dante; he believed *The Divine Comedy* and the *Vita Nuova* to be full of esoteric meanings, and he would spend hours going through them in search of hidden references to Freemasonry, cabbalism, alchemy, and the like. The children naturally shied away from writings apparently so difficult and abstruse, *libri mistici*. Their reaction to his Dante cult was typical of their general attitude towards their father; for them he was not a person to be taken very seriously. They loved him, but they did not respect him. Through all the years of his English exile Gabriele remained indelibly Italian, a typical Neapolitan, emotional, undisciplined, demonstrative. His uninhibited displays of emotion embarrassed his anglicised children. To call two baby girls 'lovely turtle-doves in the nest of love' is a not impossible conceit, sounding less sentimental in the original Italian; but when those babies grow into big girls they fight shy of such endearments. Gabriele doted on his children, especially when they were very young. If they were away from home he was miserable, if they were ill he was distraught. Though he knew well enough that their mother forbade sweet-eating he would come home of an evening with his pockets full of lollipops. Of course the children ate the sweets and despised the indulgent parent who could encourage such a breach of discipline. As they grew older they compared him with their mother and saw his failings even more clearly; for William at least his father came to represent self-applause, his mother self-effacement. Of the four Maria was the one most in sympathy with Gabriele, who loved her for her resemblance to his mother, Christina the one who found him least congenial. All the children loved their mother better than their father; but Christina's devotion to her was peculiarly strong.

Frances Rossetti was solely responsible for the early education of all four children, a task for which she was admirably fitted, being a highly intelligent woman with much experience of teaching. In 1836 Dante Gabriel went off to day school, William following the year after. The two girls had a few lessons in singing and dancing from outside masters, two subjects for which they had neither interest nor aptitude. They learnt a little German—Christina was afterwards to describe herself as 'a smattering linguist'[9]—from a German colleague of their father who offered to teach them in return for lessons in Italian. Every other subject they learnt from their mother who encouraged them to read widely in three languages.

Two small volumes survive to give us some idea of the nature of this reading. The first is an anthology of religious verse entitled *The Sacred Harp*. It is inscribed 'Presented by the Revd. T. W. Paule to Master W. Rossetti for his improvement in good behaviour, Oxford House Establishment, June 1837'. Underneath is a second inscription, 'Christina G. Rossetti from William, December 1844'.[10] The poems are copiously annotated in a childish hand, but unfortunately the pencil is so faint and the writing so unformed that it is impossible to tell whether the writer is William or Christina. The second volume, a manuscript book now in the Bodleian, is more interesting. In her governess days Frances Rossetti had kept a commonplace book for the benefit of her pupils, copying out most of the extracts herself but sometimes asking a pupil to write in some special passage. She continued the practice with her own children. The first extract in Christina's hand, written when she was about thirteen, is George Herbert's poem, 'Sweet day, so cool, so calm, so bright'. Because critics have seen a resemblance between Christina's own poetry and the writings of the seventeenth-century metaphysical poets it is interesting to note that the book contains only two poems by Herbert, none by Vaughan, and of Crashaw only the famous line descriptive of the miracle at Cana of Galilee, 'The modest water saw its Lord and blushed'.

Quotations from Shakespeare are few, perhaps because a knowledge of Shakespeare was taken for granted. Wordsworth is represented by extracts from *The Excursion*, but by none of the shorter poems; Dryden, Southey, Crabbe, Tennyson, Poe, Tom Moore, Lamartine, and Camille Desmoulins are some of the many poets included. There are a surprising number of Byron's poems, and, more surprising still, a translation of a poem by Sappho. The collections included writers as various as Dickens, Edward Irving, Machiavelli, Doctor Johnson, Robert Burton, Voltaire, Thiers, Monckton Milnes, Samuel Taylor Coleridge and his son Hartley. Among the many religious passages are 'a song composed and sung by Mr Nicholas Ferrar's family at Little Gidding', and the Commendatory Prayer from the Roman Breviary. Remembering how preoccupied Christina was to be in her own poetry with thoughts of death the large number of epitaphs is perhaps significant. Altogether, the choice is a wide and in some ways an unusual one, a clear indication of the varied nature of Christina's reading as a young girl.

Frances Rossetti encouraged the children's own literary efforts, helping with the production of a family magazine called 'Hodge Podge'. A few numbers survive; but unfortunately nothing in them is signed, so that it is impossible to identify Christina's contributions. Some of the articles are clearly by Frances herself. In one she explores the possibilities of a holiday spent at home:

'If we cannot do all that we would like let us do all we can'. Taking this as my motto I will hint how it may be profitably applied if it is out of our power to repair to the sea-side or to the country.[11]

Though lack of means put the seaside out of reach until 1839 the Rossetti children enjoyed fairly frequent country holidays at the home of their Polidori grandparents at Holmer Green, half-way between Amersham and High Wycombe. To little Christina these visits were the greatest joys life had to offer. Though they came to an end in the year of her ninth birthday she believed that they were nevertheless a major influence on her development as a poet:

> If one thing schooled me in the direction of poetry it was perhaps the delightful liberty to prowl all alone about my grandfather's cottage grounds some thirty miles from London, entailing in my childhood a long stage-coach journey. The grounds were quite small, and on the simplest scale; but to me they were vast, varied, and well worth exploring.[12]

In this description, given years later to Edmund Gosse, the key-words are perhaps 'all alone'. Occasions for solitude are essential for the growth of the poetic talent, and such occasions were not to be found in Charlotte Street. 'All four of us were constantly together in infancy and childhood', wrote William: 'Wherever one was there the other was—and that was almost always at home.' Sometimes Dante Gabriel would go by himself to visit his grandparents at Holmer Green, where he too would be perfectly content, wandering about a little, doing nothing in particular. A small pond was a favourite spot with both sister and brother. Unlike most small boys, Dante Gabriel never thought to build a raft or even to sail a boat; instead, he caught frogs.

Neither of the Rossetti boys took any interest in outdoor games or sport. They had no wish to go riding or even to shoot in the unsporting manner of Grandfather Polidori, who enjoyed taking pot shots at sitting pigeons out of his bedroom window. Their sisters were equally unenterprising. In spite of cumbersome clothes, little girls of the Victorian age could be agile and venturesome creatures. Enveloped in strong overalls—'encased in brown holland', as Miss Yonge puts it—they would join the boys in making mud pies, climbing trees, jumping ditches, rolling down banks and generally running wild as children who have any element of the tomboy in them will always do if turned loose in the country.

There was nothing tomboyish about Christina. She did not want to explore distant fields and woods or to make friends with such large and alarming animals as cows and horses. It was the small creatures of the countryside which fascinated her, birds, rabbits, squirrels, frogs, toads, mice. She would pick up and fearlessly handle beetles, caterpillars and worms which even country-bred children might find repulsive. She enjoyed playing at funerals and on one unforgettable occasion she buried a dead mouse in a moss-lined grave, planning to dig it up again a few days later. When she did so, expecting to find the little furry body as whole and beautiful as ever, she saw a loathsome black insect emerging from the decaying corpse and fled in horror from the sight. It was her first, never to be forgotten, experience of corruption.

This horrid episode, which haunted her for years, was almost the only blot on her happy memories of that enchanted garden. Within doors Holmer Green had nothing of much interest or excitement to offer a little girl. Grandmother Polidori was a permanent invalid spending all her time upstairs in a bedroom which William described as having 'all the dignity of a presence-chamber which I entered at sparse intervals with a certain awe.'[13] The household was managed by her daughter Eliza Harriet, 'only partially amiable' and with no interests outside domesticity. However, after her mother's death Eliza was to have her hour of glorious life. In 1854 she volunteered to go out to the Crimean war with Florence Nightingale. Arrived at Scutari, to her deep disappointment she was not allowed to nurse but only to act as store-keeper; nevertheless she had the satisfaction of returning to England wearing a Turkish medal. Another daughter, Charlotte, worked as a governess. A brother, Henry, a not very successful solicitor, had anglicised his name to Polydore; his daughter Henrietta was later to become very friendly with Christina. The two remaining members of the family lived at home with their parents: a son, Philip, a gentle, harmless creature, slightly retarded mentally, and a daughter, Margaret, who suffered from 'nervous tremors' and on occasion would burst into loud shrieks of hysterical laughter. It was Margaret who, on the rare occasions when her sister Frances was ill or enjoying a much needed rest at Holmer Green, came to Charlotte Street to supervise the family there. In a letter to Frances on one such occasion in 1836 she gives a charming picture of the five-year-old Christina struggling with the complicated fastenings of Victorian-style frocks.

Christina has taken Maria's place in performing the office of dressing me, which she does not do amiss for so young a tyro in the art. I fancy she feels no small degree of awe, whilst in the act of hooking her Aunt, and her Aunt is obliged to stand like patience upon a monument.

Christina is to have a red book as a reward for her progress in lessons—'it has to be red because she wishes it so'.[14] Yet another aunt, or rather great-aunt, a sister of Mrs Polidori, lived in London and was known to the children as Granny. Called Mrs rather than Miss Pierce, she was rumoured to be secretly married to the Earl of Yarborough. (No one seems to have so much as hinted that she might not have been Lord Yarborough's wife but his mistress.) She lived in greater comfort and luxury than any other member of the family and was in a position to give generous presents to her favourite niece, Frances Rossetti.

From a child's point of view by far the most interesting person at Holmer Green was Grandfather Polidori. A great reader, he also enjoyed working with his hands at many different crafts and would invite the children into his workshop. Christina loved him as she never loved her own father. She was his favourite grandchild; '*Avra piu spirito che tutti,*' he would say to her, a remark not calculated to make Maria any less jealous.

In 1839 Grandfather Polidori sold the Holmer Green house and moved his family back to London. Christina never saw real country again until she was 'a great girl of fourteen', when the sight of a mass of primroses growing on the slope of a railway cutting brought back something of the old rapture. The Polidori house in London was within easy walking distance of Charlotte Street; the two families met almost daily and the children would often play in their grandfather's garden which sloped down to the Regent Canal. This they found a poor substitute for the delights of Holmer Green, but they consoled themselves with the discovery that Uncle Philip's library contained books more horrid than any to be found on their own shelves, and they shuddered most enjoyably over his copies of *The Newgate Calendar* and *Legends of Terror*.

The earliest of Christina's surviving poems dates from this period of late childhood. In April 1842 she presented her mother with the birthday gift of a nosegay accompanied by a short poem which Grandfather Polidori had printed for her on his private press:

> To-day's your natal day;
>   Sweet flowers I bring:
> Mother, accept I pray
>   My offering.
>
> And may you happy live,
>   And long us bless;
> Receiving as you give
>   Great happiness.

Though it falls off in the last line the little poem has none of the faults of rhythm and scansion usually to be found in children's verse. Another set of verses written by Christina in this same year of 1842 are in comic vein, describing a Chinaman's grief at the loss of his pigtail. These two childish poems are typical of the two sides of Christina's character both as child and adult, the one essentially serious, loving and deeply involved with the loved person, the other detached, smiling, gently satirical.

Chapter Two

Change and Crisis

Christina at the age of eleven is a quick-tempered but very affectionate little girl, full of whims and fancies, and just beginning to show a real talent for putting those fancies down on paper. She is not particularly talkative but neither is she shy; she is used to receiving praise and affection from grown-up people and she is not lacking in self-confidence. Then towards the end of 1842, about the time of her twelfth birthday, darkness falls over this attractive, open-hearted child. For four years she vanishes from view to emerge again in 1847 changed almost beyond recognition. The sixteen-year-old Christina is retiring, introverted, mistrustful of the world and of her own self. The tempestuous child has become an almost painfully controlled young girl; she, who was once so confiding and confident, now shuts herself away from outside contacts behind a screen of shyness and almost impenetrable reserve.

What brought about this strange metamorphosis so very much more marked than the changes common in adolescence? No one can answer that question with any certainty. Because of this change the years from 1842 to 1847 are a crucial period, perhaps *the* crucial period, in Christina's life—and precisely at this important moment the would-be biographer runs up against a blank wall. None of Christina's own letters survive; she is mentioned in no reminiscence or correspondence; in the Memoir which her brother William attached to the collected edition of her poems he passes over these years completely except for a brief and inexplicit reference to her health. Where facts are not to be found guesswork can hardly be avoided; but such guesswork can only produce tentative conclusions which must not be substituted for fact or used as the basis for further speculation.

The search for clues to the change in Christina must begin with an examination of the outward circumstances of her life. Though we know nothing of Christina as an individual we are not short of information about the Rossetti family during this period. Up to 1842 their lives had been happy, healthy, and on the whole prosperous. Money had been in short supply but sufficient for their simple needs. In 1843 a dismal change took place. Gabriele fell so seriously ill that for a time his life was thought to be in danger. He survived but only to become a permanent invalid, querulous, depressed, and suffering from various physical ills, including partial blindness. Though he never went totally blind he could not see well enough to continue teaching. He resigned his post at King's College and abandoned the much more lucrative practice of taking private pupils. (One of the last of these pupils was a schoolfellow of Dante Gabriel's, a gifted linguist called Charles Bagot Cayley, who was later to play a very important part in Christina's life-history.)

When Gabriele's earnings ceased the family were left almost penniless. Thanks in great part to Frances Rossetti's courage and good management they succeeded in remaining solvent and paying their way, but they learnt what it meant to pinch and scrape and do without things which other people considered necessities. Clothes were threadbare: elbows had to be darkened with ink or prussian blue if the boys' coats were to look even moderately respectable. The children were not unhappy, being too unworldly to be seriously troubled by such difficulties and deprivations; but the experience was certainly an unpleasant one.

Both girls had always known that when they grew up they would be expected to follow their mother's example and go out as governesses. Maria now took a post with the family of Lord Charles Thynne, but though the situation was considered an exceptionally good one she did not find the life enjoyable. At the age of fifteen William left school and became a clerk in the Excise Office. Frances Rossetti went back to her old trade of teaching, giving lessons to pupils in their own homes. Only Dante Gabriel and Christina were exempt from the necessity to earn money, Dante Gabriel because everyone agreed that he must devote himself to the business of becoming an artist—paying for his artistic training was one of the biggest drains on the family resources—Christina because she was at first too young and afterwards too delicate. Many years later she was to hint at another reason for this exemption. 'I feel myself like an escaped governess,' she wrote to Swinburne on November 19th 1884, 'for had I only learnt my lessons properly at the proper age I too might have taught someone something—and doubtless I should have had to do so.'[1] She was writing in jest for she knew well enough that it was not lack of knowledge but lack of health that had saved her from the necessity of becoming a governess, a fate she had always dreaded.

With Maria away and her mother and brothers out of the house for the greater part of the day Christina was left alone with her invalid father. Of Christina's personal reaction to this depressing situation we know nothing. One thing, however, is certain; all his children were deeply distressed by Gabriele's state. 'In all those years,' William was to write, 'the threatened blindness of my father, followed by various forms of illness, including paralytic strokes and enfeeblement, saddened our thoughts far more than did the material straits of our condition.'[2]

It was during this time of stress and anxiety that a new influence was brought to bear upon Christina. The religious education which Frances Rossetti had given her children had been of a somewhat conventional nature though thorough and sincere. The family had first attended Holy Trinity Church Marylebone, then St Katherine's Chapel Regent's Park, two respectable but not particularly inspiring places of worship. In or about 1843 they started to attend Christ Church Albany Street where the services and preaching were of a very different kind from that to which they had been accustomed. The incumbent, William Dodsworth, described by Manning in his Anglican days as 'showing a good Catholic temper', was a supporter of the High Church Oxford Movement, a well-known follower of Keble, Pusey, and Newman.

These were difficult days for the Tractarians, as the men of the Oxford Movement were called. Tract Ninety had been condemned; Pusey had been suspended from preaching; Newman was in retirement at Littlemore whence he was only to emerge after joining the Church of Rome, (Dodsworth himself was later to go that same way). But if the times were troubled they were also stirring; the Church of England, which had seemed so safely moribund, was coming dangerously alive.

Frances Rossetti and her daughters embraced Tractarianism, or Anglo-Catholicism as it was later to be called, with all the fervour of converts. At fourteen William had turned agnostic; but for a brief time Dante Gabriel seems to have been attracted to this new type of religion.

The Church Porch, an early sonnet addressed to his sister Maria, ends thus:

> But having entered in, we shall find there
> Silence, and sudden dimness, and deep prayer,
> And faces of carved angels all about.

For Christina this form of religion came to be, quite simply and without question, the most important thing in her life. This being so, a proper understanding of Christina is impossible without a proper understanding of the religion which meant so much to her.

It is too commonly supposed that the Oxford Movement was primarily concerned with what were known as 'ritualistic practices', vestments, lights, incense and the like, and that the Tractarians looked to the medieval Church for model and exemplar. This is not so. Though the second, Anglo-Catholic, phase of the Movement can rightly be called ritualistic the earlier generation of Tractarians, of whom Dodsworth was one, knew little and cared less about such matters. 'I do not even know what constitutes the difference between High and Low Mass,' Keble once wrote—and he certainly did not care. They were concerned with doctrine rather than with ceremonial and liturgy. In contradistinction to the Evangelicals, who understood religion simply in terms of the relationship between God and the individual soul, and the old-fashioned Erastians, who saw the Church merely as the state in its ecclesiastical aspect, they believed the Church of England to be a valid part of the Catholic Church, a society founded by Christ himself and invested by him with divine authority. They looked not to the Middle Ages but to primitive Christianity as representing the golden age of the Church, and they laid great stress on the study of the writings of the Early Fathers.

Such a creed demands assent from the head rather than from the heart. Of course the Oxford Movement had its emotional side just as it had a link with the Romantic Movement through the Ecclesiological Society and the cult of Gothic architecture. Christina herself came into contact with this aspect because Benjamin Webb, Secretary of that Society and one of the greatest enthusiasts for Gothic, was curate at Christ Church in the late eighteen-forties. This pseudo-medievalism appealed to Dante

Gabriel and to a lesser degree to Christina. But to call Tractarianism an emotional creed as some recent historians have done is to make a bad mistake. In his preface to *The Christian Year*, the book which became the bible of the Oxford Movement, Keble wrote of the importance of 'a sober standard of feeling in matters of practical religion'. William described Christina as 'an Anglo-Catholic, and, among Anglo-Catholics, a Puritan'.[3] Many Anglo-Catholics were Puritans, not only in matters of morals but also in matters of religion. Ritualistic services may have appealed to the emotions; but where personal religion was concerned the emphasis was on inner discipline, and any display of emotion was immediately suspect.

The best picture of what Anglo-Catholicism—she herself would not have used that term—could mean to a girl of Christina's age is to be found in the books of Miss Charlotte Yonge. In her early teens Charlotte came under the influence of John Keble, and from then onwards she devoted herself to the practice and propagation of the type of religion she had learnt from him—'I have always viewed myself as a sort of instrument for popularising Church views'. Fortunately she was also an excellent story-teller. Religion as it appears in Miss Yonge's innocuous but entrancing stories has very little in common with, say, the Anglo-Catholicism of Compton Mackenzie in *Sinister Street*. Hers is a world of squires and professional people, with a peer or two thrown in for good measure, where closely-connected families, whom we come to know as intimate friends, live their lives according to 'Church principles'. The word 'God' occurs seldom if ever; nobody lays bare their soul; no one tries to convert anyone else; characters like Clement Underwood who are addicted to 'extreme' religious practices are subjected to gentle mockery. Religion is neither obtruded nor obtrusive; but, as a matter of course, children break off skating to attend week-day evensong; or two girls meeting at a picnic find themselves discussing fasting and self-denial: 'I mean, one can do little secret things—not read story books on those days —or keep some tiresome work for them.' 'Little secret things'—there lies the heart of the matter. Anything verging on the dramatic is to be discouraged; there is to be no release of the emotions in outward acts of piety.

This form of religion exactly suited Miss Yonge's most avid readers, young ladies like Lucy Lyttelton or Elizabeth Wordsworth, brought up in English nurseries and schoolrooms and trained from childhood to repress rather than to express their feelings. It was not so well adapted to the needs of a girl, by blood three-quarters Italian, reared on a diet of romantic literature, and just beginning to feel the urge to express herself in poetry. 'I have often thought that Christina's proper place was in the Roman Catholic Church,' her brother William was to write, adding that 'Her satisfaction in remaining a member of the English Church may have been partly due to her deep affection for her mother,'[4] an interesting comment when it is remembered that her mother represented the English strain in Christina's ancestry. Her Pierce blood would not have allowed her to feel at ease in the Church of Rome. She never showed any inclination towards that Church, but with all the strength of her very strong will she struggled to guide her life and shape her character in conformity with a type of Anglicanism whose *ethos* was alien to one side of her nature. 'Her temperament and character,' says William, 'naturally warm and free, became "a fountain sealed".'[5] That Anglo-Catholicism brought her profound satisfaction and at times a very great happiness no one familiar with her poems can possibly doubt; but just because religion was of such supreme importance to her, the tension between the type of religion she practised and the natural bent of her temperament was peculiarly acute. The change from a passionate, confident child to a repressed and reticent adult was partly self-induced; and the spectacle of Christina Rossetti trying to turn herself into a Miss Yonge heroine is a strange one.

In this context it is perhaps worth noting that for a Miss Yonge hero or heroine Confirmation was always a major turning-point in life. (One of her books is actually sub-titled *The Deferred Confirmation*.) Nothing is known about Christina's Confirmation except that it almost certainly took place between 1842 and 1847. If this is correct, an occasion which is often one of psychological crisis came upon her at a time when she was already under considerable mental strain.

The physical change in Christina was as marked as the mental and spiritual one. Mind and body are very closely allied; it is a well-known fact that psychological troubles can and do cause physical illness. Anxiety over financial difficulties, the absence from home of her brothers and sister, the illness of her father and his threatened blindness, the excitement and enthusiasm of what amounted to religious conversion, and the tension between this newly-adopted form of religion and one side of her own character, add up to sufficient cause for a breakdown which could have had lasting effects both physical and psychological. Did such a breakdown in fact take place?

In 1963, when Mrs Packer's biography was published, the only available evidence as to the state of Christina's health during the hidden years between 1842 and 1847 was a sentence or two in William Rossetti's Memoir and a short passage in the official biography by Mackenzie Bell, published in 1898. William begins by describing Christina as 'a tolerably healthy child'. 'She was not fully fifteen when her constitution became obviously delicate,' he continues. 'She always received excellent medical advice, and was treated at different times for a variety of maladies.'[6] He then lists these maladies which all occurred after 1850 and are therefore irrelevant to the period in question, and finishes with the often-quoted description of Christina as 'an almost constant and often a sadly-smitten invalid, seeing at times the countenance of Death very close to her own,'[7] but he cannot or will not say what it was that changed the tolerably healthy child into a sorely smitten invalid.

Her first biographer, Mackenzie Bell is slightly more helpful. 'Dr. Charles J. Hare first attended her professionally in November 1845', he records; 'and she remained more or less constantly under his care until 1850.' The date November 1845 bears out William's statement that Christina's serious ill-health began when she was not 'fully fifteen' (her fifteenth birthday occurred on December 5th 1845); and the fact that she was under medical supervision until 1850 proves that throughout her adolescence she was ill, or at least unwell. Mackenzie Bell quotes a description of Christina's physique written by Doctor Hare after this first visit:

Fully the middle stature; appears older than she really is—15; hair brown; complexion is brunette, but she is now pale (anaemic). Conformation good.

Doctor Hare also records that before he saw her Christina had been under the care of 'several very distinguished physicians—Drs. Locock and Watson, and, I think, Latham'.[8] Watson and Latham were well-known physicians; Locock was a fashionable gynaecologist who had attended Frances Rossetti in all her confinements. (In spite of their lack of means the Rossettis always went to the best doctors; Christina was later to become a patient of Sir William Jenner, physician-in-ordinary to Queen Victoria and to the Prince of Wales.)

Another small but perhaps significant piece of evidence as to Christina's state of health has come to light since Mrs Packer's book was published. In the November 1968 issue of *Notes and Queries* James A. Kohl quoted a note written by Mackenzie Bell's friend, Godfrey Bilchett, at the back of his copy of Bell's book:

> The doctor who attended on Christina Rossetti when she was about 16–18 said she was then more or less out of her mind (suffering, in fact, from a form of insanity, I believe a kind of religious mania).

The doctor in question is almost certainly Hare. Third-hand evidence of this nature is suspect, but in the absence of anything more authoritative it deserves some consideration. The reference to religious mania— whatever may be implied by that term—is interesting, remembering that Christina's preoccupation with religion dates from this period. The use of the word insanity is probably an exaggeration; but it might be borne in mind that the milder term, hysteria, is used in connection with Christina three or four times at various stages in her life.*

Genius must be paid for; and the price demanded is nearly always a marked degree of psychological imbalance. Christina's uncle John Polidori committed suicide; her father Gabriele was an unusually volatile character; her brother Dante Gabriel is a classic example of what used to be called 'the artistic temperament'. She herself was one of the most brilliant members of this gifted family but with their gifts she may also have inherited a measure of their instability. True that she showed few

---

*Another possible piece of evidence as to Christina's state comes from William Sharp, quoting information received from Dante Gabriel: 'When she was still a child (not more than twelve, if Rossetti was right), Christina became poignantly melancholy whenever alone.' Dante Gabriel was speaking many years later and his dating is suspect. (*Atlantic Monthly*, Vol. LXXV, pp. 738–9)

signs of it in adult life; but adolescent psychological and mental disturbances, like such physical woes as acne and puppy-fat, often prove to be temporary troubles. If boys or girls, already preoccupied with the difficulty of adjusting themselves to the physical and mental changes of puberty—and the mention of Locock suggests that Christina may have suffered from some physical trouble—are subjected to any severe strain the result may be a breakdown, physical, mental, or both combined.

If Christina did in fact suffer from such a breakdown and if in her case it was predominantly a mental one, this would explain the absence of information and the studied vagueness of William's references to her health. In the eighteen-forties all mental and psychological troubles were classed together as insanity and regarded with the horrified alarm which that term inspires. If Christina's family agreed with Doctor Hare in believing her to be 'more or less out of her mind' they would have been at pains to keep her condition a secret both at the time and afterwards.

A mental breakdown, however, would not explain the permanent physical deterioration in Christina's physical health. It is therefore more probable that she suffered from one of those obscure adolescent illnesses which are today thought to be psychosomatic in origin but which produce physical effects that are often permanent. Mrs Packer believes this to be true; she argues that Christina's illness was self-induced, an unconscious attempt to avoid the horrid necessity of going out as a governess. Such a motive has something in common with the dread of growing up which is today supposed to underlie much adolescent ill-health. All this, however, is mere conjecture. We know that between 1842 and 1847 Christina Rossetti's character underwent far-reaching changes while her health deteriorated severely. We know that during those years she was suffering from strain and anxiety severe enough to cause a mental breakdown or a psychosomatic illness of a type common in adolescence; but to put these two statements together and come to anything but a tentative conclusion is to commit the cardinal error of adding up two and two to make five.

But if facts about Christina's adolescence are scarce she herself has left us a guide to her feelings at this age. In 1850, when she was nineteen, she wrote a long 'short-story' in which she is clearly looking back at her adolescent self. *Maude* was not published till 1897 when it appeared prefaced by a 'prefatory note' by William Rossetti in which he stresses the autobiographical nature of this little tale:

> It appears to me that my sister's main object in delineating Maude was to exhibit what she regarded as defects in her own character, and in her attitude towards her social circle and her religious obligations. Maude's constantly weak health is also susceptible of a personal reference, no doubt intentional: even so minor a point as her designing the pattern of a sofa-pillow might apply to Christina herself.[9]

At the beginning of the story Maude is fifteen. Her failings are so small as to be almost invisible to the naked eye, the only obvious defects of character being a certain degree of pride and a liking to hear her verses praised. (Like Christina, Maude is a poet.) Her social faults amount to no more than a dislike of boring people, though even here she tries to behave better, 'resolved on doing her best not only towards suppressing all appearance of yawns but also towards bearing her part in the conversation'. Maude is depicted as shy and a little haughty with strangers, but as a leader in her own circle, capable of becoming the life and soul of the party:

> Maude now exerted herself to amuse the party; and soon proved that ability was not lacking. Game after game was proposed and played at, and her fund seemed inexhaustible, for nothing was thought too noisy or too nonsensical for the occasion.

Like Maude, shy Christina could blossom out among congenial people, even congenial strangers; like Maude, she was good at parlour games and especially at *bouts rimés*, the game at which Maude also excelled. The Rossetti brothers and sisters delighted in giving one another a series of rhyme endings, *bouts rimés*, to be used in the construction of a sonnet. All the family were remarkably quick and clever at this game; in six or seven minutes they could reel off a very passable sonnet, Christina's contributions being especially noteworthy. Some of her *bouts rimés* appear in *Maude*, the best being the one which begins 'Vanity of vanities, the Preacher saith,' while another sonnet is concerned with Maude's failure to fulfil her religious obligations:

> I listen to the holy antheming
> That riseth in thy walls continually,
> What while the organ pealeth solemnly
> And white-robed men and boys stand up to sing.
> I ask my heart with a sad questioning:
> 'What lov'st thou here?' and my heart answers me:
> 'Within the shadows of this sanctuary
> To watch and pray is a most blessed thing.'
> To watch and pray, false heart? it is not so:
> Vanity enters with thee, and thy love
> Soars not to Heaven, but grovelleth below.
> Vanity keepeth guard, lest good should reach
> Thy hardness; not the echoes from above
> Can rule thy stubborn feelings or can teach.

In plain language, Maude has been guilty of the heinous sin of forsaking her parish church for another where the services are aesthetically attractive and more to her liking. Clearly she is afflicted with the scrupulosity which was Christina's besetting sin. William saw his sister's fault clearly enough, describing Christina as being 'by far over-scrupulous' and writing of 'this one serious flaw in an otherwise beautiful and admirable character'. Christina herself knew her own failing. Writing of 'scrupulous persons,— a much tried and much trying sort of people', she described some of the troubles these unfortunates inflict on themselves and on other people and ends with the confession 'These remarks have, I avow, a direct bearing on my own case.'[10]

Maude-Christina is not, however, so scrupulous or so foolish as to suppose that these tiny sins afford sufficient justification for her refusal to come to Holy Communion on Christmas Day. She knows that the real fault is more serious and fundamental. 'You are trying to correct your faults,' she says to her friend Agnes. 'I am not trying.'

One of the characters in *Maude* enters a convent, an episode which gives Christina a pretext to include a poem describing the motives which induce three girls to become nuns. The first girl hopes to find in the convent the safe innocence of lost childhood:

> Sing, that in thy song I may
> Dream myself once more a child

The second girl has been unhappy in love:

> I loved him, yes, where was my sin?
> I loved him with my heart and soul.

The third girl yearns for the joys of Heaven, and in the intensity of her longing she comes very close to Christina herself:

> Oh for the grapes of the True Vine
> Growing in Paradise,
> Whose tendrils join the Tree of Life
> To that which maketh wise,
> Growing beside the Living Well
> Whose sweetest waters rise
> Where tears are wiped from tearful eyes.

It would be tempting to treat *Three Nuns* as an autobiographical poem reflecting three facets of the author's character but that Maude, who is also Christina, specifically declares that none of the three girls in any way represents herself—'I never did anything half so good as to profess.' (Rather surprisingly, Christina at no time showed any inclination towards the religious life.) Taken as a whole, however, *Maude* is clearly an attempt at a self-portrait; and therein lies its chief interest. The poems scattered throughout its pages are the only readable parts of the book. Poetry was the medium in which Christina excelled; she was never to achieve either skill or success in the writing of prose.

Much of Christina's adolescent poetry has been preserved, thanks to Grandfather Polidori. On moving to London he had set up a private printing press on which he had already printed a ballad by Dante Gabriel. Maria too had appeared in print with a pious allegory entitled *The Rivulet*. Now it was Christina's turn. In the summer of 1847 Polidori produced a little book of her poems, adding a preliminary 'Word to the Reader' in which he speaks of himself as 'silencing the objections raised by her modest diffidence'. The little volume circulated within the Rossetti circle of friends and relations, where it did not meet with unmixed approval, to judge by a letter from Dante Gabriel to his mother:

> As to the nonsense about Christina's *Verses*, I should advise her to console herself with the inward sense of superiority (assuring her more-over that she will not be the first who has been driven time after time to the same alternative), and to consign the fool and his folly to that utter mental oblivion to the which, I doubt not, she has long ago consigned all those who have been too much honoured by the gift of her book.[11]

The most remarkable point about these early poems is their technique. Christina is already using short couplets and feminine rhymes, the metre she was to make peculiarly her own. A poem written as early as 1844 begins:

> Water calmly flowing,
> Sunlight deeply glowing,
> Swans some river riding
> That is gently gliding

Already she shows a liking for long descriptive lists:

> Heap up flowers, higher, higher—
> Tulips like a glowing fire,
> Clematis of milky whiteness,
> Sweet geraniums' varied brightness,
> Honeysuckle, commeline,
> Roses, myrtles, jessamine;

The Martyr is written entirely in feminine rhymes:

> See, the sun has risen—
> Lead her from the prison;
> She is young and tender,—lead her tenderly;
> May no fear subdue her,
> Lest the saints be fewer—
> Lest her place in Heaven be lost eternally.

The poetic value may be small, the sentiment almost ludicrously over-strained; nevertheless, to produce nine technically flawless verses in this difficult metre is no mean achievement for a fifteen-year-old.

The subject matter of these verses is less remarkable than the style. Poems such as *Tasso and Leonora*—'A glorious vision hovers o'er his soul Gilding the prison and the weary bed'—or *Will these Hands ne'er be clean?*—'And who is this lies prostrate at thy feet, And is he dead, thou man of wrath and pride?'—are clearly echoes of the horrific romances which were the young Christina's favourite reading. Adolescent authors positively enjoy writing gloomy and tragic poems; Christina's pre-occupation with change, death and decay does not necessarily reflect 'the dark mood of hopelessness the conditions of her life suggested to her',[12] though of course the conditions of her life may well have increased the 'inspissated gloom' common to teenage poets.

Very young writers take their subjects not from their experience of life but from their reading of literature. Christina would borrow a character or a situation from a novel by Maturin or Lady Georgina Fullerton or from a poem by Crabbe and use this as the basis for meditation on whatever general theme it might suggest to her. Thus in *Imalee* and in *Isidora* the title and the heroine are taken from Maturin's *Melmoth the Wanderer* but the finished poems have only the faintest connection with that novel. As Mrs Hatton writes, 'The way in which Christina's imagination seized upon these portrayals of frustrated love and conflicts between sacred and profane love and in which she transmuted (no doubt unconsciously) the novelists' materials for her own purposes, indicates that the tendencies were lying dormant within her; the novels merely awoke latent sympathies and gave them definite shape.'[13] What is remarkable about Christina's early verse is the way in which she can on occasion turn this second-hand material into the stuff of real and memorable poetry. In September 1847 she wrote two poems, *Heart's Chill Between* and *Death's Chill Between*—the choice of titles was Dante Gabriel's—in which she deals with a tragedy of thwarted love. If ever poems read like a cry from the heart these are they; yet it is all but certain that the sixteen-year-old Christina had never been in love. To attempt to set bounds to the strength and scope of the creative imagination is a big mistake.

These two linked poems should be sufficient warning of the danger of reading an autobiographical meaning into Christina's early poetry as Mrs Packer has done. In her opinion, Christina's adolescent love poems reflect 'both her new interest in sex and her uncertain state of mind concerning it'.[14] Christina was not an American teenager but a Victorian young lady. The Victorians were not so prudish as many people suppose but they certainly did not encourage their daughters to think or talk about sex. They were also possessed of an enviable ability to separate sex from love. No one was more adept at this exercise than Dante Gabriel, whose influence with his sister was very great. Sex played a small part in his ten-year courtship of Elizabeth Siddal. Later, he lived for many months in the same house as Jane Morris, whom he openly adored, but though he shared her home it is doubtful whether he also shared her bed. Fanny Cornforth and others were his for sexual pleasure, Lizzie and Janey were his for love. Against this must be set the fact that he is the author of one of the most notable poems of sexual love ever written in English; but it is sexual love within the context of marriage—'*nuptial sleep*'.

Two literary influences, both of them particularly powerful in the Rossetti circle, tended to encourage this idea of asexual love. All educated Victorians read Dante; but once they had overcome their childish revulsion, the Rossettis elevated him to the position of a family totem, to borrow a phrase from William Gaunt.[15] The Dante-Beatrice relationship, if relationship it can properly be called, became their ideal of love between man and woman.

The other influence was that of the poets and novelists of the Romantic Movement, with their highflown talk of knights and ladies. Christina's contemporaries had been reared on the novels of Scott and his imitators.

They knew nothing of the squalid realities of medieval life; they saw the Middle Ages simply as the Age of Chivalry. At art school Dante Gabriel was known as 'a clever sketcher of chivalric subjects'. Girls in the school-room would search out pictures of 'true knights' to copy into their albums as enthusiastically as today's scholgirls collect photographs of pop stars. Whatever may have been stirring in Christina's subconscious her conscious mind was concerned not with sex but with chivalry. She was looking for a knight in shining armour; what she found was a plump, middle-class young man called James Collinson.

Chapter Three

First Love and the Pre-Raphaelite Brotherhood

Glamour was not James Collinson's most notable characteristic. The son of a bookseller in Mansfield, he spoke with a slight Midlands accent, and he did not shine in conversation. He was short and rather rotund—'dumpy' was William's word for him—and his face was intelligent rather than handsome. For Christina, however, he was invested with a double halo of romance: he was her first suitor, and after his name he could write the mysterious initials, P.R.B.

The Pre-Raphaelite Brotherhood sprang from the friendship existing between a handful of gifted and enthusiastic young men. Its nature and origin have been admirably described by Rosalie Glynn Grylls:

> Although, wise after the event, we know the movement was to have its place in history, it was at the time much like any other that is formed any term at any university. It was started as a lark, or whatever may be the current slang of the time, and kept going from some unacknowledged need to hold fast the unrelenting minute, to bank up the fires of mutual admiration against a colder world outside. And it followed the usual course: run with a fervour only equalled by casualness and inevitably breaking up as those who started it were the first to outgrow it, but keeping the loyalty of lesser spirits.[1]

Dante Gabriel was the moving spirit within the group. His apprenticeship to art had run anything but smoothly. After four years spent at Sass's Art School, where the pupils were expected to concentrate on drawing casts from the antique, he followed the established practice for would-be artists and entered the Royal Academy School. Once more faced with the tedious discipline of drawing from the antique, he idled away the days, spending more time in writing verse than in studying the elements of his chosen profession. In March 1848 he removed himself from the Academy School and persuaded Ford Madox Brown, an artist whom he greatly admired, to accept him as a pupil. The arrangement lasted no more than five months. Madox Brown expected his pupil to work hard at drawing and painting still-life subjects; Dante Gabriel found bottles and pickle-jars even less to his taste than casts. Leaving Madox Brown, with whom, however, he was always to remain on excellent terms, he arranged to share a studio with a young artist of his own age, William Holman Hunt. Through Holman Hunt he met and made friends with the boy wonder, John Everett Millais, who had been a fellow-pupil with him at the Academy School; and from the friendship between these three young men grew the Pre-Raphaelite Brotherhood.

Quite properly, since they were none of them over twenty-one, Dante Gabriel, Hunt and Millais derided established standards of excellence and poured scorn on the idols of the Academicians. Raphael they considered overrated; Sir Joshua Reynolds was 'slosh'. Inspiration must be sought elsewhere, perhaps in the works of Madox Brown, whom they regarded with great esteem, perhaps in Italian Art of the pre-Renaissance period, certainly in a closer and more painstaking study of nature. In the late summer of 1848, after an evening spent in admiring a set of engravings of the frescoes in the Campo Santo at Pisa, they decided to band together in a brotherhood vowed to pursue these new ideals in art. Soon they were calling themselves the Pre-Raphaelites, though no one seemed to know for sure how the term came into being or what might be its exact significance.

A brotherhood presupposes brothers; the three members debated as to which of their friends and relations should be invited to join them. Dante Gabriel wished to include writers as well as artists; he even went so far as to suggest that Christina should be admitted as a kind of honorary brother on the strength of her poetry. Not surprisingly, Hunt and Millais objected to the idea of a woman joining their masculine coterie. In vain did Dante Gabriel protest that he had never supposed that Christina would be present in person at their meetings, he had merely intended to read aloud her poems. Finally Christina herself vetoed the whole suggestion, fearing that any such reading of her poetry might come dangerously near to undesirable 'display'. A horror of anything which might be thought to savour of ostentation or self-advertisement was typical of the Tractarian attitude to which she was committed.

Four more members were ultimately admitted, Frederick George Stephens, Thomas Woolner, William Michael Rossetti, and James Collinson. Of these four Stephens was an art critic who was later to have a few pictures to his credit, Woolner a sculptor, William Michael a Civil Servant; only Collinson was a professional painter. Dante Gabriel's description of him as a 'stunner' did not at the time appear so ludicrously off the mark as with hindsight we now see it to have been. Unlike Hunt and Dante Gabriel, Collinson had already exhibited his work at the Academy. *The Charity Boy's Debut*, a *genre* picture in the manner of Wilkie, had won some favourable notice; he could look forward to a reasonably successful career as a professional artist. He was a poet too after a fashion; in September 1848 he had all but finished a long and extremely dull religious poem entitled *The Child Jesus* which Dante Gabriel described as 'a very first-rate effort'.

Collinson may have been a worthy rather than an interesting character but he was not unpopular with his fellows. Holman Hunt admitted to liking 'that meek little chap', believing that 'with higher inspiration', presumably to be supplied by Pre-Raphaelitism, 'he might do something good'.[2] Dante Gabriel himself was always apt to take up a person or an ideal with more enthusiasm than judgement. Collinson was his latest discovery and as such Collinson must certainly be made a member of the P.R.B. Hunt described Dante Gabriel as 'having taken possession of Collinson', adding that 'it appears the Rossetti family are much attached to him'.[3]

Christina already knew James Collinson well by sight since he was a devout and regular member of the Christ Church congregation. He had however ceased to attend service there and joined the Roman Catholic Church some little while before Dante Gabriel first brought him to the Rossetti home. The exact dating of events is difficult. According to William, Collinson's introduction to the Rossetti family took place 'about the time of the formation of the P.R.B.'[4] The meeting over the Campo Santo engravings which is usually regarded as the beginning of the Brotherhood took place some time in September 1848; yet in August and early September of that year when William, Christina, and Mrs

Rossetti were at Brighton, Dante Gabriel was writing letters to them full of news of Collinson, who was obviously already known to them. Always regarded as a slow mover, James Collinson pursued Christina with uncharacteristic speed. Though we do not know the exact date of his first proposal to her it must have occurred almost immediately after her return from Brighton. Dante Gabriel strongly favoured acceptance. She herself was intrigued and a little in love yet nevertheless she refused him, her reason being that he was a Roman Catholic. She would marry no one who was not a convinced and practising Anglican. Collinson thereupon reconsidered his religious position and decided to return to the Church of England. He proposed once more; and this time Christina accepted him. By mid-autumn they were officially engaged, though with no immediate prospect of marriage. Christina was still a few weeks short of her eighteenth birthday.

The engagement has caused more dismay to Christina's biographers than ever it did to her friends and relations. 'It is difficult to understand why Christina fell in love with him,'[5] writes Mary Sandars. D. M. Stuart agrees with her: 'What must always remain incomprehensible, and, indeed, almost inconceivable, was her response to his wooing.'[6] Mrs Packer finds the explanation of Christina's acceptance of Collinson in her supposed reluctance to remain at home. Since she was both unable and unwilling to become a governess marriage was the only alternative course open to her. As a promising artist, a poet of sorts, a friend of her much loved brother, and once again an adherent of her own type of religion he was a man with whom she might be expected to find much in common. She therefore accepted him as a means of escaping from the necessity of remaining at home as a financial burden on her already hard-pressed family.

A girl of seventeen does not weigh up her first suitor in this cold-blooded manner. Pleased and flattered by his attentions she has no eye for his deficiencies but on the contrary invents for him merits which he does not possess. She is waiting on tiptoe as it were, eager to find out what love is all about; her family usually have considerable difficulty in pointing out to her that she is not in love with this not very desirable man but with love itself. In Christina's case, however, her family, in the person of Dante Gabriel, stressed Collinson's good points rather than his demerits and encouraged her to believe herself in love with him. Is it therefore surprising that she decided to accept his proposal?

Financial questions cannot have weighed very heavily with her because she knew well enough that if she accepted Collinson who had no private means her family would have to continue to support her for a long and indefinite period until he was earning sufficient money by his painting to make marriage a possibility. Though home was no longer the happy place it had once been it was still the dearest spot on earth to her. She might feel herself to be a financial burden on her family but she knew that she was loved and cherished by every member of that family. Even Maria had ceased to feel jealous and had become a close and dear companion. 'She used to be pitiful of her younger sister, who was delicate and rather demure,' Dante Gabriel was to say of Maria, 'and Christina simply worshipped her.'[7] Though she could contribute little or nothing to the family income she knew herself to be a useful and valued member of the family circle. She had not chosen James Collinson in order to rid that family of a financial burden; she had chosen him because she was in love, or fancied herself to be so.

If there was some unreality about Christina's love for Collinson he himself, at least in these early days, was deeply and seriously in love with her. 'Well he might be,' wrote William acidly, 'for in breeding and tone of mind, not to speak of actual genius or advantages of person, she was markedly his superior.'[8] Advantages of person the seventeen-year-old Christina certainly possessed. She was at this period sitting to Dante Gabriel for the figure of Mary in his first picture in the Pre-Raphaelite manner, *The Girlhood of Mary Virgin*. Between 1847 and 1849 he did some half-dozen drawings of her and a portrait in oils. Collinson also painted a portrait but an unsuccessful one in which she appears to be ten or twenty years older than her actual age at the time.

The most attractive of these portraits of Christina and also, according to contemporaries, the best likeness, is the figure of the Virgin in Dante Gabriel's picture. She is shown in profile, busy at an embroidery frame under the supervision of her mother, Saint Anne, for whom Frances Rossetti was the model. The face is the face of a young girl, expectant of a future which she looks forward to with joy but also with dread. When Holman Hunt first met Christina he described her as 'exactly the

The Girlhood of Mary Virgin by Dante Gabriel Rossetti

William Bell Scott

pure and docile-hearted damsel that her brother portrayed God's Virgin pre-elect to be'.[9] The girl in the picture is not docile but rather self-controlled, almost self-repressed. She will accept what is coming—*Fiat volontas tua*—but the acceptance will be her own choice and it will only be made after a painful struggle.

Of the other likenesses of Christina, Dante Gabriel's oil portrait shows the same brooding withdrawn girl as Mary Virgin, but with the sweetness gone from her face. A pleasant drawing, described by William as 'more matter-of-fact in expression'[10] gives yet another aspect of its subject, Christina as she may have appeared every day at the breakfast table. The drawing which William himself preferred and which he twice selected for reproduction is a delicate profile sketch, showing Christina not as a girl but as a beautiful and mature young woman. In all these drawings and paintings the physical features are so precisely the same, the likeness so identical, that we come to recognise Christina's face in its varying moods as easily as if we had seen her in the flesh. The slightly tip-tilted nose, the over-long chin which does not spoil her profile but instead gives it individuality, the wide apart, marvellous eyes, changing like Dante Gabriel's from dark grey to hazel, the thick coils of straight brown hair (two earlier drawings show her with incongruous and very unbecoming curls) add up to a beauty of a quiet understated type which might be expected to attract rather than to alarm a shy and retiring individual such as Collinson.

No record of their engagement survives, no love-letters, no diaries, nothing but short and casual references in letters to or from other people. Living close at hand in London and being a family friend as well as Christina's accepted suitor, it would seem probable that Collinson would be a frequent visitor at the Rossettis' home; yet there is no mention of any visits nor, curiously enough, of any meeting between the lovers except for half-a-dozen banal words in a letter from Christina to William dated 19th September 1849, 'last night we saw Mr Collinson'. The two are never seen, as it were, face to face.

From the first it was clear that the engagement must be a long one since Collinson could not possibly support a wife on the allowance which he received from his family. This was, however, large enough to entertain his fellow P.R.B.s comparatively lavishly in his lodgings in Somers

Town. Unfortunately, like Alice in Wonderland's dormouse, whom he physically resembled, being short and round and thick-necked, he was all too apt to fall asleep at his own parties. However, not only did he entertain the Brotherhood but he performed the more serious duty incumbent on him as a Pre-Raphaelite by forsaking the genre style of painting and embarking on a large religious picture entitled *The Renunciation of Saint Elizabeth*, a subject taken from Charles Kingsley's *The Saint's Tragedy*, a poem illustrated by Kingsley himself with unpublished and unpublishable erotic drawings. There was nothing erotic about Collinson's picture, which had for background the interior of a recently built London church in the correct ecclesiological Gothic style, complete with encaustic tiles.

In November 1848 William, and not as might have been expected, the newly-engaged Christina, visited Collinson's mother and sister at their home at Pleaseley Hill near Mansfield. There Christina wrote to him saying nothing of James Collinson but asking for information about her mother-in-law and sister-in-law to be:

> I had fancied Mrs. Collinson the very reverse of *prim*; but, as you conjecture, kind-hearted. I am glad you like Miss Collinson, but have a notion that she must be dreadfully clever. Is either of these ladies *alarming*? not to you, of course, but would they be so to me?

Though they had not yet met, Mary Collinson had already made the friendly gesture of asking that she might be called by her Christian name, a familiarity which Christina was too shy to practise easily:

> Pray, if you think it expedient, present my respects to Mrs. Collinson and love to Miss C. Why I have left off calling the latter Mary is not easily explained except on the score of feeling awkward.[11]

In the spring of 1849 Christina's health broke down again. Not until August could she visit Pleaseley Hill, and then she went without James Collinson who chose instead to go on holiday with William to the Isle of Wight. Her stay with his family was only a qualified success—'my visit was very pleasant for some reasons, but not exclusively so.'[12] Her future sister-in-law proved more congenial than she had expected. 'Do you know, I rather like Mary;' she informed William with some show of surprise, 'she is not at all caressing, but seems real.'[13] Nevertheless she was disappointed to find that Mary, whom she had believed to be 'dreadfully clever', took no interest in the books and poems which she herself found so absorbing. She was bored by local gossip and by continual talk of *beaux*, although the Collinsons were sensitive enough to realise that she must not be teased about her own lover. The most enjoyable part of the visit proved to be the time spent at Mansfield with James's brother Charles, whose wife she described as 'delightful, the most to my taste of anyone I have met down here'.

Back at Pleaseley Hill with no more interesting occupations than gardening and crochet—'In my desperation I knit lace with a perseverance completely foreign to my nature'—she suffered from boredom and homesickness—'Ah, Will! if you were here we would write *bouts rimés* sonnets and be subdued together.' And here lay the root of the difficulty. The Collinsons failed to understand her longing to be 'subdued', mistaking her shyness for a form of pride. Other people were apt to make the same mistake; one friend told her to her face that she 'seemed to do all from self-respect, not from fellow feeling with others or from kindly consideration for them.'[14] This criticism was to haunt Christina for the rest of her life. In the spring of 1850 she wrote a poem entitled *Is and Was*, which shows how much she had taken it to heart. The last verse runs thus:

> Now she is a noble lady
> With calm voice not over loud;
> Very courteous in her action,
>   Yet you think her proud;
> Much too haughty to affect;
> Too indifferent to direct
> Or be angry or suspect;
> Doing all from self-respect.

Christina herself was apt to conceal her natural shyness under an air of pride and reserve. 'She was in fact extremely shy,' wrote William: 'Most people probably perceived as much; but she preserved a calm and collected demeanour, which may perhaps have imposed on some of the unwary, and induced them to fancy her distant.'[15]

On returning home she naturally thought to continue correspondence with Mary Collinson, but to this Mary would not agree. 'My correspondence with Mary Collinson has come to an end by her desire,' Christina wrote to William. 'Do not imagine we have been quarrelling: not at all: but she seems to think her brother's affairs so unpromising as to render our continuing to write to each other not pleasant. Does this sound extraordinary?'[16] Charles Collinson, at whose house she had spent the happiest hours of her visit, also failed to reply to a letter on some business matter—'C.C.'s silence astonishes me; perhaps he wishes the acquaintance to cease.'[17] Maybe Collinson's family were aware that he was once more veering in the direction of the Church of Rome; certainly they must have known that since his allowance had been either stopped or considerably reduced he was now in serious financial difficulty, pawning his watch and begging an odd pound or so from his fellow P.R.B., Stephens.

Though all was not going well between the two families Dante Gabriel remained on good terms with James Collinson. On holiday with Holman Hunt in Paris and Belgium he was writing long descriptive letters addressed sometimes to William, sometimes to the P.R.B. in general, sometimes to Collinson himself. He is anxious to know what Collinson thinks of the poem later known as *The Staff and Scrip*—'Let me also have Collinson's verdict.'[18] Disillusion, however, is beginning to set in; writing to William about the cost of a magazine to be produced by the P.R.B. he remarks, 'I cannot see why old Collinson should not be made to take a share. Endeavour to impress this on the amount of mind he possesses.'[19] Nevertheless he still thinks well of Collinson's work; one letter written to him ends 'I long to see what you have done to your picture, and shall rush down at once to Brompton* on my return.'[20]

The proposed magazine was in effect the work of the Rossetti family rather than of the Brotherhood as a whole. The original idea had been Dante Gabriel's and he it was who collected contributions not only from P.R.B.s but from outsiders such as Coventry Patmore. William under-

*Collinson was at this time sharing a studio at Brompton with Holman Hunt.

took to be editor and Christina acted as general assistant to both her brothers. Meanwhile Dante Gabriel was planning to start work on a picture of the Annunciation to be called *Ecce Ancilla Domini*—Hunt made the horrible howler of calling it *Ecce Angelus Domini*—with Christina once more his model for the Virgin Mary. 'The Virgin is to be in bed but without any bedclothes on,' wrote William, excusing this lapse from Pre-Raphaelite principles of accuracy by 'consideration of the hot climate'.[21] Clearly the Rossettis had not been to Palestine in the month of March. In the finished picture the Virgin is shown dressed in a long white nightgown and crouched down on her bed against the wall as if shrinking away from the angelic visitant.

The first number of *The Germ*, as the P.R.B. magazine was rather unfortunately named, appeared on New Year's Day 1850, a year which was to be an unhappy one both for the P.R.B. and for Christina. The contributions included a prose story by Dante Gabriel and one of his finest poems, *My Sister's Sleep*, a remarkably bad sonnet by William who also produced a review of Arthur Hugh Clough's poem *The Bothie of Tober-na-Vuolich*, and two poems by Christina, *Dreamland* and *An End*. Both are Pre-Raphaelite paintings in verse, archaic in tone and suffused with a gentle melancholy. *An End* is a lament for dead love:

> Love, strong as Death, is dead.
> Come, let us make his bed
> Among the dying flowers:
> A green turf at his head;
> And a stone at his feet,
> Whereon we may sit
> In the quiet evening hours.

Here is no touch of the passionate personal emotion which was to characterise all her best work. She had available some half-dozen better poems including the well-known sonnet, *Remember me when I am gone away*, but these she kept to herself, probably fearing that they might be construed as referring to her love for Collinson. In April of the previous year, when Thomas Woolner had asked to see some of her poems she had replied thus to William:

To please you, Mamma not objecting, Mr. Woolner is welcome to any of my things which you may have the energy to copy. Only I must beg that you will not fix upon any which the most imaginative person could construe into love personals [*sic*]; you will feel how more than ever intolerable it would *now* be to have my verses regarded as outpourings of a wounded spirit; and that something like this has been the case I have too good reason to know.[22]

Seven hundred copies of this first number of *The Germ* were printed but only two hundred were sold. Financial ruin threatened its promoters; nevertheless Dante Gabriel decided to bring out a second number which contained *The Blessed Damozel*, soon to become the best-known of all his poems. Christina contributed the song beginning 'Oh roses for the flush of youth', *A Pause of Thought* (later to be reprinted as the first part of the trilogy, *Three Stages*) and *A Testimony*, a long religious poem much admired by Coventry Patmore, who himself provided a poem for publication. To this galaxy of talent Collinson added his not very notable contribution in the shape of *The Child Jesus* which he had at last completed. Judged by any standards this number of *The Germ* was a distinguished production, yet only forty copies were sold. Two more issues were attempted under a different title before, in May 1850, the magazine gently expired, leaving the P.R.B. to face a considerable load of debt.

Other and more serious trouble now overtook the Brotherhood. The secret meaning of the initials P.R.B. leaked out in the press; and the artistic world took umbrage at what it considered to be a slight on Raphael and others of its established idols. The critics who had praised the pictures exhibited by Millais, Dante Gabriel and Holman Hunt the previous year now united in a fierce attack on 'the preposterous Pre-Raphaelite works' appearing in the 1850 Academy exhibition. Millais's *Christ in the House of His Parents* was a chief target for abuse—'revolting', 'disgusting', 'a pictorial blasphemy'—but Dante Gabriel's *Ecce Ancilla Domini* came in for a fair share of vituperation. The only praise, and that very faint, was for the head of the Virgin for which Christina had been the model—'A certain expression in the eyes of the ill-drawn face of the Virgin affords a gleam of something high in intention.'[23]

James Collinson did not exhibit at the 1850 Academy. He had not yet finished his St Elizabeth picture, perhaps because other matters were now absorbing his attention. Once again he was considering leaving the Church of England for the Church of Rome, a step which would surely mean the end of his engagement to Christina.

Collinson was not alone in contemplating such action. Today, even among devout Anglicans, not one in a thousand has so much as heard of the Gorham Judgment, an issue which Gladstone described as 'going to the very root of all life and all teaching in the Church of England'. The details of the affair have nothing to do with the history of Christina and Collinson; sufficient therefore to say that what began in 1847 as a theological argument ended three years later as a full-blown controversy involving the authority of the State over the Church in matters of doctrine. Bishop Philpotts of Exeter refused to institute a parson called George Gorham to a living in the diocese on the ground that Gorham held heretical views on the subject of baptismal regeneration. Gorham was indicted for heresy before the ecclesiastical Court of Arches and found guilty. He appealed, and by a curious quirk in the British legal system, the appeal lay to a secular court, the Judicial Committee of the Privy Council, which quashed the previous finding and declared that Gorham's view of baptism was an admissible one in accordance with the teaching of the Church of England.

This assertion of the authority of the State in matters of belief sent a shudder of alarm through the 'Puseyite' party, and helped many waverers to decide that the time had definitely come to join the Church of Rome. The most important of these secessionists was Henry Manning, afterwards Cardinal Archbishop. Another was William Dodsworth of Christ Church, Albany Street, whose defection brought the affair close to home for the Rossetti family. Neither Manning nor Dodsworth actually joined the Roman Church until 1851, to be followed in the next few years by other notable characters such as George Ryder and the Wilberforce brothers. And preceding them all in 1850, like a minnow leading a shoal of whales, went James Collinson

As he must have anticipated, Christina immediately broke off their engagement. Being the child of a happy 'mixed' marriage she might have been expected to have no very great objection to the idea of marrying a Roman Catholic. William for one was puzzled by her attitude. A declared agnostic, he had little or no understanding of the change in religious climate between 1826, the year of the marriage of Gabriele Rossetti and Frances Polidori, and the period of Christina's engagement to Collinson. In 1826 Roman Catholics had been a small and powerless minority and conversions to Rome were so rare as to be negligible; twenty years later with public office and position opened to them by the Emancipation Act of 1829, they were asserting themselves and making converts in a manner calculated to arouse that terror of Popery inbred in so many Britons. Ironically enough, the adherents of the Oxford Movement, while stressing the Catholic nature of the Church of England, were especially horrified when any of their number went over to Rome. As well as being a denial of the catholicity of the Church of England such a conversion gave substance to the charge that the 'Puseyites' were Papists in disguise. A friend had turned traitor and denied the fundamental tenet of the Movement; he had given the enemy cause to blaspheme.

The controversy over the Gorham Judgment served to exacerbate such feelings. When Newman went over to Rome in 1845 Keble and Pusey saw him go with great grief but without bitterness. Six years later the reaction to Manning's secession was a very different one. Gladstone, who had been Manning's intimate friend since Oxford days, returned all his letters and broke with him completely; and even the kindly Keble admitted to 'indulging in a subtle sort of spleen towards him'. Other conversions provoked similar feelings among those near and dear to the converts. Christina was only doing what many another young woman would have thought it right and proper to do in similar case.

But if the break was inevitable it was none the less painful. The decision to break an engagement is always a difficult one to take and a hard one to carry through. Christina suffered the more acutely because she was a peculiarly sensitive person. The two sides of her nature were once again in conflict, Italy pulling against Miss Yonge. Her instincts, and what Mackenzie Bell calls 'her underlying sensuousness', prompted her to opt for Collinson and marriage; her reason and her sense of religious duty told her that he must be let go. Though she was not, and never had been, seriously in love with him, and though the long and not very satisfactory engagement may have left her a little disillusioned, he was none the less her first love and her accepted suitor. On him centred her present happiness and her hopes for the future. Moreover, she believed him to be in love with her, and she shrank from the thought of the suffering she must cause him.

There is no means of telling whether Collinson was in fact much grieved by the ending of the engagement. He cut himself off from his former friends, resigned from the P.R.B. and joined the Jesuit community at Stonyhurst as a lay-brother. Having found that he had mistaken his vocation, he soon emerged again and went back to his old trade of painting *genre* pictures. He married a niece of the Academician, J. R. Herbert, and died in 1881, not having made much success of his career as an artist.

Christina's distress over Collinson's dismissal was apparent to all her family. In a state of physical collapse she was packed off to Brighton to benefit by the effects of sea air, always a favourite Rossetti remedy for anything wrong with either health or spirits. From there she wrote sad little letters to William, timidly begging for news of Collinson:

Have you seen the *St. Elizabeth* lately? and do you yet know what is to be done with the figure of the old woman whose position was not liked? Whilst I am here, if you can manage without too much trouble, I wish you would find out whether Mr. Collinson is as delicate as he used to be: you and Gabriel are my resources, and you are by far the most agreeable.

I direct this to the Excise that Mamma may not know of it. Do not be shocked at the concealment, this letter would not give her much pleasure. Do have patience both with the trouble I occasion you and with myself. I am ashamed of this note, yet want courage to throw it away; so must despatch it in its dreary emptiness with the sincere love of Your &c.[24]

In another letter she refers to 'an unhappy little fragment which so totally disgusted Mamma that I very speedily made away with it'.[25] As William put it, 'a blight was on her heart and spirits'[26] which she could not speedily shake off. In the autumn of 1850, several months after the break, she chanced to see Collinson in the street and fell down in a dead faint.

Chapter Four

Enter William Bell Scott and Elizabeth Siddal

The years of Christina's engagement to James Collinson also saw the beginning of her lifelong friendship with another man, William Bell Scott. Though shy she was not by nature a solitary person but someone with many friends of both sexes, though none of them perhaps very close to her. Her friendship with Scott would therefore be of no particular significance were it not that upon this base Mrs Lona Mosk Packer chose to build an airy fabric of romance. Because Mrs Packer was a scholar of repute and because her book, the fruit of long and extensive research, is the only full-scale biography of Christina still in print, her theory must be given serious consideration.

The known facts about the early period of Christina's friendship with Scott are few and simple. William Bell Scott was a Scotsman born in Edinburgh in 1811. A minor poet remembered today only for one poem in *The Oxford Book of English Verse*, he was also a professional artist and head of the Government School of Design at Newcastle-upon-Tyne. In 1846 he published a long poem entitled *The Year of the World*, which was either ignored or castigated by the critics. He was therefore the more pleased to receive a letter from an unknown admirer signing himself Gabriel Charles Rossetti, full of extravagant praise of this 'dignitous' work. Scott sent a warm reply and in return received a bundle of poems headed 'Songs of the Art-Catholic'. The contents were more promising than this peculiar title since they included both *The Blessed Damozel* and *My Sister's Sleep*. Scott was sufficiently interested to make a call at Charlotte Street the next time he was in London. He was shown into the front parlour where he found not Dante Gabriel but Gabriele and Christina. His description of the scene has often been quoted:

I entered the small front parlour or dining-room of the house, and found an old gentleman sitting by the fire in a great chair, the table drawn close to his chair, with a thick manuscript book open before him, and the largest snuff-box I ever saw beside it conveniently open. He had a black cap on his head furnished with a great peak or shade for the eyes, so that I saw his face only partially. By the window was a high narrow reading-desk, at which stood writing a slight girl with a serious regular profile, dark against the pallid wintry light without. This most interesting to me of the two inmates turned on my entrance, made the most formal and graceful curtsey, and resumed her writing, and the old gentleman signed to a chair for my sitting down, and explained that his son was now painting in the studio he and a young friend had taken together: this young friend's name was Holman Hunt, a name which I had not heard before. As the short day was already nearly spent, I could not go there at once. The old gentleman's pronunciation of English was very Italian, and though I did not know that both of them—he and his daughter—were probably at that moment writing poetry of some sort and might wish me far enough, I left very soon. The girl was Christina, who had already at seventeen written, like her brother, some admirable lyrics, nearly all overshaded with melancholy.[1]

This meeting, at which it might be noted that Christina spoke not one word, marked the beginning of a friendship between Scott and the entire Rossetti family. 'We all took to him most cordially and he to us.'[2] William wrote, while Scott declared that 'Dante Gabriel Rossetti, Christina and Maria his sisters and William his brother, from that day to this have all been very near and dear to me'.[3] Newcastle, however, was a long way off; and Scott appears to have paid only one more visit to London before September 1850. In that month William spent part of his holiday with Scott in Newcastle and discovered, somewhat to his surprise, that his host was a married man.

Out of this skeleton of fact Mrs Packer elaborated a fantasy of frustrated love. Her version of the story runs thus. Christina met Scott again during a visit he paid to London in the winter of 1848-9. (Such a meeting is indeed highly probable though no record of it exists.) She fell in love with him, although by this time she was engaged to Collinson, hence the feeling of guilt which characterises so much of her love poetry of this period. When in the spring of 1850 she broke off her engagement, she felt herself free to indulge in dreams of love between herself and Scott, only to discover, a few months later, that he was a married man. Meanwhile Scott, who had flirted with Christina as he flirted with every pretty woman he met, found himself in his turn falling in love with her. Mrs Packer thus sums up the supposed situation in the autumn of 1850:

> . . . she had already managed to engage herself to a man she was not in love with, and, having plighted her troth to him, had been further mortified to realize that she could feel desire for another man. After the painful ordeal of breaking off the engagement, normally she could have anticipated a natural development of the more attractive relationship. Instead, she learned that all the while their underground romance had been spreading strong roots, the man had been married and hence inaccessible. What had flourished with such fertility had to be killed. The rich bloom of life was not to show itself; the deeply harmonious chord was not to be sounded. the sketch not to be completed with the loving brush strokes of fulfilling detail.[4]

The roots of this underground romance must indeed have been deeply buried since from that day to this no shoot from them has appeared on the surface. According to Mrs Packer the supposed romance began in the winter of 1848–9 and lasted until 1857. A man and a woman who are in love for as long as eight years must be either preternaturally lucky or extraordinarily discreet (which Christina was but Scott was not) if they are to keep their love secret. Yet no breath of gossip, no whisper of family tradition hints at the existence of any such romance. The only full-length study of Scott is an unpublished thesis by Miss Vera Walker, who has recently stated that she found 'no shred of evidence' to suggest any idea of love between Scott and Christina. Yet, in face of this total absence of confirmatory evidence, Mrs Packer believed that this hopeless business dragged on, Scott either openly or implicitly asserting his love, and Christina denying hers for him, until in 1857 he finally put an end to the affair.* Christina nevertheless continued to love on in secret, and

*Although today they are generally taken to imply a sexual relationship, it is impossible

in 1866 she at last admitted that she loved him—too late, because he was by that time deeply attached to Alice Boyd and living with her as her lover.

At first sight Mrs Packer's theory is an alluring one. James Collinson seems a ludicrously inadequate character to fill the role of the Great Lover; and Christina's love for him can provide no explanation of the theme of guilt which underlies much, though by no means all, of her love poetry. The married man Scott, with his Mephistophelean face and his well-known attraction for women, fills the bill in a much more satisfactory manner. Admittedly, Christina's love-poetry presents an insoluble problem if it is assumed that poetry is of necessity the fruit of personal experience. Writing of her poem which begins 'I took my heart in my hand' an authority as considerable as Sir Maurice Bowra declares that 'No woman could write with this terrible directness if she did not to some degree know the experience she describes.'[5] To some degree, yes—but to what degree? Genius can make bricks of the poorest quality straw or sometimes of no straw at all:

> My love for Heathcliff resembles the eternal rocks beneath, a source of little visible delight, but necessary. Nellie, I *am* Heathcliff—he's always in my mind—not as a pleasure any more than I am always a pleasure to myself—but as my own being.

So far as we can be sure of anything to do with love we can be sure that the woman who wrote those words was never in love with any man nor was any man ever in love with her. *Wuthering Heights* was written by a poet; and no limit can be set to the poetic imagination, as Christina herself well knew. In 1865 she wrote a poem originally called *Under the Rose* but later re-titled *The Iniquity of the Fathers upon the Children.* In it she describes the reactions of an illegitimate child to the stigma of illegitimacy and her feeling toward the mother who loves her but has never owned her as a daughter. Justifying her choice of subject in a letter to Dante Gabriel, Christina argued thus: 'whilst it may truly be urged that unless white could be black and Heaven Hell my experience

not to use the terms 'affair' and 'love affair', which in Christina's day did not necessarily have this meaning. Mrs Packer never suggests that Scott and Christina were lovers in the physical sense of that word.

(thank God) precludes me from hers, I yet don't see why "the Poet Mind" should be less able to construct her from its own inner consciousness than a hundred other unknown quantities.'[6] From that inner consciousness Emily Brontë evolved *Wuthering Heights* and Christina constructed the best of her love-poetry.

One point is perhaps worth mention—both Emily and Christina saw passionate love very near at hand. They both watched a dearly-loved brother in the grip of an overwhelming love-affair, Branwell Brontë in love with Mrs Robinson, Dante Gabriel with Lizzie Siddal. But, unlike Emily Brontë, Christina had at least had some first-hand experience of love; she had been loved, she had thought herself to be in love, she had been engaged, and she had broken the engagement. No more than this was needed to set her poetic imagination alight. Why then go to immense lengths to provide her with another supposed lover?

For the theory that Christina was in love with Scott is based entirely on supposition. It is not impossible, but not one jot or tittle of factual evidence exists to prove it true. To read Mrs Packer's book is to be reminded of the old saying 'If ifs and ans were pots and pans there'd be no need for tinkers'—or for biographers who believe in the importance of historical facts. The expressions 'must have', 'could have', 'would have' bespatter her pages, and the rhetorical question is one of her favourite devices—'Christina must have responded to "the singularly penetrating and deliberate gaze" of the magnetic blue eyes'; 'He would certainly have wanted to see her again'; 'It could not have taken Christina long to discover Scott's new friendship'; 'Was it at Penkill that Christina told Scott that she loved him?' And so on and so forth.

Mrs Packer explains and excuses this total absence of historical proof on the ground that William, the primary authority for everything concerning Christina, knew of her love for Scott, and deliberately omitted or falsified any evidence which might point in that direction. One of the great difficulties in the way of Mrs Packer's theory is that in order to believe her it is necessary to disbelieve William, and that he appears on balance to be the more credible of the two:

William Rossetti never said a cruel thing, not even an unwise one. In his comments on life he had something of the gentle pessimism of

Thomas Hardy; he did not share his sister Christina's faith. Yet his own sweetness and rich humanity gave me an added belief in men, as talent and character never fail to do.[7]

So William Rothenstein wrote in 1932. Those people still alive who remember William describe him as an essentially honest and truthful man who would have found it all but impossible to tell a lie. But a man who never says a cruel thing or an unwise one, though he may speak nothing but the truth, cannot always speak the whole truth. William could and did deliberately omit facts as he himself admitted in his preface to his Memoir of Dante Gabriel:

> Some readers of the Memoir may be inclined to ask me—'Have you told everything, of a substantial kind, that you know about your deceased brother?'—My answer shall be given beforehand, and without disguise: 'No; I have told what I choose to tell and have left untold what I do not choose to tell'.[8]

There is however a world of difference between omitting facts and putting up a smoke-screen of untruths and semi-truths to conceal facts. William omits, but he does not falsify; and this is as true of his statements about emotions as of his statements about fact. When, for instance, he declares that Collinson 'struck a staggering blow at Christina Rossetti's peace of mind'[9] he is saying what he believes to be true; he is not explaining away or covering up the inconvenient fact that 'the staggering blow' was in reality struck by another man. Had Christina been in love with Scott, William would certainly not have recorded that love in any of the many books he wrote or edited. He might have destroyed some letters, he might have cut out passages from others as in fact he cut out various passages referring to Collinson,* but he would not have made a mis-statement nor would he have deliberately encouraged his readers to believe something which he knew to be untrue.

Since Mrs Packer has no facts on which to base her theory she must find some other proof of its truth or at least of its probability. This proof she finds in Christina's poetry. Unlike Ford Madox Ford, who maintained that 'She did not sit down to "poetise" . . . on her vicissitudes',[10]

*See Princeton Papers.

Mrs Packer believes that Christina's poetry closely reflects her changing emotions and circumstances. Much of her love poetry cannot be made to fit either in mood or content with either of her acknowledged love affairs; therefore, says Mrs Packer, she must have had a third, unacknowledged love—and who so suitable to fill that role as William Bell Scott? She then sets out to prove from the poetry and the poetry alone that this guess is a correct one. She looks about for some occasion, such as a hypothetical meeting between Scott and Christina during one of Scott's visits to London, or William's discovery that Scott had a wife, which might have marked a crisis in the supposed relationship, and then searches the poetry which Christina was writing at that date for traces of an emotional reaction appropriate to such a crisis. Conversely, she sometimes starts from the poetry and works backwards to a supposed event. For instance, she points out that the well-known poem beginning 'When I am dead, my dearest' was written in December 1848, approximately at the time of Scott's visit to London: therefore, she argues, it can have no connection with Collinson but expresses Christina's reaction to a meeting with Scott which must have taken place during this visit.

> When I am dead, my dearest,
>   Sing no sad songs for me;
> Plant thou no roses at my head,
>   Nor shady cypress tree:
> Be the green grass above me
>   With showers and dewdrops wet;
> And if thou wilt, remember,
>   And if thou wilt, forget.
>
> I shall not see the shadows,
>   I shall not feel the rain,
> I shall not hear the nightingale
>   Sing on as if in pain:
> And dreaming through the twilight
>   That doth not rise nor set,
> Haply I may remember,
>   And haply may forget.

This plaintive, enchanting song, which reads more like a poetic exercise than an expression of heartfelt emotion, is described by Mrs Packer as 'an odd lyric to be written by a girl presumably in the first flush of triumphant love.'[11] Leaving aside the fact that by December 1848 Christina had been engaged to Collinson for over a year and was therefore not in the first flush of any kind of love, the poem seems to express very clearly the feelings of a young girl who, on recovering from a long period of ill health and, to repeat William's phrase, still seeing at times 'the countenance of Death very close to her own', finds herself for the first time loved by a man and returns his love with tenderness, though not with passion. If the poem is not simply a flight of fancy it is easily applicable to the relationship between Christina and Collinson.

Apart from the interpretation of a particular poem, a subject on which opinions may rightly differ, this method of deducing fact from poetical references is not a legitimate one. To quote Rosalie Glynn Grylls again, 'as biographical material poetry is very misleading'.[12] And it is particularly misleading over any question of dates. Of course a series of poems in a persistent mood is indicative of an emotional crisis; but poetry cannot be used to date such a crisis with any degree of certainty. In a review of Mrs Packer's book appearing in *Victorian Studies* (University of Indiana) Professor Fredeman has pointed out that letters in the Penkill Papers which were not available to her now show many of her dates to be completely erroneous. To the examples he gives might be added another from the period of Christina's engagement to Collinson. Mrs Packer maintain that 'the blight on her health and spirits' to which Williams refers was caused not by the breaking of this engagement but by the discovery that Scott was a married man. The dates, however, contradict this supposition: Christina had collapsed both in health and spirits and had been sent to Brighton to recover from this breakdown some weeks before William ever went to Newcastle; the 'blight' on her therefore cannot have been caused by his discovery of the fact that Scott had a wife.

Even supposing that it is both possible and permissible to use poetry as biographical material Mrs Packer is sometimes a little disingenuous in the deductions she draws from the poems. Writing of the years from 1847 to 1850 she argues that because 'the theme of guilt and sin' dominates the poetry of this period Christina must have been indulging in what might have been considered a guilty love, that is, a love for Scott rather than for Collinson to whom she was engaged. The theme of guilt and sin is, however, in no way peculiar to this period but a constant one in Christina's poetry; 'Once my heart was gladsome, now my heart is broken; Once my love was noble—now it is a crime' are lines occurring in a poem she wrote at the early age of sixteen. To sum up—though Mrs Packer's theory provides a plausible answer to some otherwise insoluble problems it is a theory which rests on no factual basis whatsoever, and therefore it cannot be taken seriously. The best that can be said for it is the old Scottish verdict, 'not proven'.

In the spring of 1850, as the love between Christina and James Collinson withered, for the first time in his life Dante Gabriel fell in love. A few months later, in September of this same year, Christina wrote a poem describing a golden-haired beauty:

> Her hair is like the golden corn
>   A low wind breathes upon
> Or like the golden harvest moon
>   When all the stars are gone,
> Or like a stream with golden sands
>   On which the sun has shone
> Day after day in summer-time
>   Ere autumn leaves are wan.

The Pre-Raphaelites were so enamoured of red-gold hair that if they saw an unknown girl in the street with hair of that desirable colour they would accost her and ask her to sit as a model. Now Dante Gabriel fell in love with a golden-haired girl called Elizabeth Siddal,* a milliner's apprentice. She was his Lady Lilith:

> All the threads of my hair are golden,
> And there in a net his heart was holden.

*The name was originally spelt 'Siddall', but Dante Gabriel made her drop the second 'l'.

This sketch of me was made by my
Sister Christina when I was about 19
                                D G Rossetti

Sketch of Dante Gabriel
Rossetti by Christina,
when she was seventeen

William Michael Rossetti by Christina

Dante Gabriel Rossetti by Holman Hunt

So it was that his mother and sisters saw 'Lizzie'; they thought of her as the baleful Lilith, never the fruitful Eve. She was 'La Belle Dame Sans Merci' who had his heart in thrall.

This view was unfair to Lizzie, a respectable girl who appears to have disliked the idea of an illicit love-affair and yearned for matrimony. Bessie Parkes, who was later to be the mother of Hilaire Belloc, said of her that 'She had the look of one who read her Bible and said her prayers every night, which she probably did.'[13] In the early stages of their love Lizzie made Dante Gabriel very happy; they played together like children, giving each other ridiculous nicknames, 'Gugs' and 'Guggums' (Dante Gabriel had a great liking for nicknames; he would, for instance, address his mother in irreverent but affectionate manner as 'the Antique' or 'Teaksicunculum'). What was more important, she was the spark which set his artistic genius alight; he was forever drawing or painting her in an endless variety of characters and poses. But there was about her an air of physical delicacy and mental depression; she painted sad, sinister little pictures, and she wrote sad, sinister little poems which made Christina's gloomiest efforts appear comparatively cheerful. 'Perhaps this is merely my overstrained fancy, but their tone is to me even painfully despondent;' Christina herself was to write years later to Dante Gabriel, 'talk of my bogieism, is it not by comparison jovial?'[14] Instinctively the Rossetti family seem to have felt that though Lizzie might be an inspiration to Dante Gabriel as an artist she was an incubus to him as a man.

The general consensus of opinion is that among Dante Gabriel's relations it was Christina who particularly objected to his involvement with Lizzie. Though the direct evidence is slight—there is no mention of Lizzie in any of Christina's letters of this period—it is probable that whatever she may have said and done a year or so later, in these early days she at least gave no open sign of disapproval. Christina had been attempting to draw likenesses, and hearing of this, on August 4th 1852 Dante Gabriel wrote asking her to send him some of her work:

. . . will you enclose a specimen, as I should like to see some of your handiwork? You must take care however not to rival the Sid,* but keep within respectful limits. Since you went away, I have had sent me,

*One of D.G.R.'s nicknames for Lizzie.

among my things from Highgate, a lock of hair shorn from the beloved head of that dear, and radiant as the tresses of Aurora, a sight of which may perhaps dazzle you on your return. That love has lately made herself a grey dress, also a black silk one, the first bringing out her characteristics as 'a meek unconscious dove', while the second enhances her qualifications as a *'rara avis in terris'*, by rendering her *'nigro simillima cygno'*.[15]

The happy, light-hearted tone of this letter does not suggest that Christina had as yet expressed any dislike or disapproval of Lizzie, whatever her private feelings may have been.

It is also supposed that Dante Gabriel's relations disapproved of Lizzie on snobbish grounds. Certainly at that date no one with any pretensions to gentility could have regarded a milliner's apprentice, daughter of a working cutler living at Newington Butts, as a desirable daughter-in-law. The Rossettis were, however, curiously free of class-consciousness. The Pierces and Polidoris were of gentle blood but the Rossettis themselves came of peasant stock, and as Italians they were more or less outside the English class system. Lizzie, it seems, could behave, as Dante Gabriel's friend Deverell put it, 'like a real lady'; characters such as Bessie Parkes and Barbara Bodichon,* Dr.† and Mrs Acland, even Ruskin's extremely conventional parents, all accepted her without a qualm.

The Rossettis may well have been less distressed by Lizzie's lack of breeding than by the ambiguous nature of her relationship with Dante Gabriel. Ambiguous it remains to this day; no one can say with absolute certainty whether she was or was not his mistress. With his family Dante Gabriel always behaved as if he and Lizzie were officially engaged, expecting them to treat her as his promised bride. Marriage, however, was out of the question because he had not the means to support a penniless wife. He was frequently borrowing money from his aunt Charlotte Polidori and still more frequently from the long-suffering William, who

---

* A pioneer of the Women's Movement.

† Doctor—afterwards Sir Henry—Acland was a member of the famous Devonshire family. He and his wife were well-known Oxford characters.

was also falling in love after his own quiet manner. William's work on *The Germ* had brought him into contact with literary journalists, and he had been asked to write art criticism both for *The Critic* and *The Spectator*. He was soon on friendly terms with the Editor of *The Spectator*, Robert Rintoul, at whose house he found himself 'almost as much at home as at my own',[16] and he proceeded to fall in love with Rintoul's daughter, Henrietta. Although he knew that she returned his love, typically enough he said nothing either to her or to her parents 'as the moderate scale of my income and the general position imperatively demanded a prudent reserve'.[17] He did, however, go so far as to introduce Henrietta to Christina, who struck up a friendship with her which was to last for many years.

Through her brothers and their many contacts both literary and artistic Christina had the opportunity to meet many interesting and well-known people. She was a guest at the parties given by Mrs Orme, 'a lady of rich physique and luminous dark eyes',[18] who much enjoyed playing the hostess to celebrities. At her house Christina could meet and talk with such characters as William Allingham, G. H. Lewes, Douglas Jerrold and Herbert Spencer. Here too she met Tennyson's brother Frederick and his sister Mrs Jesse, who had once been engaged to Arthur Hallam, the 'hero' of *In Memoriam*. This lively outspoken woman, a person of great character, took a marked liking to Christina, but as William sadly remarked, nothing came of this. Christina was in fact too shy to profit much by these encounters.

Another guest at Mrs Orme's parties also took a liking to Christina and paid her considerable attention. John Brett is remembered today as the painter of *The Stone Breaker*, but in his lifetime he was best known for his seascapes. Brett is the 'John' of Christina's poem *No thank you, John*, apparently written in 1860 but, according to William, referring to an episode which took place some eight years earlier. Christina herself told Dante Gabriel: 'As to "John", no such person existed or exists,'[19] a statement which William, knowing that the poem referred to John Brett, was at some pains to square with his belief that in all her life Christina had never told a deliberate lie. Christina herself must have known well enough that she was not telling the truth in her letter to Dante Gabriel since against her own copy of *No thank you, John* she had scribbled the cryptic remark, 'The original John was obnoxious, because he never gave scope for "No thank you!" '20

Dante Gabriel objected to the poem on the ground that 'everything in which this tone appears is utterly foreign to your primary impulses'.21 From childhood, however, Christina had written comic verse tasting slightly bitter on the tongue. She addresses John thus:

> I never said I loved you, John;
>   Why will you tease me day by day,
> And wax a weariness to think upon
>   With always 'do' and 'pray'?

Why, she asks, must he be so foolish as to continue pestering a woman who has never shown any sign of loving him?

> I have no heart?—Perhaps I have not;
>   But then you're mad to take offence
> That I don't give you what I have not got;
>   Use your own common sense.

> Let bygones be bygones:
>   Don't call me false, who owed not to be true:
> I'd rather answer 'No' to fifty Johns
>   Than answer 'Yes' to you.

Such humour as this was in fact one of Christina's 'primary impulses', not the jollity and joking which delighted Dante Gabriel, but an odd, wry humour, sometimes nonsensical, sometimes caustic. 'You were not a pure saint by any means,' Virginia Woolf wrote of her: 'You pulled legs, you tweaked noses, you were at war with all humbug and pretence.'22 So Christina mocks lovelorn John, obviously suspecting that an element of humbug lurks beneath his protestations of a broken heart.

When asked to write an entry in the album of Mrs Orme's daughter, instead of concocting something in this humorous vein Christina produced a set of verses beginning

Do you hear the low winds singing,
     And streams singing in their bed?—
Very distant bells are ringing
     In a chapel for the dead:—

Undeterred by this lugubrious effort the young Miss Orme made friends with Christina. Together the two girls attended an art class run by Madox Brown primarily for working men, where, instead of copying casts, the pupils drew such everyday objects as shavings picked up from the floor of a carpenter's shop. Christina herself still sat occasionally as a model for her brother and also for Holman Hunt, then working on his famous picture *The Light of the World*. He had used many models for the head of Christ, taking some feature or characteristic from each one. Appreciating 'the gravity and sweetness of her expression'[23] he asked Christina to sit for him and she agreed to do so, chaperoned by her mother. Unfortunately Hunt worked direct on to the canvas without making preliminary sketches, so that we have no likeness by him of Christina to compare with the many drawings by Dante Gabriel.

At this period, therefore, Christina was enjoying a reasonably full social life although financial stringency and her father's worsening condition had meant the abandonment of the simple, pleasant entertaining which had once been a feature of life in the Rossetti household. In 1851, presumably to save expense, the family moved from Charlotte Street to Number Twenty-eight Arlington Street in North London. Here, in an attempt to add to their tiny income, Frances Rossetti opened a small day-school. Although Maria had given up her post as a governess and was now living at home she was already fully occupied teaching Italian to private pupils. It therefore fell to Christina to act as her mother's assistant. Although she had no natural talent for teaching she was willing and prepared to help in any way she could, but she found the task an uncongenial one. The school attracted very few pupils; and the business of educating a handful of girls, daughters of local tradesmen, proved to be both dreary and unremunerative.

Two country visits provided a break from schoolteaching though to a person as shy as Christina such visiting was often more of a pain than a pleasure. In July 1851 she stayed at Longleat, where her Aunt Charlotte was acting as companion to Lady Bath, and the following summer she spent some time at Darlaston Hall in Staffordshire, the home of a Shakespearean scholar called Swynfen Jarvis, a friend of her father, whom she had known when she was a small child. Here, though the ostensible purpose of her visit was to teach Italian to his daughters, she was treated not as a governess but as a guest and family friend.

At home matters went from bad to worse. Gabriele's health continued to decline and the little school was proving a failure. Aunt Charlotte's employer, Lady Bath, now suggested a possible solution to these problems. As patron of the living of Frome, a market town in Somerset, she had recently appointed to that living a cleric who was something of a hero to the Anglo-Catholics, as the one-time Tractarians had begun to call themselves. As priest-in-charge of St Paul's Knightsbridge, W. J. E. Bennett had won the love and respect of his poorer parishioners by his work in the slums of Pimlico during the cholera epidemic of 1849. When, however, the new church of St Barnabas was opened in this poor district the nature of the services Bennett conducted there gave rise to loud cries of 'No Popery'. The storm of protest took the form of quite serious rioting which continued until, at the request of his bishop, Bennett agreed to resign. Lady Bath thereupon offered him the living of Frome, where he was to work for many years and make himself much beloved.

It was now suggested that a school at Frome, run under Bennett's auspices, might prove more successful than the moribund venture in Arlington Street. Gabriele's health might benefit from the change from London, while Christina and her mother would find themselves in congenial Anglo-Catholic surroundings. The Rossettis decided to make this experiment, taking a house in Frome in Brunswick Terrace and moving there in March 1853. Dante Gabriel had already set up for himself at Chatham Place near Blackfriars Bridge in a picturesque if unhealthy house overlooking the river. Here Lizzie could spend all day with him though at night she returned to her own lodgings. Maria was left behind to continue with her teaching of Italian and to keep house for William, whose work kept him in London.

The year spent at Frome was not a happy time for the Rossetti family.

Hardly had they settled into their new home than Frances Rossetti was recalled to London to the death-bed of her mother. Left in charge of her invalid father and of the newly-opened school Christina wrote bravely, 'I am managing very well and doubt not I shall continue to do so.'[24] Old Mrs Polidori had been bedridden for so long that her death caused no great feeling of loss or shock. A far more poignant grief came eight months later with the death of Gaetano, Christina's much-loved grandfather. Though over ninety this remarkable old man remained physically active and mentally alert until the very end. Once again Frances Rossetti rushed to London; once again Christina was left in sole charge at Frome. On receiving a letter telling her that there was no hope and that Gaetano was actually dying she broke down completely, weeping and crying, 'Oh, my dear grandfather! Oh, my dear grandfather!'

She had always loved this grandfather better than her own father, shrinking from Gabriele's overwhelming exuberance. Now, however, she could have wished some of that old enthusiasm and spirit back again. He who had once been so absorbed in politics and philosophy now had little or nothing to say on such subjects—'Papa now hardly ever makes a remark or expresses an opinion on public affairs,'[25] Christina told William. She was in bad need of mental stimulus. Frome could provide her with no intelligent talk of books and pictures, no interest or hobby to take the place of Madox Brown's art classes, no social life to compare with the gatherings at Mrs Orme's home. Most of all she missed Maria and her two brothers:

> A pair of brothers brotherly,
>   Unlike, and yet how much the same
> In heart and high-toned intellect,
>   In face and bearing, hope and aim:
> Friends of the self-same treasured friends,
>   And of our home the dear delight,
> Beloved of many a loving heart,
>   And cherished both in mine, Goodnight.

When the cholera raged in London in the summer of 1853 she hoped 'vividly' that her brothers would be spared, but scrupulously honest as ever where her feelings were concerned, she admitted to feeling no real alarm—'I am not very timid, so shall not (in fact cannot) make myself miserable on spec.'[26]

The break-up of the home circle was a grief to all the members of this closely-knit family, and to none more so than to Dante Gabriel. Although he had been the first to set up on his own he sadly missed the neighbourly presence of his family and the chance to visit them whenever he felt so inclined. 'I want to find my way to Frome, and see your dear face again before long,' he wrote to his mother, '—also as much as is visible of the governor's and Christina's almost stereotyped smile.'[27] Christina had found little at Frome to make her smile; if she smiled at all it must be from formal politeness—hence the epithet 'stereotyped'. Her studied politeness had in fact become a joke with both her brothers. 'Christina's gratitude will be oppressive but you must prepare yourself for it,'[28] William wrote to Stephens, who had sent her some cuttings for the garden. This exaggerated expression of politeness or gratitude was her answer to the old accusation of hauteur, 'doing all from self-respect', which had so much troubled her. In an effort to combat her ingrained shyness and reserve she rushed to the other extreme and forced herself to become almost fulsomely polite, especially to strangers. She herself was well aware of this exaggeration and would joke about 'my un-liveable-with politeness'.[29] With her brothers, however, she could be her natural self; 'I really do remember absent friends though I do not gush,' she wrote to William on September 10th 1853, and again, thirteen days later, 'I know you are not one to whom to address long sentences of gush.'[30]

In her exile at Frome news of the P.R.B. was always welcome to Christina. The Brotherhood, however, was fast breaking up. Collinson had resigned on becoming a Roman Catholic; Woolner was about to leave for Australia, hoping that prospecting for gold might prove more profitable than sculpture; Holman Hunt planned a long visit to Egypt and Palestine in search of material for the biblical scenes which were his favourite subjects. Meanwhile, Millais had gone over to the enemy's camp and had allowed himself to be elected an A.R.A. Christina wrote a sonnet in comic valediction:

The P.R.B. is in its decadence:
For Woolner in Australia cooks his chops
And Hunt is yearning for the land of Cheops;
D. G. Rossetti shuns the vulgar optic;*
While William M. Rossetti merely lops
His Bs in English disesteemed as Coptic;
Calm Stephens in the twilight smokes his pipe;
But long the dawning of his public day;
And he at last the champion great Millais,
Attaining academic opulence,
Winds up his signature with A.R.A.
So rivers merge in the perpetual sea;
So luscious fruit must fall when over-ripe;
And so the consummated P.R.B.

Although as late as December 1853 Christina was gallantly maintaining that 'I really think the school may yet succeed' it was clear that what she had described as 'the Frome forlorn hope' had been a failure from the very start. The financial prospects of the family were, however, improving. William was now earning a good salary and with typical generosity he offered to take a house in London and to make a home for the whole family. After the death of her parents Frances Rossetti had inherited some small legacies which made it the more possible to accept this welcome proposal. The exile at Frome was at an end; in March 1854 all the family except Dante Gabriel found themselves once more living together under one roof at Number Forty-five Upper Albany Street.

*A reference to D.G.R.'s dislike of exhibiting his pictures in public.

Chapter Five

Charles Cayley

In her biography of Christina, Dorothy Stuart describes the eighteen-fifties as 'the grey years': perhaps they seem grey because we know so little about them. Interest has inevitably centred on other members of the family, in particular on Dante Gabriel. It is difficult to trace the sequence of events where Christina herself is concerned: very few letters survive; and printed authorities differ as to facts and dates.* One all-important fact, however, is clear; during these years she was writing much poetry.

'I doubt if you developed very much,' Virginia Woolf wrote of Christina: 'You were an instinctive poet.'[1] D. M. Stuart makes the same point—'She had no earlier and later style.'[2] But though they differ very little either in style or subject from the early 'Juvenilia' these poems of the eighteen-fifties show a less literary approach, a deeper feeling of personal involvement. Like all poets, Christina must write of love and death, but she writes of them with a difference. For her the common position is reversed; death is the bringer of joy, love the bringer of grief. Only two of all the poems written during this period celebrate love happy and fulfilled. The first is the song beginning 'It is not for her even brow', the second the much more considerable sonnet, *A Pause*:

> They made the chamber sweet with flowers and leaves,
>   And the bed sweet with flowers on which I lay;
>   While my soul, love-bound, loitered on its way.
> I did not hear the birds about the eaves,

---

*Mackenzie Bell, for instance, mentions three visits to the Scotts in Newcastle; but Mrs Packer has it that 'the record reveals only the one visit', without specifying what that record may be.

Nor hear the reapers talk among the sheaves:
   Only my soul kept watch from day to day,
   My thirsty soul kept watch for one away:—
Perhaps he loves, I thought, remembers, grieves.
At length there came the step upon the stair,
   Upon the lock the old familiar hand:
Then first my spirit seemed to scent the air
   Of Paradise; then first the tardy sand
Of time ran golden; and I felt my hair
   Put on a glory, and my soul expand.

Otherwise the best she can say for love is to describe it thus:

   A bitter dream to wake from,
   But oh how pleasant while we dream!
   A poisoned fount to take from,
   But oh how sweet the stream!

The poem from which these lines are taken was printed under the short and cryptic title *What?* but in manuscript it is given a longer and more revealing one—*What Happened to Me.* 'In blank autumn,' she cries, 'who can speak of love?'

Death, on the contrary, is infinitely to be desired. Sometimes it is an almost pagan desire, a Swinburnean wish that even the weariest river may run somewhere safe to sea:

   The wind shall lull us yet,
     The flowers shall spring above us:
   And those who hate forget,
     And those forget who love us.

   The pulse of hope shall cease,
     Of joy and of regretting:
   We twain shall sleep in peace,
     Forgotten and forgetting.

> For us no sun shall rise,
> Nor wind rejoice, nor river,
> Where we with fast-closed eyes
> Shall sleep and sleep for ever.

But, more often and more characteristically, she longs for the Christian heaven:

> O celestial mansion,
> Open wide the door:
> Crown and robes of whiteness,
> Stone inscribed before,
> Flocking angels bear them;
> Stretch thy hand and wear them,
> Sit thou down for evermore.

Somewhere in the course of her religious education Christina must have been taught, just as other good little Anglo-Catholics are taught in Sunday School, that the Church is divided into three parts, the Church militant, expectant and triumphant. Only this division between expectant and triumphant can explain the contradictory nature of her view of life after death. In poem after poem she writes of the dead as asleep:

> Underneath the growing grass,
> Underneath the living flowers,
> Deeper than the sound of showers:
> There we shall not count the hours
> By the shadows as they pass.

So she writes in a poem dated February 1854. But the sleeping dead are only waiting 'in darkness for beatitude to be'. A pair of sonnets entitled *Two Thoughts of Death*, although of no great literary merit, are worth study as illustrative of her very individual attitude towards death, at one and the same time extraordinarily morbid and unusually joyful. The first sonnet, crammed full of worms and corruption, is a production nasty enough to turn a squeamish stomach (it is tempting to remember the dead mouse in the garden at Holmer Green); the second is a triumphant answer to all this grisly horror:

> Her heart that loved me once is rottenness
>   Now and corruption; and her life is dead
>   That was to have been one with mine, she said.
> The earth must lie with such a cruel stress
> On eyes whereon the white lids used to press;
>   Foul worms fill up her mouth so sweet and red;
>   Foul worms are underneath her graceful head;
> Yet these, being born of her from nothingness;
> These worms are certainly flesh of her flesh.
>   How is it that the grass is rank and green
> And the dew-dropping rose is brave and fresh
> Above what was so sweeter far than they?
> Even as her beauty has passed quite away,
>   Theirs too shall be as if it had not been.
>
> So I said underneath the dusky trees:
>   But, because still I loved her memory,
>   I stooped to pick a pale anemone,
> And lo my hand lighted upon heartsease
> Not fully blown: while with new life from these
>   Fluttered a starry moth that rapidly
>   Rose toward the sun: sunlighted flashed on me
> Its wings that seemed to throb like heart-pulses.
>   Far far away it flew, far out of sight,—
> From earth and flowers of earth it passed away
> As though it flew straight up into the light.
>   Then my heart answered me: Thou fool, to say
>   That she is dead whose night is turned to day,
> And no more shall her day turn back to night.

Unlike Keats, Christina is not languidly 'half in love with easeful death'. For her, death is not to be desired as an escape from this naughty world but as an entry to another and incomparably better one. In her poetry she writes very precisely of the joys of heaven, a place full of flowers and trees and singing birds:

> I heard the songs of Paradise;
> Each bird sat singing in his place;
> A tender song so full of grace
> It soared like incense to the skies.
> Each bird sat singing to his mate
> Soft cooing notes among the trees:
> The nightingale herself were cold
> > To such as these.

Birds of Paradise—she was to treat this theme again later and with more imaginative power.

But the core and meaning of heaven is of course the presence of God. The most remarkable of the many remarkable religious poems of this period is written as a dialogue between the soul and God, slightly reminiscent of Herbert's dialogue poem beginning 'Sweetest Saviour if my soul were but worth the having':

> I will accept thy will to do and be,
> > Thy hatred and intolerance of sin,
> > Thy will at least to love, that burns within
> > And thirsteth after Me:
> So will I render fruitful, blessing still,
> > The germs and small beginnings in thy heart,
> > Because thy will cleaves to the better part.—
> > Alas, I cannot will.
>
> Dost not thou will, poor soul? Yet I receive
> > The inner unseen longings of the soul,
> > I guide them turning towards Me; I control
> > And charm hearts till they grieve:
> If thou desire, yet it shall come to pass,
> > Though thou but wish indeed to choose My love;
> > For I have power in earth and heaven above.—
> > I cannot wish, alas!

What, neither choose nor wish to choose? and yet
  I still must strive to win thee and constrain:
  For thee I hung upon the cross in pain,
How then can I forget?
If thou as yet dost neither love nor hate
  Nor choose nor wish,—resign thyself, be still,
  Till I infuse love, hatred, longing, will.—
I do not deprecate.

In spite of the unfortunate last line—schoolmistress Christina should have known that 'deprecate' cannot be used as an intransitive verb—these verses have an immediacy hitherto lacking in her religious poetry; it is as if she was turning slowly, painfully but with deliberate intention, away from human love, *eros*, to *agape*, the love of God. This remarkable poem was written on June 13th 1852; three days later she returned to her earlier, more mannered style in a little poem on Saint Elizabeth, interesting only as showing that her thoughts were still running on James Collinson and the picture which should have been, but certainly was not, a masterpiece. Of all the tensions which tore her apart and shaped both her character and her poetry by far the most acute, and the most fruitful, was the tension between the two loves, human and divine. As Maurice Bowra wrote, 'it was this conflict between her human self and her divine calling which created her most characteristic poetry'.[3]

Gabriele Rossetti did not long enjoy his pleasure at the reunion of his family. By the beginning of April 1854 he was so weak as to be hardly able to move. He lingered for a few weeks, confused in mind and pitifully frail in body, then on April 25th died quietly without a struggle. The last words of this one-time agnostic were '*Ah Dio, aiutami me*—O God, help me.' Towards the end of his life he had turned towards Christianity, not the Catholicism of his childhood but a vague Evangelical form of religion. His last published work had been a collection of Italian hymns, *Arpa Evangelica*, some of them translated into English by Christina.

At the time of his father's last illness Dante Gabriel was at Hastings, where he had gone with Lizzie, 'very unwell indeed', in the hope that sea-air might prove beneficial to her health. He returned to London in time to be present at his father's death-bed but hurried back to Hastings immediately after the funeral. Though he would not marry Lizzie he could not live without her. Defying convention, he had taken rooms for himself in the house where she lodged so that they could spend all day together. (As to the nights, who can say?)

The practical difficulty in the way of marriage was, of course, money. On his return to London Dante Gabriel saw much of John Ruskin, who, admiring Lizzie's artistic gift and wishing to be of help in this difficult situation, offered to settle £150 a year on her on condition that she sent him all her pictures to sell or keep as he wished, giving her any surplus over £150 that they might fetch.

On Lizzie's behalf Dante Gabriel accepted this generous offer. The financial obstacle had been at least partially removed; why then was there still no talk of marriage? The query remains unanswered and—as yet— unanswerable. Already some members of Dante Gabriel's family were treating Lizzie with kindness and familiarity, Aunt Charlotte Polidori, for instance, sending her the present of a shawl and Maria making en- quiries about Florence Nightingale's 'sanatorium' in Harley Street where it was suggested she might go for treatment for her increasing ill-health. On April 15th 1855, two days after Ruskin had made his welcome offer of help, Dante Gabriel took Lizzie to Albany Street for her first meeting with his mother. From now onwards Frances Rossetti was on reasonably good terms with her future daughter-in-law, accompanying her, for instance, on visits to the doctor, and having her to stay for the night—'I told her that I would ask you to give her a bed overnight, which I am sure you will do like a good old buncum'[4] Dante Gabriel wrote persuasively.

Christina, however, does not appear to have accepted Lizzie with any show of willingness. Almost immediately after her return from Frome Dante Gabriel invited her to meet Lizzie. 'Tell Christina that if she will come here on Thursday Lizzy will be here and she can also see that Gug's emanations' he wrote to William. 'I shall be glad if she will come, as I have told Lizzy [sic] she mentioned her wish to do so.'[5] Of this meeting between Lizzie and Christina no record remains. As a preliminary to possible publication Dante Gabriel was planning to show Christina's poems to William Allingham, best known as the author of 'Up the airy mountain, Down the rushy glen'.

> Allingham has been looking over her poems, and is delighted with many of them. I am going to lend them him (trusting in her permission to do so) that he may give his opinion as to which will be the best for a volume. Lizzy will illustrate and I have no doubt we shall get a publisher.[6]

This plan was never carried out, perhaps because Christina failed to show proper admiration for Lizzie and Lizzie's 'emanations'. William tells how Dante Gabriel 'was at times a little put out with the latter [Christina], thinking that her appreciation of Lizzie was not quite up to the mark'.[7] A passionate regard for truth made it impossible for her to make a tactful show of liking what in fact she did not like; and the result was a temporary coldness between brother and sister.

In March 1855 Christina collapsed with one of her mysterious illnesses, sometimes tentatively diagnosed as angina, sometimes as consumption. Perhaps because of this illness she was not present at the April meeting between Frances Rossetti and Lizzie. Later in the summer she was sent to Hastings to recuperate, and on her return to London spent a few days with the Madox Browns. 'There is a coldness between her and Gabriel because she and Guggums do not agree,' Brown noted in his diary. 'She works at worsted ever and talks sparingly.'[8] A postscript to a letter which Dante Gabriel wrote to Brown that same month of September might have provided another and valuable clue to Christina's feelings about Lizzie: 'I don't know about bringing Christina as . . . I don't encourage her'[9] this tantalising sentence reads, the missing words being obliterated by an ink-smudge.

Lizzie spent the winter of 1855–6 abroad for the sake of her health. Dante Gabriel sent her some charming verses on Saint Valentine's day:

> Come back, dear Liz, and looking wise
> In that arm-chair which suits your size,
> Through some fresh drawing scrape a hole.

Your Valentine and Orson's soul*
Is sick for those two friendly eyes.[10]

On Lizzie's return, however, there was still no talk of marriage, only a
constant and ever more noticeable decline in her health. Christina may
not have shown any great enthusiasm for Lizzie but in December 1856
she wrote a poem which summed up the situation in an unexpectedly
sympathetic and perceptive manner. It is headed *In an Artist's Studio*:

> One face looks out from all his canvases,
>   One selfsame figure sits or walks or leans:
>   We found her hidden just behind those screens,
> The mirror gave back all her loveliness.
> A queen in opal or in ruby dress,
>   A nameless girl in freshest summer-greens,
>   A saint, an angel—every canvas means
> The same one meaning, neither more nor less.
> He feeds upon her face by day and night,
>   And she with true kind eyes looks back on him,
> Fair as the moon and joyful as the light:
>   Not wan with waiting, not with sorrow dim;
> Not as she is, but was when hope shone bright;
>   Not as she is, but as she fills his dream.

Lizzie wept and stormed, took refuge with the Madox Browns or
wandered from place to place, ostensibly in search of health. Meanwhile,
in the summer of 1857, Dante Gabriel went down to Oxford, and with
two new friends of a younger generation of artists, William Morris and
Edward Burne-Jones, set about the business of covering the walls and
ceiling of the Union hall with frescoes which vanished almost as soon as
painted. At Oxford he met the daughter of a groom, a 'stunner' who was
to play a vital part in his life-history. Jane Burden was as dark as Lizzie
was fair. William Morris was another of her admirers, and he it was who
married her in April 1859; but that was not to be the end of the story.

*D.G.R. had been the model for Valentine and Lizzie for Silvia in a picture by Holman
Hunt illustrative of a scene from *The Two Gentlemen of Verona*.

At length, in 1860, Dante Gabriel made up his mind to marriage with his ailing and querulous Lizzie. The letter in which he told his mother of this decision carried the ominous date of Friday the thirteenth of April. Touchingly, and with typical generosity, he took all the blame on himself:

Like all the important things I ever meant to do—to fulfil duty or secure happiness—this one has been deferred almost beyond possibility. I have hardly deserved that Lizzie should still consent to it, but she has done so.[11]

The wedding took place on May 23rd; at last, after ten troubled years, Elizabeth Siddal and Dante Gabriel Rossetti were man and wife.

In this same year of Dante Gabriel's marriage William's long-drawn-out love affair came to an unhappy end. He had been quietly but deeply devoted to Henrietta Rintoul—'In refinement of mind, character, and demeanour she stood on a level which I have seldom known equalled, never surpassed.'[12] Because of financial difficulties William did not propose to Henrietta until January 1856; his family, however, were well aware of his attachment to her. Christina often mentions Henrietta in her letters to him while in a bantering letter dated March 3rd 1854 Dante Gabriel makes clear that he knows all about his brother's feeling:

I forgot to mention yesterday that MacCrac's daub* will be going on *Monday* . . . If therefore HENRIETTA wishes to see it (or rather if you cannot be put off bringing her) it must be before then.[13]

When at last William felt himself free to propose Henrietta accepted him without hesitation. However, although they had given him much tacit encouragement, both her parents objected to the match. Knowing that her father was in failing health Henrietta gave way and broke off the engagement, only to renew it almost immediately. Her father died in 1859, her mother in October 1860. In November of that year Henrietta told William that grief for her mother's death 'made her view with dismay

*The picture *Ecce Ancilla Domini*, bought by Francis MacCracken, a Belfast shipping agent.

the idea of forming any new ties',[14] and she asked him to release her from the engagement. William was naturally both puzzled and distressed, the more so because the vacillating Henrietta made no complaint against him personally but on the contrary appeared to be still much in love with him.

Christina's view of William's love for Henrietta differed greatly from her attitude towards Dante Gabriel and his Lizzie. She had made a friend of Henrietta, sending her messages in letters to William, and sometimes writing to her on her own account. Now both William and Henrietta turned to her for help in their unhappy predicament. In a letter to William dated November 30th 1860, almost immediately after the breaking of his engagement, she describes a meeting with Henrietta:

> I think you may like to see the note which I enclose; it reached me on Wednesday, and in consequence of it and of what you had told me I went yesterday to Henrietta and remained a considerable time with her.
>
> I never saw anything like her misery. She held me fast kissing me and crying, and I could feel how thin she is and how she trembled in my arms. It seemed some relief to her to tell me a great deal about what is past and what now is; poor dear, I pity her beyond what words can express, and would give much to comfort her effectually; but this is indeed not in my power. She has begged me to spend [a] great part of Thursday with her; and then if I can do nothing more I can at least pity and love her for your sake. If her happiness and yours were compatible, I would make a sacrifice to secure hers; but if otherwise, she cannot be dust in the balance with me, weighed against my most dear brother whom I love better than any man in the world and who has bought my gratitude by life-long kindness. . . . Of course, by the way, I took the little books back. I wish it were something better, but don't despise the love even a sister has to offer.[15]

Reading this warm-hearted letter, completely free from the embarrassingly sprightly, deliberately impersonal tone so characteristic of much of her surviving correspondence, it seems the more regrettable that many of her private letters must have disappeared, presumably destroyed in an all-too-successful attempt to preserve her privacy.

Badly hurt by Henrietta's puzzling defection, William determined to remain single, a resolution which he kept for a dozen years. Meanwhile Maria had also had her taste of unhappy love. The object of her affection was John Ruskin. In 1855, when Dante Gabriel was seeing much of Ruskin, Christina was first incapacitated by illness and then away from London at Hastings. Maria was therefore the only available Miss Rossetti, and it was Maria who was asked to dine in Ruskin's company, and Maria to whom he sent messages and paid some slight attention. Unused to the ways of men, Maria took this for more than it was worth. When she discovered that Ruskin meant nothing serious she reacted in typical manner. 'One of the most genuine Christians I ever knew, once took lightly the dying out of a brief acquaintance which had engaged her warm heart, on the ground that such tastes and glimpses of congenial intercourse on earth wait for their development in heaven.'[16]—so Christina wrote many years later in *Time Flies*, and in the margin of the copy she gave to her Aunt Eliza she scribbled the words, 'Maria with Ruskin'. Later, Maria was to be attracted in similar fashion to the artist Charles Allston Collins, again with no serious response on his side.

In the late eighteen-fifties love seemed to be the chief concern of the Rossetti family and their friends:

> All the world is making love:
>   Bird to bird in bushes,
> Beast to beast in glades, and frog
>   To frog among the rushes:
> Wake, O south wind sweet with spice,
>   Wake the rose to blushes.

So Christina wrote in June 1858 in one of her least successful poems. (Those frogs are surely not among her happier inventions.) As so often in her poetry *Today and Tomorrow* is written in two parts, the second one being in a different metre:

> I wish I were dead, my foe,
> My friend, I wish I were dead,
> With a stone at my tired feet
> And a stone at my tired head.

In the pleasant April days
Half the world will stir and sing,
But half the world will slug and rot
For all the sap of Spring.

According to the dictionary the verb 'slug' cannot be used as Christina uses it to suggest a horror of sliminess and unclean decay; but of all her many unorthodox and unusual words this is perhaps the most effective.

While Dante Gabriel, Maria, and William were all in pursuit of love Christina continued in her usual round of home duties and pleasures. In the autumn of 1854, however, she made an application which might have changed the whole course of her life had it met with success. She applied to go out to Scutari with her Aunt Eliza to nurse the wounded from the Crimea, but she was rejected as being too young. It would be interesting to know more about this abortive scheme, which is recorded only in one brief sentence of the *Memoir* which William attached to the *Collected Poems*.

For Christina the year 1855 had been a time of illness, but by November she was sufficiently recovered to take a temporary post as a governess with a family at Hampstead. Not surprisingly, her health gave way; and much to her relief it became clear that she was not strong enough for such work. 'I know I am rejoiced to feel that my health does really unfit me for miscellaneous governessing'[17] she wrote to William. Never again was she to attempt to work either as governess or schoolmistress; instead she did her best to contribute to the family income by literary hack-work such as articles for an encyclopedia or translations from the Italian.

Christina's life, though quiet, was neither uninteresting nor solitary. Immediately after telling us that 'like her mother, Christina went very little into society' William lists some fifty well-known personages whom, he says, 'she knew and appreciated'.[18] The list includes such characters as C. L. Dodgson ('Lewis Carroll'), Browning, Swinburne, Jean Ingelow, Edmund Gosse, Coventry Patmore, John Clayton of the stained glass firm of Clayton and Bell, and Lady Mount-Temple, wife of William Cowper-Temple, later Lord Mount-Temple, who gave his name to a

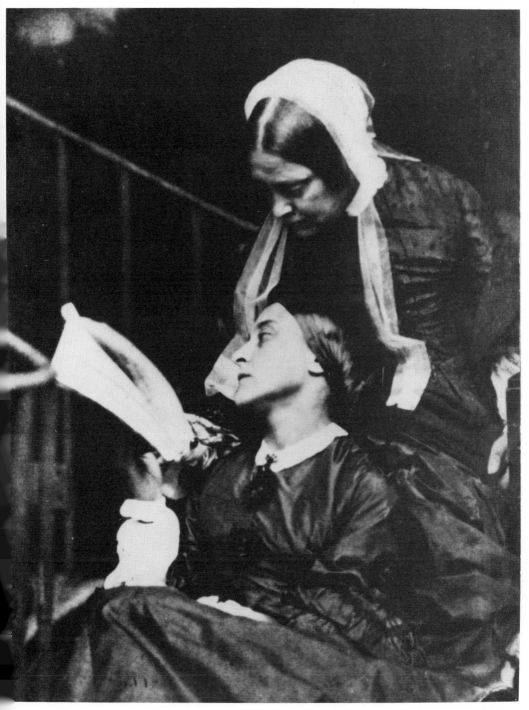

Christina and her mother. Photograph by Lewis Carroll

Three studies of animals from the Zoo, by Christina

famous clause in the 1870 Education Act and, more profitably, inherited Broadlands from his stepfather, Palmerston. She was also in touch with all the members of the Pre-Raphaelite circle, and with old friends such as Ann Gilchrist, widow of Blake's biographer, Mary and William Howitt, both of them authors in their own right and well-known in literary circles, and of course, William Bell Scott and his wife Letitia.

In June 1858 Christina spent a happy holiday in Newcastle with the Scotts. She was taken on expeditions and picnics, and introduced to interesting local characters such as Thomas Dixon, a cork-cutter of Sunderland who dabbled in literature, and Dora Greenwell the poetess, who came of a well-known Durham family whose most notable member was the eccentric fisherman and archaeologist, Canon Greenwell. Though now forgotten, in her own day Dora Greenwell was a minor celebrity, a writer who, in William Rossetti's phrase, 'produced some work both refined and of genuine feeling to which her appearance and manner corresponded'.[19]

Perhaps the most interesting part of Christina's Newcastle visit was the twenty-four hours she spent with Letitia Scott at Wallington, the home of Sir (Walter) Calverley Trevelyan and his wife Pauline. William Bell Scott did not accompany them but came next day to escort them back to Newcastle. He had already started on the work which he hoped would prove to be his *magnum opus*, the series of large frescoes depicting scenes from Northumbrian history, which were to decorate the newly-built great hall at Wallington.

In the train on her way back from Newcastle to London Christina wrote a short poem:

> Parting after parting
> All one's life long;
> It's a bitter pang, parting
> While love and life are strong.
>
> Parting after parting
> Sore fear and sore sore pain
> Till one dreads the pang of meeting
> More than of parting again.

When shall the day break
When this thing shall not be?
When shall the earth be born
That hath no more sea:
The time that is not time
But all eternity.

'The intensity of feeling here expressed really originated in a very slight occurrence—' writes the obviously puzzled William, 'the occurrence merely served the poet's turn as a suggestion of highly serious matters.'[20] Following her curious habit of adapting old poems to fit new subjects Christina resurrected this poem nearly thirty years later and printed part of it in *Time Flies*, applying it to the parting between the martyrs Saint Sixtus and Saint Laurence. This was the version printed in *Collected Poems*, much toned down from the original and with a final verse added which completely altered the emphasis:

To meet, worth living for;
Worth dying for, to meet;
To meet, worth parting for,
Bitter forgot in sweet;
To meet, worth parting before,
Never to part more.

Back home again, Christina was at pains to keep in touch with the Scotts and with the new friends she had made in the North, writing fairly frequently to Dora Greenwell, with whom she had struck up a real friendship, and also to Pauline Trevelyan. Reading these letters to Pauline it is clear that the two women were on more familiar terms than might be supposed from the formal opening, 'Dear Madam'. The Trevelyans owned a property in Devonshire where Pauline was anxious to encourage the traditional craft of lace-making. Christina succeeds in selling some lace collars for her, and buys some more to be given away as Christmas gifts. She enquires in detail about the progress of Scott's plan for the decoration of the great hall, she tells how she has shaken hands with the Bishop of London—'I cannot help suspecting he may have taken me for someone else, which tempers my elation at the incident'—and she asks warmly after Pauline's pet dog. Finally, she makes a significant request; she begs Pauline to accept a special present:

> You have several times and in various ways given me pleasure: let me now ask you to please me once more but in quite a novel fashion, by accepting a new metrical version of the Psalms, just published by our old friend Mr Cayley.[21]

The Rossettis first met Charles Cayley when, as a young man in his twenties, he came to their house to learn Italian from Gabriele. He was a brilliant linguist, mastering any language easily, and translating not only Dante—his translation of *The Divine Comedy* into the same metre as the original was something of a *tour de force*—but also Homer, Aeschylus, Petrarch, and the Hebrew Psalms (this was the book which Christina planned to give to Pauline Trevelyan). Even Red Indian tongues presented him with no insuperable difficulties; he superintended a translation of the New Testament into the language of the Iroquois tribe.

Cayley started life as a Civil Servant, but having adequate private means he abandoned this career in favour of literary work and scholarship. Unfortunately, he invested all his capital in an advertising venture which went bankrupt, leaving him penniless. Money, however, meant nothing to this gentle scholar. He came of a well-to-do family and with kind relations at hand to see that he did not want for absolute essentials he was completely content. What other people regarded as necessities were to him pointless luxury. His clothes, for instance, were of great age and shabbiness, though William maintained there was always an air of 'prim decorum' about his dress. Madox Brown, however, describes Cayley's manner of dressing as neither prim nor decorous—'I forgot Cayley, who looked mad, and is always in a rumpled shirt with no collar, and an old tail coat.'[22] His speech was so badly articulated as to be barely intelligible. When spoken to he would pause for a long time before answering, then let his words come tumbling out in a flustered rush.

Charles Cayley had dark hair and eyes and a massive forehead. As a young man he is said to have been good-looking but the few surviving likenesses seem to show that his looks did not last. Clearly he was not a man with any great liking for society nor was he an ornament to any party—William tells how his arrival was always greeted with apprehension because 'some degree of embarrassment was sure to ensue'.[23] Yet this shy, awkward person was very much a gentleman, notably punctilious and polite, and meticulously observant of small social conventions such as morning calls which were already regarded as old-fashioned. Above all, he was unworldly, the perfect example of the abstracted scholar. Unlike the unworldly Christina he was not preoccupied with dreams of heaven—he seems to have been an agnostic—but he was so sunk in his own thoughts as to be oblivious of people and surroundings. Mrs Packer tells how he went with a friend and her children to the British Museum to see the bones of an ichthyosaurus. The skeleton had not been completely assembled and was therefore not on public view. An official let them into a locked room, and when they had gazed their fill at the monster, let them out again, locking the door behind them. They had gone some way when one of the children exclaimed, 'But where is Mr Cayley?' Back they had to go and persuade the keeper to unlock the room once more. There they found Charles Cayley, 'like Jonah, deep in the interior of the whale, hands folded behind his back, gazing meditatively at the exhibit, totally unaware that the others had gone and he had been left behind.'[24]

Such a man was not, on the surface, attractive to women; but he might hold a strong appeal for a woman, no longer very young, who valued the things of the mind and who was not to be put off by his unworldliness but who was on the contrary drawn to him by that very quality. 'I have met many men who had a larger share of the active virtues than Charles Cayley,' William was to write, 'but none who seemed freer from aught that savoured of the wrongful or the mean—none who loved the intellectual life with so little obstruction from the world, the flesh, and the devil.'[25] In short, Charles Cayley was an oddity, but for a woman who troubled to look below the surface, an oddity with a brilliant brain and a very loving heart.

Immediately after Gabriele's death, all his family, as the custom then was, had written an account of his last days, to which Christina had contributed one sentence, 'Mr Cayley called twice at the very last, and waited, but did not see my father, much endearing himself to us.'[26] In years to come Cayley was to endear himself greatly to Christina, but they were not to see much of each other for another six years. It is possible, however, that during that time Christina's thoughts were turning towards Cayley; perhaps she recognised the small, secret beginnings of love before he did. Two poems written in the winter of 1857 deal with the theme of a woman's secret:

> Now if I could guess her secret
> 　Were it worth the guess?
> Time is lessening, hope is lessening,
> 　Love grows less and less. . . .
>
> I will give her stately burial,
> 　Stately willow branches bent
> Have her carved in alabaster
> 　As she dreamt and leant
> While I wondered what she meant.

A month earlier she had written some other verses, in a different, light-hearted mood but basically on this same theme. This time it is the woman who speaks:

> I tell my secret? No, indeed, not I:
> Perhaps some day, who knows?
> But not today; it froze, and blows, and snows,
> And you're too curious: fie!
> You want to hear it? well:
> Only my secret's mine, and I won't tell. . . .
>
> Perhaps some languid summer day,
> When drowsy birds sing less and less,
> And golden fruit is ripening to excess,
> If there's not too much sun nor too much cloud,
> And the warm wind is neither still nor loud,
> Perhaps my secret I may say,
> Or you may guess.

Chapter Six

Goblin Market

In 1860 Christina began a work which she was to continue for the next ten years. The problem of prostitution weighed heavily on the Victorian conscience. Dante Gabriel showed his preoccupation with it in his poem *Jenny* and in the painting, *Found*, to which he returned again and again without succeeding in producing a finished version. Women were as much concerned as men; Mrs Gladstone, for instance, helped her husband with his rescue work and on occasion did some 'rescuing' on her own account. Christina herself worked from 1860 to 1870 at the House of Charity at Highgate, a penitentiary run by Anglican nuns. There is no record of the exact nature of the work she was called upon to do; but whatever she did she must have done well since William says that she was offered some sort of position as superintendent, an offer she wisely declined. She would sometimes stay for quite long periods at the House of Charity; Letitia Scott describes her dressed in the habit of an Associate of the Order, 'very simple, elegant even; black with hanging sleeves, a muslin cap with lace edging, quite becoming to her with the veil'.[1]

The inmates of the House of Charity are described as 'fallen women'. Many were certainly prostitutes; but others would have been merely unmarried mothers, girls who had been, in the language of the day, 'ruined' by some unscrupulous man. Some of Christina's poems of this period seem to be connected with her preoccupation with these women. In *Cousin Kate* a 'cottage maiden' loves and is betrayed by a 'great lord':

> He lured me to his palace home—
> Woe's me for joy thereof—
> To lead a shameless shameful life,
> His plaything and his love.
> He wore me like a golden knot,

He changed me like a glove:
So now I moan an unclean thing
Who might have been a dove.

She is in fact forsaken for her equally plebeian but more virtuous, or perhaps more prudent, cousin Kate, who could not be had without a wedding-ring:

Because you were so good and pure
He bound you with his ring:
The neighbours call you good and pure,
Call me an outcast thing.
Even so I sit and howl in dust,
You sit in gold and sing;
Now which of us has tenderest heart?
You had the stronger wing.

The discarded mistress, however, holds the ace of trumps:

Yet I've a gift you have not got
And seem not like to get:
For all your clothes and wedding-ring
I've little doubt you fret.
My fair-haired son, my shame, my pride,
Cling closer, closer yet:
Your sire would give broad lands for one
To wear his coronet.

Seldom does Christina descend to these depths of bathos; but the poem is interesting as showing her concern for the unmarried mother and her child.

Under the Rose, written in 1865 and in 1872 clumsily retitled *The Iniquity of the Fathers Upon the Children*, deals with the same situation from the point of view of the child rather than the mother. This time it is the woman who is the aristocrat, and who dares not acknowledge the daughter she bore to an unnamed lover. Mrs Packer justly praises this poem not for its literary merit but for its remarkable insight into a situation which Christina could only know at second-hand. 'Christina's treatment of the subject, which is frank, realistic, unsentimental, and psychologically convincing, seems decades ahead of the mid-century Victorian novelists on the same subject.'[2]

In her manuscript book Christina wrote the words 'House of Charity' against another poem written this same year of 1865:

> Go from me, summer friends, and tarry not:
>   I am no summer friend but wintry cold;
>   A silly sheep benighted from the fold,
> A sluggard with a thorn-choked garden plot.
> Take counsel, sever from my lot your lot,
>   Dwell in your pleasant places, hoard your gold;
>   Lest you with me should shiver on the wold,
> Athirst and hungering on a barren spot.
> For I have hedged me with a thorny hedge,
>   I live alone, I look to die alone.
> Yet sometimes when a wind sighs through the sedge
> Ghosts of my buried years and friends come back,
>   My heart goes sighing after swallows flown
> On sometime summer's unreturning track.

William was puzzled by the connection between this sonnet and the House of Charity, thinking it too personal in tone to be regarded as an utterance put into the mouth of one of the women there. Obsessed as usual by the notion that Christina was in love with Scott, Mrs Packer sees it as evidence that 'she did not consider the gap between herself and the Highgate penitents so wide as to appear incomprehensible'[3]—not, be it noted, because she was a compassionate and humble Christian but because she had herself known the temptation of a guilty love. A more reasonable explanation of the connection with the House of Charity is to see this poem as yet another example of Christina's gift of allowing her imagination to dwell upon some experience, perhaps even a mere hint or suggestion, taken from her reading or from her daily life, in this case from her work among 'fallen women', and turning it over and over until it changed into something personal to herself and grew into the stuff of poetry.

Another and very moving poem which appears to be the fruit of this same process was written in June 1861 and headed *Wife to Husband*. 'I am not aware that this poem has any individual application', wrote William. 'If any, it might perhaps be to my brother's wife, whose constant and severe ill-health permitted no expectation of her living long.'[4] Like the sonnet *In an Artist's Studio*, a poem more obviously connected with Lizzie, *Wife to Husband* stresses the tragedy of change and decay in love:

> Pardon the faults in me
>   For the love of years ago:
>   Good-bye.
> I must drift across the sea,
>   I must sink into the snow,
>   I must die.
>
> You can bask in the sun,
>   You can drink wine, and eat:
>   Good-bye.
> I must gird myself and run,
>   Though with unready feet:
>   I must die.
>
> Blank sea to sail upon,
>   Cold bed to sleep in:
>   Good-bye.
> While you clasp, I must be gone
>   For all your weeping:
>   I must die.
>
> A kiss for one friend,
>   And a word for two,—
>   Good-bye:—
> A lock that you must send,
>   A kindness you must do:
>   I must die.

> Not a word for you,
> Not a lock or kiss,
> Good-bye.
> We, one, must part in two;
> Verily death is this:
> I must die.

'The love of years ago' between Dante Gabriel and Lizzie had indeed all but vanished. In January 1861 she had given birth to a stillborn daughter, and from then onwards she declined rapidly in health and spirits. Though Dante Gabriel showed compassion and patience her bouts of black depression and her difficult behaviour put a heavy strain on their already fragile relationship.

Christina's reaction to her brother's marriage had not been an enthusiastic one. Writing to a friend she pointed out that she herself had known the bride but slightly and that several years ago, and she stressed the drawback of Lizzie's poor health. In the two years between the wedding-day and Lizzie's tragic death there is no record of any meeting between the two women though both of them must have been present at some at least of the family tea-drinkings and other occasions mentioned in Dante Gabriel's letters.

Both Christina and Lizzie were, in their different ways, very shy creatures, so that a *rapprochement* between them would have been difficult in any case. The coldness between Dante Gabriel and Christina caused by her attitude towards Lizzie had, however, proved to be only a temporary cloud. He was deeply interested in her writing and much occupied with efforts to get some of it published. Her poems circulated from hand to hand among an admiring circle of friends and acquaintances, but apart from Grandfather Polidori's volume of juvenilia the only ones which had as yet appeared in print were two published many years previously in the *Athenaeum* and the few which had appeared in the short-lived *Germ*.

Dante Gabriel's first idea was to approach John Ruskin. 'I asked Ruskin whether he would say a good word for something of Christina's to the *Cornhill*,' he wrote to William on January 18th 1861, 'and he promised to do so if she liked. If so, would she send me by book-post the book containing the poem about the two Girls and the Goblins?'[5] (This, incidentally, is the first mention of Christina's best-known poem, *Goblin Market*.) He was also anxious to show Ruskin a story entitled 'Folio Q', which William regarded as the best of her prose tales; but unfortunately Christina herself destroyed this possible masterpiece—most of her prose stories are uncommonly dull—for the improbable reason that it appeared to raise 'dangerous moral problems'. Ruskin, however, proved singularly unhelpful and obtuse. His letter dated January 24th 1861 was justly described by Dante Gabriel as 'most senseless':

> I sat up till late last night reading poems. They are full of beauty and power. But no publisher—I am deeply grieved to know this—would take them, so full are they of quaintnesses and offences. Irregular measure (introduced to my great regret, in its chief wilfulness by Coleridge) is the calamity of modern poetry. The *Iliad*, the *Divina Commedia*, the *Aeneid*, the whole of Spenser, Milton, Keats are written without taking a single licence or violating the common ear for metre; your sister should exercise herself in the severest commonplace of metre until she can write as the public like. Then if she puts in her observation and passion all will become precious. But she must have the Form first.[6]

Dante Gabriel now proposed to send *Goblin Market* to Mrs Gaskell the novelist, 'who is good-natured and appreciative, and might get it into the *Cornhill*',[7] but nothing seems to have come of this idea. He had already approached Alexander Macmillan, an up-and-coming young publisher whose Thursday evening 'tobacco parliaments' were frequented by the new generation of authors and artists, including the Rossetti brothers and other members of the now defunct P.R.B. Macmillan agreed to publish *Up-hill* in the February number of *Macmillan's Magazine*. The success of what Dante Gabriel described as 'your lively little Song of the Tomb'[8] was instantaneous and complete; Macmillan was much congratulated on his discovery of a new poet. His choice had been a wise one; *Up-hill* appeals to a wide variety of readers and it has remained a steady favourite, to be found today in many anthologies:

Does the road wind up-hill all the way?
   Yes, to the very end.
Will the day's journey take the whole long day?
   From morn to night, my friend.

But is there for the night a resting-place?
   A roof for when the slow dark hours begin.
May not the darkness hide it from my face?
   You cannot miss that inn.

Shall I meet other wayfarers at night?
   Those who have gone before.
Then must I knock, or call when just in sight?
   They will not keep you standing at that door.

Shall I find comfort, travel-sore and weak?
   Of labour you shall find the sum.
Will there be beds for me and all who seek?
   Yea, beds for all who come.

Delighted with the success of this poem Macmillan printed *A Birthday* in the April number of the magazine and *An Apple Gathering* in the August one. Once again he had chosen well. *A Birthday* is the only one of Christina's better-known poems to deal with the happy fulfilment of love; nearly all her work is sorrowful in tone, but this piece overflows with joy:

My heart is like a singing bird
   Whose nest is in a watered shoot:
My heart is like an apple-tree
   Whose boughs are bent with thickset fruit;
My heart is like a rainbow shell
   That paddles in a halcyon sea;
My heart is gladder than all these
   Because my love is come to me.

An Apple Gathering will not stand comparison with either *Up-hill* or *A Birthday*. It is a simple enough parable—pick the apple-blossom and you will have no fruit—but though melancholy it is in no sense morbid, an accusation often brought against Christina's poetry.

Eighteen sixty-one was, on the whole, a happy year for Christina. For the first time she achieved a measure of real success as a writer, and though she could tell Mrs Heimann, an old family friend, that of necessity she was 'husbanding my not exuberant strength'[9] she was nevertheless enjoying what was for her a period of good health. 'Perhaps the least unhealthy years of her womanhood were towards 1861,'[10] William was to write. Then, in June, she had the treat of a first holiday abroad, when she went with William and her mother to France, visiting Paris, and from there going on to Rouen, Saint Lô, Avranches, Coutances (where they stayed for nearly three weeks) and home by way of Jersey.

In the autumn came what must always be one of the most thrilling moments in an author's life, the acceptance of her first book for publication. Alexander Macmillan planned to bring out her poems in 'an exceedingly pretty little volume', but he did not appear to be particularly enthusiastic about this project. 'I quite think a selection of them would have a chance—or to put it more truly that with some omissions they might do', he wrote to Dante Gabriel. 'At least I would run the risk of a small edition.'[11] The book was to be called *Goblin Market* and was to include a selection of lyrics as well as the title-poem. Dante Gabriel was to supply two woodcuts as illustrations. So speedy was the publishing process in 1861 that *Goblin Market* was planned as a Christmas book for that year, but in the event it did not appear until March 1862, less than a month after Lizzie Rossetti had died of an overdose of laudanum.

Of Christina's reaction to this tragedy we know nothing. As so often at a crucial moment in her life no letters survive, no scrap of notes or diary, no word of oral tradition to tell us something of her thoughts and feelings. She had few intimate friends and no regular correspondents apart from the members of her own family, who were all at home at the time of Lizzie's death; no need, therefore, for letter-writing. Unable to face the house at Chatham Place with its memories of Lizzie, Dante Gabriel came back to the family home and remained there until he could find rooms for himself in Lincoln's Inn Fields. In October he moved to

Tudor House, Cheyne Walk, an old house overlooking the river which he had loved so well at Chatham Place. At the back of the house was a large garden where he could keep a menagerie of strange birds and animals, peacocks, racoons, an armadillo, a zebra, and a furry wombat which was Christina's favourite. (It was she, and not Dante Gabriel, who had first discovered one of these charming little creatures at the zoo.)

Like the good brother that he was Dante Gabriel took real pleasure in the success of Christina's book, sending her copies of reviews, which were on the whole enthusiastic although the sales were at first slightly disappointing. Reading these poems the first impression is one of freshness. Here is a new and very individual voice. Christina has two gifts invaluable to any singer whether poet or musician, a clear, pure tone, and a very acute ear. 'Your instinct was so clear, so direct, so intense,' Virginia Woolf wrote of her, 'that it produced poems that sing like music in one's ears—like a melody by Mozart or an air by Gluck.'[12] The irregularity which so much displeased Ruskin is of the greatest charms of her poetry; in her verse 'it is this quality of the unexpected, the avoidance of the *cliché* in metre, the fact that here and there you must beat time in a rest of the melody, that gives it its fascination and its music,'[13] said Ford Madox Ford.

Nowhere is her technical skill more apparent than in the title poem, *Goblin Market*. Maurice Bowra speaks of 'her command of a rippling metre';[14] but sometimes she ripples so much that she approaches perilously near to a Gilbert and Sullivan patter-song:

> It suffices. What suffices?
> All suffices, reckoned rightly;
> Spring shall bloom where now the ice is.

In *Goblin Market*, however, this short, tripping metre exactly suits the fairy-tale subject, and here Christina varies it with a skill that amounts almost to genius:

> Come buy, come buy:
> Our grapes fresh from the vine,
> Pomegranates full and fine,

> Dates and sharp bullaces,
> Rare pears and greengages,
> Damsons and bilberries,
> Taste them and try:
> Currants and gooseberries,
> Bright-fire-like barberries,
> Figs to fill your mouth,
> Citrons from the South,
> Sweet to tongue and sound to eye;
> Come buy, come buy.

Goblin Market is perhaps the best known and most admired of Christina's poems, and with good reason, for *Goblin Market* is that rare thing, a wholly satisfactory narrative poem. Christina's poetic invention never flags; she manages to hold our attention from beginning to end. The story is a fairy-tale with overtones. Day after day two sisters, Laura and Lizzie, hear the goblins crying their wares. Lizzie flees from temptation but Laura is less prudent. One evening she buys the goblin fruit with a curl from her golden head and eats her fill. When she returns home Lizzie gently upbraids her:

> Dear, you should not stay so late,
> Twilight is not good for maidens;
> Should not loiter in the glen
> In the haunts of goblin men.
> Do you not remember Jeanie,
> How she met them in the moonlight,
> Took their gifts both choice and many,
> Ate their fruits and wore their flowers
> Plucked from bowers
> Where summer ripens at all hours?
> But ever in the moonlight
> She pined and pined away;
> Sought them by night and day,
> Found them no more, but dwindled and grew grey;
> Then fell with the first snow.

Laura now begins to pine away as Jeanie had pined, craving the magic fruit which no one may taste twice. Those who have fallen victim to the goblins' wiles can never again hear them calling, never again buy their wares. But Lizzie hears them:

> Beside the brook, along the glen,
> She heard the tramp of goblin men,
> The voice and stir
> Poor Laura could not hear;
> Longed to buy fruit to comfort her,
> But feared to pay too dear.

At length Lizzie masters her fear and seeks out the goblins, begging them to sell her their fruit so that she can take it back to Laura. This they will not do unless she first tastes it herself and when she refuses they set upon her:

> Their tones waxed loud,
> Their looks were evil.
> Lashing their tails
> They trod and hustled her,
> Clawed with their nails,
> Barking, mewing, hissing, mocking,
> Tore her gown and soiled her stocking,
> Twitched her hair out by the roots,
> Stamped upon her tender feet,
> Held her hands and squeezed their fruits
> Against her mouth to make her eat.

But she is not to be moved: and at last the goblins tire of tormenting her and vanish. With her face covered with fruit pulp and running with juice she hurries home to Laura and cries to her to make haste:

> Hug me, kiss me, suck my juices
> Squeezed from goblin fruits for you,
> Goblin pulp and goblin dew.

Eat me, drink me, love me:
Laura, make much of me;
For your sake I have braved the glen
And had to do with goblin merchant men.

Laura is saved by Lizzie's self-sacrifice; she will never forget 'how her sister stood, In deadly peril to do her good. And win the fiery antidote'. Some readers may feel that the poem falls away at the end and that the last six lines sound a note of bathos:

For there is no friend like a sister
In calm or stormy weather;
To cheer one on the tedious way,
To fetch one if one goes astray,
To lift one if one totters down,
To strengthen whilst one stands.

Others may be reminded of the last scene of *Don Giovanni* when after the statue of the Commendatore has dragged the Don down to hell the remaining characters step forward and in a brief finale bid the audience consider the all-too-evident moral of the tale. Perhaps both Christina Rossetti and Mozart thought some drop in tension was advisable before the return to everyday life; or perhaps they feared that, left to ourselves, our sympathies would be with the reprehensible Laura and Don Giovanni rather than with the virtuous but slightly boring Lizzie and Don Ottavio.

The moral of Christina's fable must not be pressed too hard since she herself said that in her own intention *Goblin Market* was no allegory at all. The poem can be read at many levels of meaning, as a straightforward fairy-story, as a parable of temptation, sin and redemption, as a hymn in praise of sisterly devotion, or as a sexual fantasy. The sexual interpretation has been applied ribaldly in an article in the magazine *Playboy*, and in all seriousness by Mrs Packer, and by Maureen Duffy in *The Erotic World of Faery*. Mrs Packer provides 'an analysis of the poem in the light of the emotional facts of Christina's life,'[15] that is to say, in the light of the 'fact' of her 'outlawed love' for Scott.

A month before Christina finished *Goblin Market* Scott, while painting at Wallington, met Alice Boyd, a handsome woman in her thirties and herself something of an artist. From this meeting sprang what Scott himself described as 'friendship at first sight', a friendship which soon developed into a thoroughgoing and lifelong love-affair. 'That Scott could have "turned from one love to another" with such apparent ease must have been a serious shock to Christina,' Mrs Packer writes. 'His behaviour would have shown her the unstable nature of his earlier attachment to her, would have revealed the depth of the abyss into which she had almost plunged, the peril of the temptation from which, like Laura, she had been saved.'[16] (Laura, by the way, had not been saved from temptation but had yielded to it.)

Maureen Duffy does not connect the poem with any actual love of Christina's but instead sees it as an erotic fantasy, a collection of sexual symbols. Thus the goblins 'are mostly in phallic bird and fish forms'[17] and the two sisters, Laura and Lizzie, are an example of 'the double female image' which is 'an interesting component of the period's eroticism'.[18] Dante Gabriel's woodcut of the sisters folded in each other's arms certainly bears out this theory. According to Maureen Duffy 'two girls entwined "cheek to cheek and breast to breast Locked together in one nest" are no longer individuals but duplicate images ripe for polygamy'.[19] Christina herself, however, did not see them thus; whatever notions may have been floating about in her subconscious mind, consciously she may well have remembered her father's description of herself and Maria as 'lovely turtle-doves in the nest of love', a description which of course can have been itself an unconscious piece of eroticism.

The sexual undertones in *Goblin Market* are fairly obvious. Even small children, too young to be aware of sex, sometimes find themselves, for no reason that they can understand or explain, obscurely puzzled and embarrassed by the poem. A sexual interpretation is a legitimate and convincing one, but it must not be pushed too far nor must it be regarded as the only permissible meaning. Readers instinctively equate the goblin fruit with illicit sexual experience and, because this fruit can only be enjoyed once, they connect it, though less definitely, with the loss of virginity. Almost certainly this is what Christina herself understood and intended; but further than this she did not go, nor did she, consciously at least, read any sexual significance into the details of her parable. Of course she was interested in love and sex, and of course she was strongly affected by the fact that her own sexual desires had not been satisfied; she would have been less than human otherwise. But if she was pre-occupied with *eros* she was far more deeply preoccupied with *agape*. The religion to which she sacrificed her hopes of sexual love was the very core and centre of her life; and although it has been almost wholly neglected by the critics, the religious interpretation of *Goblin Market* is much nearer to her own way of thought than the sexual one.

Goblin Market has obvious connections with the story of Eve, a theme which occurs frequently in Christina's poetry, in *An Afterthought* for instance, and in *Bird and Beast*. One of her most quoted poems is actually entitled *Eve*—a poem like *Goblin Market* written in the short irregular metre which is particularly her own:

> How have Eden bowers grown
> Without Adam to bend them?
> How have Eden flowers blown,
> Squandering their sweet breath,
> Without me to tend them?
> The Tree of Life was ours,
> Tree twelvefold-fruited,
> Most lofty tree that flowers,
> Most deeply rooted:
> I chose the Tree of Death.

Laura cannot resist temptation; she eats the goblin fruit, dwindles and pines, apparently 'knocking at Death's door'. So the human race, in the person of Eve, is tempted by the serpent and eats 'the fruit of that for-bidden tree whose mortal taste Brought death into the world and all our woe'. Laura is saved by the self-sacrifice of her sister, who deliberately faces temptation but does not yield to it. Lizzie stands up to the vicious attacks of the goblins, braving mockery and terror and pain, and through her suffering she wins 'the fiery antidote' which alone can save Laura. According to the Christian faith, Christ, the brother of us all, of his own will chose to face temptation, to suffer and to die, and by his sacrifice to win salvation for mankind. The parallel is obvious. Again, details must

not be pressed too hard* nor must this explanation be regarded as exclud-
ing all others; but if the sexual interpretation throws some light on
Christina's subconscious mind the Christian one is closer to her conscious
thought.

The shorter poems in the *Goblin Market* volume are divided into two
sections, religious and secular. The secular section is a well-chosen and
comprehensive selection from the poems she was writing from about
1848 to 1861. Here are two of the best of her sonnets, *Remember Me* and
After Death; here are poems reminiscent of Border ballads; and here too
is *In the Round Tower at Jhansi*, a successful experiment in the manner
of Browning, its subject an actual incident during the Indian Mutiny.
Significantly, the book contains no less than four poems listed simply as
'Song'; and many more might be so described, for the general tone is
lyrical in the strict sense of that word.

Not all the poems, however, fall into this category. Two ballads,
Sister Maude and *Noble Sisters*, tell of the treachery of a sister in contradiction of the moral so carefully explained at the end of *Goblin Market*.
That sinister little colloquy, *The Hour and the Ghost*, is a good example
of Christina's preoccupation with the occult and the macabre. (The still
more sinister poem, *A Nightmare*, was written about this time but not
published till after her death.) One longer poem is in a class by itself.

---

*It is tempting, though not perhaps permissible, to see some connection between
Christina's notion that Laura can only be saved by the same fruits which brought
about her downfall and the idea of the two trees expressed in the ancient Office-hymn
for Passion Sunday:

> When he [man] fell on death by tasting
>   Fruit of the forbidden tree,
> Then another tree was chosen
>   Which the world from death should free.

The tree of Eden has brought death; the tree of Calvary brings salvation.

> Thus the scheme of our salvation
>   Was of old in order laid,
> That the manifold deceiver's
>   Art by art might be outweighed.
> *And the lure the foe put forward*
>   *Into means of healing made.*

William describes *My Dream* as an example of 'the odd freakishness which flecked the extreme and almost excessive seriousness of her thought'.[20]

Mrs Packer treats this poem simply as a sex fantasy. She will have it that the magnificent and terrifying crocodile of Christina's dream represents Scott, her supposed lover, because 'beauty inspires terror only in a love relationship',[21] a statement of doubtful validity, to say the least. She quotes the horrifying lines describing how the crowned crocodile devours all the other crocodiles:

> An execrable appetite arose,
> He battened on them, crunched, and sucked them in.
> He knew no law, he feared no binding law,
> But ground them with inexorable jaw.
> The luscious fat distilled upon his chin,
> While still like hungry death he fed his maw;
> Till, every minor crocodile being dead
> And buried too, himself gorged to the full,
> He slept with breath oppressed and unstrung claw.

'Read symbolically,' Mrs Packer comments, 'the lines reveal their sexual significance, for what Christina is doing here is substituting one sort of sensuous appetite for another, a common form of displacement in dreams.'[22] This may make sense; but nevertheless there is no ground for identifying Christina's love, and therefore the crocodile, with Bell Scott. To put either James Collinson or Charles Cayley in the place of this regal monster is palpably absurd. If *My Dream* is to be interpreted sexually— and such an interpretation may well be the correct one—the crocodile must be taken as representing the Male in general, not any particular man.

The poem has all the nightmare inconsequence of a real dream. Standing by the river Euphrates the dreamer sees a host of young crocodiles:

> Each crocodile was girt with massive gold
> And polished stones that with their wearers grew

After this typical dream fantasy of growing jewels she describes how one crocodile grew larger and more powerful than the rest:

But special burnishment adorned his mail
And special terror weighed upon his frown

This crocodile devours all the other crocodiles and, satiated, falls asleep.
Now comes, as in a real dream, a totally inconsequent development:

In sleep he dwindled to the common size,
And all the empire faded from his coat.
Then from far off a wingèd vessel came,
Swift as a swallow, subtle as a flame;
I know not what it bore of freight or host,
But white it was as an avenging ghost.

The crocodile's reaction to this strange craft is surprising:

Lo, as the purple shadow swept the sands,
The prudent crocodile rose on his feet
And shed appropriate tears and wrung his hands.

The picture of a crocodile wringing his hands suggests a conceit out of
Alice in Wonderland, another dream fantasy which the pundits regard as
sexual in origin. Oddest of all is the epithet 'prudent'. Dante Gabriel,
for no apparent reason, borrowed this term as a nickname for William
Morris, a man who bore no resemblance to a crocodile and who was
certainly not prudent.

In the poem itself Christina emphatically declares that the dream was a
real one—'Hear now a curious dream I dreamed last night. Each word
whereof is weighed and sifted truth'—but against her own copy she
wrote the words 'Not a real dream'. What then is the origin of this
astonishing fancy? The obvious comparison is with De Quincey's
opium-induced visions of the horrible, ubiquitous crocodile: 'All the
feet of the tables, sofas etc. soon became instinct with life: the abominable
head of the crocodile and his leering eyes looked out at me multiplied
into a thousand repetitions; and I stood loathing and fascinated.' There is
no evidence, however, to prove that Christina ever read that particular
passage from *The Confessions of an English Opium-Eater*, much less that

it was in her mind when writing *My Dream*. Apart from De Quincey, the nearest literary parallel is to be found in the Bible, in the Old Testament prophets and in particular the Book of Daniel—is this the explanation of the reference to the Euphrates?—and in the New Testament Apocalypse or Book of Revelation. Christina was a great student of the Bible with a special liking for the Apocalypse (in later life she was to write a devotional commentary on that book). She had a remarkably vivid visual imagination and plenty of time for day-dreaming. Some of these day-dreams may have taken the form of quasi-visions akin to the biblical visions which were so much in her mind. So Christina may have 'seen' her crocodile fantasy, but realising that most readers would have no experience of such waking dreams or visions, she transposed it into a sleeping dream. It was for a later generation, reared on modern psychology rather than on Bible stories, to interpret her vision as an emanation from her subconscious mind, probably sexual in origin. Christina herself was at a loss as to its meaning. (Significantly enough, biblical visions were often incomprehensible to the visionary until they were interpreted.)

> What can it mean? you ask. I answer not
> For meaning, but myself must echo, What?

The puzzled reader can only re-echo that query.

The third section of the *Goblin Market* volume is headed 'Devotional Pieces'. On the whole it is disappointing, though it contains a few remarkable poems. Christina herself chose the verses to be included, with help from Dante Gabriel and from Macmillan, and therefore it is she who is herself responsible for placing *Sleep at Sea* in this section. If this haunting poem is a religious poem so too is *The Ancient Mariner*. Here also is *A Better Resurrection*, one of the most notable of her religious poems:

> I have no wit, no words, no tears;
>   My heart within me like a stone
> Is numbed too much for hopes or fears.
>   Look right, look left, I dwell alone;

> I lift mine eyes, but dimmed with grief
>   No everlasting hills I see;
> My life is in the falling leaf;
>   O Jesus, quicken me.

The cry is one of such purely human anguish that the last line strikes on
the reader with a sense of shock. For Christina there was no deep division
between *eros* and *agape*, love human and love divine; she saw the two as
very closely akin. There is a curious and touching purity in her *eros*
feeling; there is passion in her conception of *agape*.

One of the very last poems in the volume is a *tour de force*. Christina,
who was never particularly happy in her choice of titles, incongruously
lists it as an 'Old and New Year Ditty'. In it she performs the astonishing
feat of writing twenty-six lines of verse, all with the same rhyme, and
not one of them either false or far-fetched:

> Passing away, saith the World, passing away:
> Chances, beauty, and youth, sapp'd day by day:
> Thy life never continueth in one stay.
> Is the eye waxed dim, is the dark hair changing to grey
> That hath won neither laurel nor bay?
> I shall clothe myself in Spring and bud in May:
> Thou, root-stricken, shall not rebuild thy decay
> On my bosom for aye.
> Then I answer'd: Yea.
>
> Passing away, saith my Soul, passing away:
> With its burden of fear and hope, of labour and play,
> Hearken what the past doth witness and say:
> Rust in thy gold, a moth is in thine array,
> A canker is in thy bud, thy leaf must decay.
> At midnight, at cockcrow, at morning, one certain day
> Lo the Bridegroom shall come and shall not delay;
> Watch thou and pray.
> Then I answer'd: Yea.

Passing away, saith my God, passing away:
Winter passeth after the long delay:
New grapes on the vine, new figs on the tender spray,
Turtle calleth turtle in Heaven's May.
Though I tarry, wait for Me, trust Me, watch and pray:
Arise, come away, night is past and lo it is day,
My love, My sister, My spouse, thou shalt hear Me say.
Then I answer'd: Yea.

Many years later Swinburne was to write, 'The poem I put at the head of all her work and of all the religious poetry I know in any language is . . . the matchless and transcendental third of the *Old and New Year Ditties* "Passing away, saith the World, passing away". I have always thought that nothing more glorious in poetry has ever been written.'[23] Maybe this praise is an exaggerated piece of hyperbole; the poem is nevertheless a remarkable achievement.

Chapter Seven

'My lot is cast'

The success of the *Goblin Market* volume greatly pleased Dante Gabriel. Seldom has a brother been more devoted to his sister's interests or more appreciative of her genius; and seldom has a brother given his sister worse advice. Throughout 1863 and 1864 Christina was writing poetry but she was not yet prepared to consider publication. Dante Gabriel, on the contrary, was all for a new volume to follow as quickly as possible in the wake of the first one. Kindly but firmly she refused to agree with him. 'But why rush before the public with an immature volume?' she wrote on May 7th 1864. 'I really think of not communicating at all with Mac at present; but waiting the requisite number of months (or years as the case may be) until I have a sufficiency of quality as well as quantity. Is not this after all my best plan? If meanwhile my things become *remains*, that need be no bugbear to scare me into premature publicity.'[1]

The reference to 'remains' hints at the fact that once again Christina supposed herself to be looking death in the face. Some time during this year of 1864 she began to spit blood. The tentative diagnosis was of course tuberculosis; and it was proposed that she should spend the coming winter on the south coast away from London smoke and fog. In December 1864 she established herself at Hastings, where she remained until April. Part of the time she had for company her young and much-loved cousin, Henrietta Polidori, who had been definitely diagnosed as consumptive, and who, it was hoped, might also benefit from the sea air. Throughout the winter months letters flew up and down between Christina's lodgings in Hastings High Street and Dante Gabriel's house in Cheyne Walk. On December 23rd Christina wrote thanking him for what was apparently a Christmas present from both her brothers, a drawing of crocodiles by the French artist Griset. Dante Gabriel wished to send her another similar picture of a single crocodile; but much as she delighted in 'nestlings of unearthly aspect' she did not wish for any more of the kind: 'I am so happy in my nest of crocodiles that I beg you will on no account purchase the Prudent to lord it over them; indeed amongst their own number, by a careful study of expression, one may detect latent greatness, and point out the predominant tail of the future.'[2] Dante Gabriel none the less bought the second drawing and sent it her as a further remembrance of *My Dream*.

Christina had by now agreed to consider preparing a second volume of poetry. The year 1864 had proved particularly fruitful; out of the forty-seven poems which finally appeared in the new volume, fourteen date from that year. Her letters to Dante Gabriel on this subject show her to be grateful for his well-meant advice and anxious to agree with him whenever she can honestly do so. She is delighted to accept his help with practical matters—'I foresee you will charitably do the business-details'[3]—but not so happy over his interference with the choice of poems or with her methods of writing poetry. He would have had her write to order whereas she herself knew that she must wait on inspiration. Dante Gabriel was anxious that she should produce another narrative-poem somewhat in the manner of *Goblin Market* to form the title-piece. She had already written a short and beautiful dirge, 'Too late for love, too late for joy', intending it to stand as a poem by itself, but now, somewhat against her better judgement, she agreed to let it serve as the tail-piece of a long narrative-poem to be called *The Prince's Progress*.

Christina herself felt that this poem was not up to the standard she had set herself with *Goblin Market*: 'I readily grant that my *Prince* lacks the special felicity (!) of my *Goblins*,'[4] she wrote on March 6th 1865. Her instinct was right; the poem only just fails of excellence but fail it does. *The Prince's Progress* reads monotonously when compared with *Goblin Market*. There is no change of metre until the final dirge is reached although Christina seems to have provided something of the kind in an earlier, now vanished version. 'Do you know,' she wrote to Dante Gabriel on February 19th, 'I don't think it would have done to write the Alchemist without the metric jolt.'[5] In the printed version metric jolt there is none; presumably it was ironed out at Dante Gabriel's bidding. The episode of the Alchemist was a source of some trouble to her. 'True, O Brother, my Alchemist still shivers in the blank of mere possibility'[6] she had written in December 1864, a phrase which suggests that the original idea may have been Dante Gabriel's and not her own. At length the Alchemist took on shape and form but not quite in the manner expected—'Here at last is an Alchemist . . . He's not precisely the Alchemist I prefigured, but thus he came and thus he must stay: you know my system of work.'[7]

Devoted as she was to her brother, Christina would not let his demands interfere with the free working of her imagination. In particular she refused to agree to his suggestion of including a tournament scene: 'How shall I express my sentiments about the terrible tournament? Not a phrase to be relied on, not a correct knowledge on the subject, not the faintest impulse of inspiration, incites me to the tilt: and looming before me in horrible bugbeardom stand TWO tournaments in Tennyson's *Idylls*.'[8] Though her language is would-be humorous in tone her determination is serious enough; she will not be bullied into something which she knows to be an error. Finally her patience all but snaps: 'I do seriously question whether I possess the working-power with which you credit me; and whether all the painstaking at my command would result in work better than—in fact half so good as—what I have actually done on the other system.' Then, quoting a family byword, she begs of him 'please remember that "things which are impossible rarely happen"—and don't be too severe on me if in my case the "impossible" does not come to pass'.[9]

Although consciously she would certainly not have intended any reference to Dante Gabriel and Lizzie, unconsciously she seems to have had her brother's tragedy in mind when writing this poem in which he was so much interested. The description of the Prince, 'his curly black beard like silk' and his careless physical prowess as opposed to his moral weakness—'strong of limb if of purpose weak'—is Dante Gabriel to the life, while the picture of the waiting Princess pining slowly away as her lover dallies and delays suggests Lizzie and her increasing ill health during the years of waiting before her marriage. The poem tells how the Prince sets out to claim his betrothed bride. Various attractions and obstacles hinder him on his journey, an alluring milkmaid, an old alchemist who promises him the elixir of life, a desert, a torrent, a mountain range. When at last he reaches the Princess's palace he finds that he has come too late:

What is this that comes through the door,
The face covered, the feet before?
    This that coming takes his breath;
This Bride not seen, to be seen no more
    Save of Bridegroom Death?

The allegory is obvious, too obvious in fact. Part of the charm of *Goblin Market* lies in the uncertainty of interpretation, the pleasing doubt as to whether any definite parable is indeed intended or whether the poem should be enjoyed simply as a fairy-tale. In *The Prince's Progress* there can be no intriguing discovery of layer upon layer of meaning; not the most determined investigator could, for instance, find pornography here.

The volume includes only a few 'devotional pieces'. Two of her most beautiful religious poems were written in 1864 but neither is included here. She may have thought *Twice* was too personal for publication. It begins as a love-lament:

I took my heart in my hand,
    (O my love, O my love),
I said: Let me fall or stand,
    Let me live or die,
But this once hear me speak—
    (O my love, O my love)—
Yet a woman's words are weak;
    You should speak, not I.

You took my heart in your hand
    With a friendly smile,
With a critical eye you scanned,
    Then set it down,
And said: It is still unripe,
    Better wait awhile;
Wait while the skylarks pipe,
    Till the corn grows brown.

As you set it down it broke—
    Broke, but I did not wince;
I smiled at the speech you spoke,
    At your judgment that I heard:
But I have not often smiled
    Since then, nor questioned since,
Nor cared for corn-flowers wild,
    Nor sung with the singing bird.

Now the note changes:

I take my heart in my hand,
    O my God, O my God,
My broken heart in my hand:
    Thou hast seen, judge Thou.
My hope was written on sand,
    O my God, O my God:
Now let Thy judgment stand—
    Yea, judge me now.

This contemned of a man,
    This marred one heedless day,
This heart take Thou to scan
    Both within and without:
Refine with fire its gold,
    Purge Thou its dross away—
Yea hold it in Thy hold,
    Whence none can pluck it out.

I take my heart in my hand—
    I shall not die, but live—
Before Thy face I stand;
    I, for Thou callest such:
All that I have I bring,
    All that I am I give;
Smile Thou and I shall sing,
    But shall not question much.

No known episode in Christina's life fits with the situation described in this poem; to our knowledge she never offered love to a man only to have it refused. Mrs Packer, who of course connects the poem with Scott, can only go so far as to say 'We see now what may have occurred.'[10] Yet no other poem illustrates so clearly the intermingling of the two loves which lies at the root of all her feeling and all her poetry, the manner in which the passion of *eros* spills over into her conception of *agape*.

Another and very different religious poem was also written in 1864 and unaccountably omitted from the *Prince's Progress* volume. In *Birds of Paradise* she develops an old fancy dating back to some of her earliest verse and turns it into one of the loveliest of her visions of heaven:

> Golden-winged, silver-winged,
>   Winged with flashing flame,
> Such a flight of birds I saw,
>   Birds without a name:
> Singing songs in their own tongue—
>   Song of songs—they came. . . .
>
> On wings of flame they went and came
>   With a cadence clang:
>   Their silver wings tinkled,
>   Their golden wings rang;
> The wind it whistled through their wings
>   Where in heaven they sang.
>
>   They flashed and they darted
>   Awhile before mine eyes,
> Mounting, mounting, mounting still,
>   In haste to scale the skies,
> Birds without a nest on earth,
>   Birds of Paradise.

The variations of metre subtly suggest the whirling, changing rhythm of a flock of birds. No other English poet has written so often or so vividly of the joys of heaven, the birds and beasts, the trees and flowers, of the country that lies beyond death:

Oh what is that country
    And where can it be,
Not mine own country,
    But dearer far to me?
Yet mine own country,
    If I one day may see
Its spices and cedars,
    Its gold and ivory.

As I lie dreaming,
    It rises, that land;
There rises before me
    Its green golden strand,
With the bowing cedars
    And the shining sand;
It sparkles, and flashes
    Like a shaken brand.

Where the selection of shorter poems was in question Christina usually bowed to Dante Gabriel's judgement, though occasionally she insisted on having her own way. Thus she included a short poem written as long ago as 1854 and entitled *The Bourne* because it had already appeared in *Macmillan's Magazine* and had been set to music by Alice Macdonald, later to become the mother of Rudyard Kipling. Another poem, and that not a good one, she insisted on inserting because it had been praised by Charles Cayley.

For some years after his much appreciated visit at the time of Gabriele's death Christina and her mother saw little or nothing of Cayley. Both Rossetti brothers, however, were at pains to keep in touch with him, and some time in 1862, probably at Tudor House, Christina fell in with him again. Immediately he started to pay her 'marked attention'. Though she seems to have responded readily enough for at least two years he remained either too shy or too imperceptive of her feelings to be able to bring himself to propose. Christina regarded her dilatory lover with affectionate exasperation, to judge from a light-hearted poem written in August 1864:

The blindest buzzard* that I know
   Does not wear wings to spread and stir;
   Nor does my special mole wear fur,
And grub among the roots below:
He sports a tail indeed, but then
It's to a coat: he's man with men:
   His quill is cut to a pen. . . .

My blindest buzzard that I know,
   My special mole, when will you see?
   Oh no, you must not look at me,
There's nothing hid for me to show.
I might show facts as plain as day:
But since your eyes are blind, you'd say
   'Where? What?' and turn away.

If William was right in supposing that these verses refer to Cayley—and there seems no reason to think otherwise—Christina was more than a little in love with him before ever he brought himself to recognise that he was in love with her. Mrs Packer is very definite as to facts and dates, maintaining that Cayley proposed 'in September 1866 and was promptly refused'.[11] She gives no authority for this statement. William, on the contrary, is uncertain even as to the year of Cayley's proposal. In *Some Reminiscences* he writes, 'Cayley proposed to her in or about 1864'[12] but in the Foreword to his collection of Christina's letters he gives the date, with a query, as 'summer? 1866'. On balance the later date appears to be the more likely one. It is certain that Christina gave no final answer until 1866, but it is possible that the business dragged on for two years before coming to any definite conclusion.

In a letter dated February 26th 1883, one of her very few surviving letters to Cayley, Christina writes 'very likely there was a moment when —and no wonder—those who loved you best thought very severely of me, and indeed I deserved severity at my own hands'.[13] This seems to suggest that she kept Cayley dangling for some time; why should she

*Oddly enough, buzzards are particularly keen-sighted. Christina, usually so accurate in such matters, may have chosen this bird simply for the sake of alliteration.

think to blame herself if she had immediately given him an honest and straight refusal? If in fact he proposed in 1864 she may well have hesitated to give him any definite answer. At that date she was in no state to consider marriage because she was fighting a serious and maybe fatal illness. In the eighteen-sixties a diagnosis of tuberculosis was an almost certain death-warrant; and not till April 1865 was it clear that the diagnosis was a mistaken one. In any case it is unlikely that she saw much of Cayley during the winter and spring of 1864–5 because no sooner was she home from her long stay at Hastings and given a clean bill of health than she was off to Italy with her mother and William.

Their first stop was Paris, where they visited the Louvre and the Jardin d'Acclimatation (any zoo was an irresistible attraction to the Rossettis) and at the Exposition admired Whistler's *Princesse du Palais de Porcelaine* and gaped at Manet's *Olympe*, described by William as 'a most extreme absurdity'. At Basle they stopped for a few days to admire the cathedral and the famous Holbeins. On the way between Basle and Lucerne Christina had her first sight of the Alps. She, who had not even seen the mountains of Scotland or the Lake District, was at first repelled and then entranced:

> The mountains in their overwhelming might
> Moved me to sadness when I saw them first,
> And afterwards they moved me to delight.

From Lucerne they went on to Andermatt, then over the St Gotthard into the Italian-speaking region of the Ticino, and finally into Italy itself.

Christina had thought the German Swiss a hard unsympathetic race, but once among smiling Italian faces and musical Italian voices, she felt herself at home. She, whose entire life had hitherto been spent in the North, 'ice-bound, hungry, pinched and dim', had at last found what she recognised as her own country and her own people. William was so struck by the sudden blossoming of her personality in these congenial surroundings that he recorded his belief that she would have been a happier woman had she settled permanently in Italy—with her mother, of course, and within reach of an English church and chaplain. (William was very well aware of his sister's list of priorities.) Como, where she and

William rowed on the lake by moonlight and 'June that night glowed like a doubled June', Milan with its cathedral and picture galleries, dilapidated Pavia, where in a grimy hotel the animal-loving Rossettis fed sugar lumps to a tame black lamb with white skull-cap and tail-tip. Verona with its churches, monuments and Roman arena where they watched an incongruous performance by a 'clown Inglese', Bergamo, Lecco, and last of all Chiavenna—the arrival at each place was a home-coming to Christina. (Sadly enough, she was never to see the more notable Italian cities of Florence, Venice, and Rome.) Leaving Italy, she felt that she was leaving the better part of her heart behind her:

> Take my heart, its truest, tenderest part,
> Dear Land, take my tears.

Interesting though it might be, the journey home through Switzerland to Strasburg and back to Paris was inevitably something of an anticlimax. Once more in England, in or about July 1865 Christina wrote her vale-diction to the country which she knew to be her true native land:

> To come back from the sweet South, to the North
> Where I was born, bred, look to die;
> Come back to do my day's work in its day,
> Play out my play—
> Amen, amen, say I.
>
> To see no more the country half my own,
> Nor hear the half familiar speech,
> Amen, I say; I turn to that bleak North
> Whence I came forth—
> The South lies out of reach.
>
> But when our swallows fly back to the South
> To the sweet South, to the sweet South,
> The tears may come again into my eyes
> On the old wise,
> And the sweet name to my mouth.

Christina found a faint reflection of Italy in her friendship with Enrica Barile, an Italian woman of her own age who had come to London in the early eighteen-sixties and remained for a few years in the hope of establishing a teaching connection. In some verses dated July 1865 Christina contrasted the ebullient Enrica with the average Englishwoman:

> We Englishwomen, trim, correct,
>   All minted in the selfsame mould,
>   Warm-hearted, but of semblance cold,
> All-courteous out of self-respect.
>
> She, woman in her natural grace,
>   Less trammelled she by lore of school,
>   Courteous by nature not by rule,
> Warm-hearted and of cordial face.

That old reproach, 'doing all from self-respect', apparently still rankled.

The Prince's Progress should have been ready for publication in 1865. Proof-reading had been completed before Christina left for Italy but publication was delayed because Dante Gabriel was too busy with other work to find time to complete the two woodcuts he had promised as illustrations. Christina much admired the preliminary drawings for these designs. She had no criticism to make of the curiously androgynous appearance of the waiting Princess, but she suggested two corrections to be made in the other drawing:

> Do you think that two small points in the frontispiece might advisably be conformed to the text?—to wit, the Prince's 'curly black beard' and the Bride's 'veiled' face: all else seems of minor moment. Surely the severe female who arrests the Prince somewhat resembles my phiz.[14]

Dante Gabriel cunningly rectified these slips by making the Prince raise his hand to his face, and by deepening the shadows round the Bride's corpse so that the face is entirely obscured. The 'phiz' of the severe female bears little or no resemblance to Christina. Dante Gabriel

"Golden head by golden head"

Illustrations from a collected edition of Christina's poems, published 1897

Two drawings for *Sing-Song*
by Alice Boyd and Arthur Hughes

"Ferry me across the water,
   Do, boatman, do."
"If you've a penny in your purse
   I'll ferry you."

"I have a penny in my purse,
   And my eyes are blue;
So ferry me across the water,
   Do, boatman, do."

"Step into my ferry-boat,
   Be they black or blue,
And for the penny in your purse
   I'll ferry you."

could not or would not complete these drawings; as late as Christmas 1865 Christina was writing to Macmillan, 'I hardly know how to ask you to keep back *P.P.* after your "few days" advertisement;—yet if you agree with me in thinking Gabriel's designs too desirable to forego, I will try to follow your example of patience under disappointment.'[15]

Not till June of the following year did she at last receive a published copy of the volume. The book arrived when she was staying at Penkill Castle in Ayrshire, the home of Alice Boyd. The relationship between William Bell Scott and Alice had developed into a *ménage-à-trois*, Alice spending the winter with the Scotts in London, and Scott staying with her at Penkill for the whole summer, Letitia, who did not enjoy country life, coming for shorter periods.

The Rossettis being Scott's friends, Alice treated them as if they were her own, inviting Dante Gabriel, William, and Christina in turn to stay at Penkill. There seems little doubt but that Alice was Scott's mistress; in his book *A Pre-Raphaelite Circle* Raleigh Trevelyan definitely states that this was so. It is therefore at first sight a little surprising that Christina should accept the invitation to Penkill and more surprising still that she should quickly develop a deep affection and admiration for her hostess there. She had however travelled north with Letitia Scott; and Letitia's presence threw an air of respectability over the whole situation. If 'dear Mrs Scott'—so Christina always referred to Letitia—appeared perfectly satisfied with the position why should anyone else suppose it to be irregular? Christina did not necessarily suspect that Scott and Alice were lovers, and she could in all innocence enjoy a happy holiday in the company of two of her oldest and dearest friends, and of one who was soon to become as near and dear as they. To the twentieth-century mind the situation seems peculiar, to say the least; but the Victorians were expert in the useful art of turning a blind eye, and thought no worse of themselves for failing to observe what was not actually thrust upon their notice.

The medieval appearance of Penkill Castle, originally a peel tower, and the beauty of the surrounding country entranced Christina. Alice Boyd and the Scotts were at pains to entertain her, taking her for drives and showing her the neighbouring beauty-spots. She sat to Scott as a model for one at least of the figures he was painting on the walls of the

Castle stair; but because, like most of the Pre-Raphaelites, he knew little about the technique of fresco painting, these pictures have unfortunately vanished completely. Scott much enjoyed Christina's company but only if he could have her to himself, complaining that when the three women were together the conversation turned solely on religion and ailments. In spite of these occupations, however, much of her time was spent alone in her room, the topmost one in the tower, and originally known as 'the ladies' bower'. From its windows she could see the distant sea and the rocks of Ailsa Craig. She would stand for hours on end, her elbows on the window-sill, her chin cupped in her hands, looking out over the garden and the more distant landscape, 'meditating and composing'.

Christina had other things than poetry to meditate upon that summer. Whether he actually proposed before or after her seven weeks' visit to Penkill she knew well enough that the time had come to decide whether or not she would marry Charles Cayley. She was now thirty-five; if she refused him she renounced all hope of marriage. Far more important, she would be refusing a man whom she loved. But she knew that Cayley disagreed with her on matters of religion and she was convinced that it would be wrong for her to marry a man who did not share her religious views. In 'the windy room', as it was now called, she wrote a short poem which suggests that she very well knew how empty her life would be should she, of her own free will, renounce her lover:

> Oh what comes over the sea,
>   Shoals and quicksands past;
> And what comes home to me,
>   Sailing slow, sailing fast?
>
> A wind comes over the sea
>   With a moan in its blast;
> But nothing comes home to me,
>   Sailing slow, sailing fast.
>
> Let me be, let me be,
>   For my lot is cast;
> Land and sea all's one to me,
>   And sail it slow or fast.

Renounce Cayley she did, though we do not know the how, when and where of her actual refusal. By mid-September the matter was finally settled. One of the difficulties in the way of marriage had been a financial one. Apart from the charity of his well-to-do relatives Cayley had no regular source of income except the infinitesimal sums earned for him by his learned writings. The selfless William now offered the couple a home with him in his own house. Had Christina agreed to marriage on this basis William would have been obliged to maintain his sister and his sister's husband as well as contributing generously to the support of his mother and Maria and supplying Dante Gabriel's all-too-frequent demands for cash.

Firmly, though with deep gratitude, Christina refused William's generous offer. In a letter dated September 11th 1866 she explains the situation as she sees it. Although she accounts for its untidiness by the physical difficulty of writing while walking, the almost illegible scrawl seems curiously expressive of her thoughts and emotion, the words tumbling across the paper in direct, abrupt sentences very different from her usual mannered style of letter-writing:

> I am writing as I walk along the road with a party.
>
> I can't tell you what I feel at your most more than brotherly letter. Of course I am not *merely* the happier for what has occurred, but I gain much in knowing how much I am loved, beyond my deserts. As to money, I might be selfish enough to wish that were the only bar, but you see from my point of view it is not. Now I am at least unselfish enough altogether to deprecate seeing C.B.C. continually (with nothing but mere feeling to offer) to his hamper and discomfort: but, if he likes to see me, God knows I like to see him, and any kindness you will show him will only be additional kindness loaded on me.
>
> I prefer writing before we meet, though you're not very formidable.[16]

'If he likes to see me, God knows I like to see him'—Christina was not one to invoke the name of God lightly. This was not the end of what D. M. Stuart has described as 'this forlorn and yet tenacious passion'.[17] She continued to meet Charles Cayley, often over tea and a game of whist with her mother and Maria. They kept up a fairly regular correspondence though unfortunately nearly all of Christina's and most of Charles Cayley's letters have been destroyed. He sent her odd little presents, a complicated mathematical puzzle, a strange little creature preserved in spirits of wine—'it is called in Sussex a sea-mouse. But by naturalists Aphrodita aculeata, or needly Venus'.[18] To this offering Christina replied with a little poem:

> A Venus seems my Mouse
> Come safe ashore from foaming seas,
> Which in a small way and at ease
>   Keeps house.
>
> An Iris seems my Mouse
> Bright bow of that exhausted shower
> Which made a world of sweet herbs flower
>   And boughs.
>
> A darling Mouse it is:—
> Part hope not likely to take wing,
> Part memory, part anything
>   You please.
>
> Venus-cum-Iris Mouse,
> From shifting tides set safe apart,
> In no mere bottle, in my heart
>   Keep house.

Cayley also wrote poetry although his gifts in that direction were small. Christina carefully preserved all his writings, cutting out or copying any that appeared in print. The beginning of one unpublished poem he sent to her is moving, remembering the relationship between giver and receiver:

> Methought we met again, like parted mates in a bower,
>   And from between our hearts a sword
> Was lifted when a light superne streamed in around us

> And long we talked of mysteries
> And no laws of the flesh presumed any longer
> To sunder or to mingle [?] us.
> But now like glowing seraphim we lived in a region
> That love governs eternally.[19]

Here, of course, are obvious echoes of Dante and of the Dante-Beatrice theme which was such a powerful influence in Pre-Raphaelite art, life, and literature. So soaked was she in the Dante legend that Christina never seems to have thought that their innocuous but frequent meetings might be putting an undue strain on her lover, and, indeed, upon herself.

Why had she limited her intercourse with a man whom she admittedly loved to an occasional game of whist and the giving and receiving of small keepsakes? Why had she finally refused his proposal of marriage? Consciously she had reached her decision solely because of the religious difference between them; 'she enquired into his creed,' says William, 'and found he was not a Christian.'[20] Before condemning her as a bigot or looking for some hidden motive behind this cruelly painful decision it would be well to remember that she was not alone in taking up this position. Victorian ladies in fact and in fiction quite frequently refused to marry the man they loved for the very same reason which made Christina decide to refuse Charles Cayley. The actress Isabel Bateman, at one time leading lady to Irving and later Mother Superior of the Anglican sisterhood at Wantage, refused a young man whom she loved simply because he was an unbeliever. An aunt of that intrepid traveller, Isabella Bird, 'refused a clerical suitor on a doctrinal scruple and pined away',[21] a martyr-like fate which also overtook a character in Miss Yonge's story *The Two Guardians* who for the same reason broke off her engagement to a rich and eligible young man whom she sincerely loved.

It should be noted that in all these cases the man in question was a nominal member of the Church of England. Cayley was an Anglican in the sense that he had been baptised and brought up in the Church of England like the vast majority of his contemporaries; this, however, was not the sense in which Christina understood the term. She might not have been so rigid in her standards as to refuse to marry her lover because he was a Low Churchman or a Broad Churchman, but she would not marry a man who was no churchman at all, whatever may have been the church of his nominal adherence. Charles Cayley seems to have been in practice an agnostic; she therefore refused him although in so doing she went clean against the dictates of her own heart.

But although Christina herself honestly believed that she refused Charles Cayley because of his religion, or rather, his lack of religion, behind this motive, so much more easily understood by her contemporaries than by the modern reader, lay another and more subtle obstacle. As early as 1857 she had written a poem called *The Heart Knoweth Its Own Bitterness*, a poem in which her unconscious sublimation of sex is clearly apparent. Here, if anywhere, lies the key to her secret. Cayley was not asking too much of her but too little. 'Surely this refusal to marry . . . sprang from something very deep in her nature,' writes Maurice Bowra, 'something which made her shrink from the claims of the flesh.'[22] The poem makes clear that this shrinking was no commonplace dislike of sexual intercourse; it was not the nature but the inadequacy of the demands of the flesh which made her turn away to another love:

> To give, to give, not to receive!
>   I long to pour myself, my soul,
> Not to keep back or count or leave,
>   But king with king to give the whole.
> I long for one to stir my deep—
>   I have had enough of help and gift—
>   I long for one to search and sift
> Myself, to take myself and keep.
>
> You scratch my surface with your pin,
>   You stroke me smooth with hushing breath:—
> Nay pierce, nay probe, nay dig within,
>   Probe my quick core and sound my depth.
> You call me with a puny call,
>   You talk, you smile, you nothing do:
>   How should I spend my heart on you,
> My heart that so outweighs you all?

The last line shows that the pronoun 'you' is to be read in the plural; Christina is not addressing any individual but the whole breed of human lovers. To quote Maurice Bowra again, 'Only in God could she find a finally satisfying object for the abounding love which was the mainspring of her life and character.'[23] And so indeed Christina herself saw the matter:

> Not in the world of hope deferred,
>   This world of perishable stuff:—
> Eye hath not seen nor ear hath heard
>   Not heart conceived that full 'enough':
> Here moans the separating sea,
>   Here harvests fail, here breaks the heart:
>   There God shall join and no man part,
> I full of Christ and Christ of me.

Chapter Eight

A Critical Illness

According to William two groups of Christina's poems are definitely associated with Charles Cayley. Although it is impossible to date its composition with any accuracy the sonnet-sequence, *Monna Innominata*, was probably written in the sixties. These sonnets are among the finest poetry she ever produced but they have never won the fame they deserve. In her own time they were overshadowed by Elizabeth Barrett Browning's *Sonnets from the Portuguese*, and today they are all but forgotten. Scott was one of the few people to appreciate them at their proper worth. When they were published in 1881 he wrote to Dante Gabriel a letter of enthusiastic praise:

> The *Monna Innominata* is truly a great thing to have done; these fourteen sonnets are to me in a high degree noble and delightful. Perhaps knowing Christina so well makes me feel and understand them and to enter into and delight in them more than I might were they by an unknown to me. The series appears to me equal or superior to anything she has done, or anyone else has done.[1]

Cayley is but a poor peg on which to hang such poetry. Some of these fourteen sonnets, notably the fourth, agree well with the Christina-Cayley situation; others fit less exactly; others again do not fit at all. This is not surprising. In a foreword Christina explains that she is speaking not in her own person but in that of a medieval lady beloved of a troubadour and sharing her lover's poetic gift. She describes how the barrier between the lovers 'might be one held sacred by both, yet not such as to render mutual love incompatible with mutual honour'. This simple piece of camouflage not merely hides the personal reference but allows her to wander at will from the terms of that reference. Certain passages in these sonnets cannot possibly refer to Christina and Cayley. Very well—they can be taken as referring to the troubadour and his unnamed lady, or even to love and lovers in general; no need to be over-precise. The sonnets are none the less personal and immediate in tone:

> Come back to me, who wait and watch for you:—
> Or come not yet, for it is over then,
> And long it is before you come again,
> So far between my pleasures are and few.
> While, when you come not, what I do I do
> Thinking 'Now when he comes,' my sweetest 'when':
> For one man is my world of all the men
> This wide world holds; O love, my world is you.
> Howbeit, to meet you grows almost a pang
> Because the pang of parting comes so soon;
> My hope hangs waning, waxing, like a moon
> Between the heavenly days on which we meet:
> Ah me, but where are now the songs I sang
> When life was sweet because you called them sweet?

Even more personal are the Italian poems grouped together under the title *Il Rosseggiar dell' Oriente* ('the rosy light in the east'). Apparently Christina never showed these poems to anyone but kept them shut up in her desk where William found them after her death. They were written at various dates between 1862 and 1868. Christina probably regarded them as too private for publication, but in thus keeping them to herself she may also have been moved by other and less romantic motives. She had a shrewd idea as to what would and what would not please her public, and she may well have thought that Italian poetry stood little chance of success with English readers. Again, she may have had doubts as to whether her writing in Italian, which was after all only her second language, came up to the high standard which she had set herself, although in point of fact Italian scholars have judged these poems favourably, especially admiring the technical skill displayed in them.

Once again Christina writes as a woman separated from her lover by an insuperable though undefined barrier; and again, some of the poems fit her own situation more or less closely, others not so well, though the connection is more obvious than in *Monna Innominata*. The poem beginning 'Casa *felice óve piú volte omài*' matches so exactly with the life Alice Boyd and Scott lived together at Penkill and Christina's delight in the lovely surroundings there that the reader is tempted to declare Mrs Packer right after all:

> Happy house where many times my love sat talking and laughing; happy woman sitting with him, you make him happy even with what you do and say; happy garden where I walked, thinking of him, thinking and saying nothing—a happy day will it be when I go back to where I walked, thinking of him. But if he should be there when I return, if he could welcome me with his sweet laugh, all the birds would sing all around, the lovely face of the rose would blush; O God, give us that day in heaven, and make that garden our paradise.

Others, however, do not square at all with the idea of Scott, and in particular the one entitled *Per Preferenza*:

> Happy your mother, happy your sisters, who
> hear what you say, who live with you, who
> have a right to love you . . .

Cayley had a devoted mother and sisters; Scott had no sisters and his mother had died many years previously.

The woman in these poems is a devout Christian, the man an unbeliever. She prays for Christ's mercy on him:

> I have nothing but him, Lord, so do not
> spurn him, keep him lovingly in your heart
> among the things you love. Remember the day
> when you prayed to God on the cross, with
> feeble voice, with yearning heart, 'Father,
> forgive them, for they know not what they do.'
> He too, Lord, does not know what he spurns.

In spite of his disbelief she looks forward to union with her lover in the life after death:

> Lift your eyes, as I shall lift mine, to
> the kingdom where God is loved, not in vain,
> as much as it is possible to love, and all
> creation loves in charity. I loved you more
> than you loved me; Amen, if that is how God
> wills it; Amen, though my heart breaks, Lord
> Jesus. But You who know and remember every
> thing, You who died for love, in the next world
> give me that heart which I loved so much.*

Other notable poems of this period—both were probably written in 1870—are a series of sonnets entitled *By Way of Remembrance*, which read like a postscript to the *Monna Innominata* group, and *An Echo from Willow-wood*, a single sonnet written with the first of Dante Gabriel's 'Willow-wood' sequence in mind. If the first of Dante Gabriel's sonnets is put beside Christina's similar poem the notes of difference, and also the less striking similarities, can be seen very clearly. Here is Dante Gabriel's sonnet:

> I sat with Love upon a woodside well,
> Leaning across the water, I and he;
> Nor ever did he speak nor looked at me,
> But touched his lute wherein was audible
> The certain secret thing he had to tell:
> Only our mirrored eyes met silently
> In the low wave; and that sound came to be
> The passionate voice I knew; and my tears fell.
> And at their fall, his eyes beneath grew hers;
> And with his foot and with his wing-feathers
> He swept the spring that watered my heart's drouth.
> Then the dark ripples spread to waving hair,
> And as I stooped, her own lips rising there
> Bubbled with brimming kisses at my mouth.

*These extracts are taken from a literal translation by Vanessa Fox.

And here is Christina's, more slight, much less mannered, less sensual, telling the same tale in terms of a real-life occurrence, and yet alive with the same passion:

> Two gazed into a pool, he gazed and she,
> Not hand in hand, yet heart in heart, I think,
> Pale and reluctant on the water's brink,
> As on the brink of parting which must be.
> Each eyed the other's aspect, she and he,
> Each felt one hungering heart leap up and sink,
> Each tasted bitterness which both must drink,
> There on the brink of life's dividing sea.
> Lilies upon the surface, deep below
> Two wistful faces craving each for each,
> Resolute and reluctant without speech:—
> A sudden ripple made the faces flow,
> One moment joined, to vanish out of reach:
> So those hearts joined, and ah were parted so.

In 1870 Christina made the mistake of changing her publisher. Once again, with the best possible motives, Dante Gabriel gave his sister the worst possible advice. He wished her to join 'a little knot of congenial writers',[2] including such poets as Swinburne, William Morris, and Scott, to be grouped around his own publisher, F. S. Ellis, and he believed that Ellis would give her better financial terms than Macmillan had done. The arrangement did not work smoothly; and by 1874 Christina was back with 'staunch Mac', whom she was never again to forsake.

The only book of hers published by Ellis was a collection of short stories entitled *Commonplace*. (Ellis rightly objected to this dispiriting title.) Christina's prose totally lacks the technical skill so characteristic of her poetry. The stories in *Commonplace* vary in date from 1852 to 1870. The earlier ones are therefore all but contemporary with her schoolroom story, *Maude*, but none of them, whatever their date, show any advance on that immature piece of work. Christina was a most professional poet, but as a writer of prose, and especially of prose fiction, she was always to remain an amateur. The contents of *Commonplace* vary from fairy-stories—one of these, *Hero*, greatly pleased Dante Gabriel—to a moral tale on the subject of pew-rents. Reviewers were on the whole kindly and sales, though poor, were perhaps better than might have been expected. Even that most generous of critics, Dante Gabriel, could only describe these innocuous stories as 'certainly not dangerously exciting to the nervous system', adding a comment which Christina wisely laid to heart —she was to publish only one more prose story—'Of course I think your proper business is to write poetry and not *Commonplaces*'.[3]

While Christina was writing this pedestrian prose and passionate poetry her exterior life had settled into a humdrum pattern similar to the life of many another Victorian spinster. From 1866 onwards she lived vicariously in the lives of other people. What is of interest are not her own joys or sorrows but her reaction to those of her relations and friends. She was accepted, and had come to accept herself, as the spinster daughter, sister, and, later, aunt, whose concern was with her family, and in particular with her mother.

The relationship between mother and daughter had always been an unusually close one. Now that she had deliberately renounced sexual love her inner life was centring more and more upon religion and the love of God. But she also needed a centre for her ordinary, day-to-day life; she must have someone who would serve as a focus for thought and action, someone whose interests would always and unquestionably come first, someone to whom she could devote herself as she would have devoted herself to the man she loved had fate been more kind. Such a person she found in her mother—

> Blessed Dear and Heart's Delight,
> Companion, Friend, and Mother mine,
> Round whom my fears and love entwine.

Frances Rossetti was a remarkable woman; well-read, well-educated, and possessed of a quiet sense of humour, she could never be a bore. For someone of Christina's temperament she was in many ways the ideal companion. Slowly and at considerable cost to herself Christina had acquired an outward semblance of calm which, however, was completely foreign to one side of her nature. Frances Rossetti, on the contrary, had a natural stability which never failed her in the many crises and tragedies of her long life. Yet, although mother and daughter were remarkably congenial and complementary the one to the other, a life so completely bound up in the life of someone else of an older generation must be to some degree unnaturally limited and constrained; and so Christina sometimes found.

In spite of her commitment to her mother and to a quiet home life, Christina might still have made many interesting social contacts had she so wished or had her health permitted. She was a fairly frequent guest at the parties given by the Madox Browns, where Georgina Burne-Jones remembered her as a pithy conversationalist, 'gently caustic of tongue',[4] in company with Dante Gabriel, Whistler, and Swinburne. C. L. Dodgson (Lewis Carroll), a skilled photographer, took photographs of the entire Rossetti family, and in vain pressed Christina to bring her mother with her to visit him in Oxford. Every year she received an invitation to revisit Penkill; but only one of these could she accept, that for the summer of 1869. 'I mean to trim up my old hat in preparation for possible croquet,'[5] she wrote when accepting this invitation. This second visit to Penkill confirmed and deepened her friendship with Alice Boyd; from now onwards the two women addressed each other by their Christian names, in those days a sign of considerable intimacy. To Mrs Gilchrist Christina described Alice as 'perhaps the prettiest handsome woman I ever met, both styles being combined in her fine face'.[6] 'My dear Alice', she wrote sometime in the summer of 1870. 'Your letter comes like a nosegay from evergreen Penkill which blooms evergreen not only in Ayrshire but in tender memory. And your letter is like yourself—I will not further define it.'[7]

It is clear, therefore, that Christina did not lack occasion or opportunity to enjoy a full and interesting social life had she so wished. In June 1867, following the death of Aunt Margaret Polidori, who had been for some time a member of the Rossetti household, the family moved from Albany Street to Number Fifty-six Euston Square. Here they did a little quiet entertaining, in 1868, for instance, giving a small party at which Browning was a guest. A letter from Christina to William written just before her

1866 Penkill visit and telling of another meeting with Browning shows how gladly well-known people would have welcomed and made much of this rising poetess had she allowed them so to do:

> Mrs Cameron* called one day . . . with a portfolio of her magnificent photographs, of which she kindly presented five to Mamma, Maria, and self. Maria and I returned her visit at Little Holland House, where we saw the gigantic Val,† Mr Watts,‡ Mrs Dalrymple, and got a glimpse of Browning . . . I am asked to go down to Freshwater Bay, and promised to see Tennyson if I go; but the whole plan is altogether uncertain, and I am too shy to contemplate it with anything like unmixed pleasure.[8]

This last sentence pinpoints one of the difficulties which prevented Christina from making more of the social opportunities which came her way. Her fits of paralysing shyness could make social pleasures a penance to her and turn her into an awkward, even embarrassing guest. Dante Gabriel had been on intimate terms with Alexander Gilchrist, the biographer of Blake, and after Gilchrist's death he had helped his widow to complete the biography and prepare it for publication. In 1863 Mrs Gilchrist had prevailed upon Christina to come to stay; and years later the Gilchrists' daughter Grace recorded her childhood memories of that occasion. On arrival Christina was shown her room in time to prepare herself for supper:

> My mother, finding after the lapse of some time that she did not appear in the drawing-room circle, went upstairs in search of her, and, tapping at her door, found Miss Rossetti ready, but waiting, in some trepidation, too shy to venture down alone, or to be formally announced by the servant, into the expectant group in the drawing-room.[9]

Another, less well authenticated story tells how on one occasion Christina was apparently not too shy to announce herself to the assembled company. At a party given by Mrs Virtue Tebbs, wife of the Rossettis'

---

* Julia Cameron, pioneer of photography;
† Val Prinsep, artist; ‡ G. F. Watts, o.m., artist.

solicitor and family friend, a little woman dressed from head to foot in severe black suddenly rose to her feet, walked into the middle of the circle of guests, announced 'I am Christina Rossetti', and returned to her seat without uttering another word.

Perhaps even more frustrating socially than her habitual shyness was Christina's chronic ill health. Even in 1867, a period when she was in much better health than usual, she was unable to attend various evening parties 'on account of night air'—and this in mild warm weather, not in winter frost or fog. Throughout 1870 she was not so much ill as what she herself described as 'out-of-sorts and lazy'. In July she was at Folkestone with her mother. 'This expedition was undertaken with a maternal eye to my benefit, and I think it has done me good,' she wrote to Alice Boyd, 'though my persistent weariness without exertion is wonderful to contemplate. I am still in my doctor's hands.'[10] A month or so later she was back at Folkestone with Maria, and Frances Rossetti was writing anxiously bidding her 'not to forget a bulletin of health when you write'. (Apparently Cayley had been helping Christina in some way for she also comments 'I rejoice that C.B.C. uses his pen in your behalf.')[11] From now onwards Christina's health slowly declined, though as yet the doctors could find no definite disease; in February 1871, for instance, she writes to Dante Gabriel and excuses the dullness of her letter by the fact that she is suffering from an abscess. On April 28th she is again writing to him, this time in handwriting so shaky as to be almost illegible, to tell him that 'Sir W. Jenner saw me last Saturday and pronounced me seriously ill'.[12]

Jenner diagnosed neuralgia and ordered change of air and a visit to Leamington Spa. Four days later he changed his mind, realising that she was too ill to move. On May 4th William described her as 'wretchedly ill', and the next day made a longer entry in his diary:

> Christina's illness still extremely serious. I feel more alarmed about it today than heretofore. Sir W. Jenner says there is 'no immediate danger', and at his late visit today reassured Mamma a little—but only a little. He orders Christina to keep her bed strictly, which I have thought for several days would be the best thing; hitherto she has got up regularly, but done little or nothing more, save lying on a sofa.[13]

Jenner was still anxious to try what change of air might do, and since she was too weak to undertake any longer journey, on July 6th she was moved to rooms in Hampstead, where she remained for three weeks. Returning home for a few days she had the pleasure of seeing Charles Cayley at dinner before she set out for Folkestone with her mother and Maria. From Folkestone she wrote to William that, although she had gained some strength, 'Still I am weak, and less ornamental than society may justly demand'.[14] Her condition continued to puzzle the doctors. Not until November, when she developed a swelling on her throat, were they able to diagnose her trouble as a rare form of goitre, exophthalmic bronchocele.

Graves's disease, to give this complaint its common name, is a dangerous and disfiguring illness. For the next two years Christina suffered from a bewildering variety of ills, a swelling on her throat, heart-attacks, choking, frequent vomiting, sensations of intolerable heat, cough, neuralgia, fainting fits, and, not surprisingly, total exhaustion. For weeks together both her doctors and her family believed her to be at death's door. But perhaps the worst trial of all to her was the ruin of her delicate beauty. The two distinctive symptoms of Graves's disease are what William rightly described as 'the enormous protrusion of the eyes' and the darkening and discoloration of the skin. Add to these disfigurements the coarsening of her features and the loss of her abundant hair, and it is not surprising that as early as October, before the disease had done its worst, Dante Gabriel should have been shocked by the change in her appearance. In a letter he described her as 'completely altered and looking suddenly ten years older', but he added that she showed 'a great deal of courage for endurance'.[15]

She had need of all her courage because she was to have very much to endure. Graves's disease plays with its victims as a cat with a mouse, relaxing its hold for considerable periods, only to pounce again more fiercely than before. For a time Christina would be well enough to see her friends, even to go out to a small dinner-party, then she would suddenly be struck down by a worse attack than any she had previously suffered. Yet she never lost courage; at one of the worst periods of her illness William could write 'she shows a really admirable constancy, and the worst shafts of Fate find her their equal'.[16] Nor did she forget other people's troubles. In October 1871 she wrote a charming and sympathetic letter to Lucy, Madox Brown's daughter by his first wife, who was suffering from an abscess in the ear:

> It is such delightful news Maria brings me that you are relieved of your terrible pain, that I indulge in writing a line to express my love and pleasure, not forgetting how you pitied and petted me for not half the pain. I know you are too kind not to attribute my absence to its real cause, a halting convalescence, but at least I may write.[17]

That halting convalescence proved illusory. All through the winter William was reporting Christina as being 'particularly unwell', 'bad as usual', 'in a very deplorable state'. In January she suffered so severe a heart-attack that she asked Jenner if she was in danger of dying instantaneously in another and similar one; clearly she wished to prepare herself against the possibility of sudden death:

> The mystery of Life, the mystery
> Of Death, I see
> Darkly as in a glass;
> Their shadows pass
> And talk with me.

The weary winter was cheered for Christina by the appearance of her book of children's verse entitled *Sing-Song*. Its publication had been beset by frustrating difficulties. Ellis first accepted the book, and then turned it down, influenced perhaps by the comparative failure of *Commonplace* and by the problems which had arisen over the question of illustrations. Christina had wished Alice Boyd to illustrate *Sing-Song*; Alice could draw charming birds and beasts, but the designs she produced lacked the professional touch and were not judged good enough for reproduction. She withdrew in favour of the Pre-Raphaelite artist Arthur Hughes, who was a great admirer of Christina both as a person and a poet. Never was there a happier partnership between author and illustrator; pictures and poems are welded into an indivisible whole. Dante Gabriel rightly described these illustrations as exquisite, adding 'There is no man living who would have done my sister's book so divinely well.'[18]

Sing-Song is a book to enchant young and old alike. Children are captivated by such poems as *The Horses of the Sea*:

> The horses of the sea
>   Rear a foaming crest,
> But the horses of the land
>   Serve us the best.
>
> The horses of the land
>   Munch corn and clover,
> While the foaming sea-horses
>   Toss and turn over.

Older readers appreciate best the very short, very simple verses which capture the essence of babyhood and mother-love;

> Your brother has a falcon,
>   Your sister has a flower;
> But what is left for mannikin,
>   Born within an hour?
>
> I'll nurse you on my knee, my knee,
>   My own little son;
> I'll rock you, rock you, in my arms,
>   My least little one.

Or, even more short and simple:

> My baby has a mottled fist,
>   My baby has a neck in creases;
> My baby kisses and is kissed,
>   For he's the very thing for kisses.

Yet even in these childlike verses for and about children Christina cannot forget the great central themes of her poetry, love, death, and parting. A poem beginning 'A baby's cradle with no baby in it, A baby's grave where autumn leaves drop sere' is not perhaps to be accounted unusual reading for Victorian infants; but no one would expect to come across in any book of nursery rhymes this little song of love and parting and reunion:

> 'Goodbye in fear, goodbye in sorrow,
>   Goodbye and all in vain,
> Never to meet again, my dear'—
>   'Never to part again.'
> Goodbye today, goodbye tomorrow,
>   Goodbye till earth shall wane,
> Never to meet again, my dear—
>   'Never to part again.'

One curious feature of *Sing-Song* seems to have escaped the critics' notice. Angels occur some half-dozen times in this entrancing book, more obviously sometimes in the illustrations than in the text, but there is no mention of God, or of the Christian stories so familiar to Victorian children, or indeed, of religion in any form.

Though the sales were at first a little disappointing the reviews were enthusiastic and *Sing-Song* won the success it so richly deserved. Maria too was enjoying her moment of triumph as an author. Her book, *The Shadow of Dante*, reputedly still one of the best introductions to Dante studies, had appeared in August 1871 and was winning favourable notice. Otherwise the outlook for the Rossetti family in the spring of 1872 was indeed a bleak one. After a temporary improvement Christina's condition again deteriorated. Plagued by painful neuralgia and a hacking cough, she was reported as being 'excessively low'. The worst attack of all came on May 14th, when she collapsed unconscious. 'I have great apprehensions as to the result—perhaps at no very distant date' William admitted; 'for there seems to be no real rally of physical energy now for months past, and the process of exhaustion proceeds with fatal and frightful steadiness.'[19] In spite of her physical weakness, however, Christina continued to amaze him by her strength of mind and by the eagerness with which she would enter into conversation on any or every subject of interest. Everyone in the Rossetti circle was thinking and talking of her; it seemed as if her condition could hardly be worse. Then suddenly the storm centre shifted, and the alarm, fear, and desperate hope of the entire family were concentrated not on Christina but on Dante Gabriel.

Chapter Nine

The Tragedy of Dante Gabriel

May 1872 was a black month for the Rossetti family. On the fifteenth, the day after Christina's serious collapse, Dante Gabriel called at the house in Euston Square bringing with him a copy of Robert Buchanan's pamphlet, *The Fleshly School of Poetry*. This attack on his recently published book of poems had first appeared as a review in the October number of *The Contemporary*. He had not then appeared to be unduly perturbed, but now, although William reported that 'he seems sufficiently untroubled by it'[1] its reissue had in fact dealt him a near-mortal blow. In the intervening months his mind had become increasingly affected by the doses of chloral washed down with whisky which he took as a remedy for insomnia; and he was in no state to stand up against this renewed onslaught. William described Sunday, June 2nd as 'a day of extreme distress and anxiety on account of the nervous and depressed condition into which Gabriel has allowed himself to get worked'.[2] Convinced that everyone was conspiring against him and suffering from severe delusions—he believed that he heard bells ringing in the air and voices addressing him in terms of obscene abuse—Dante Gabriel was in such a condition that William rightly feared for his sanity. A mental specialist was called in, and at his suggestion the Rossettis' kindly doctor, George Hake, agreed to take the patient into his own house at Roehampton. Here, a few days later, on Whit Sunday afternoon Dante Gabriel was found in a deep coma from which he could not be roused. At once William set off for Euston Square to fetch his mother and Maria to what he believed to be his brother's death-bed. Too seriously ill to be able to leave her bed Christina had to stay behind in the care of Aunt Eliza.

On returning to Roehampton William was told that the doctors had discovered an empty bottle of laudanum. This piece of information he kept strictly to himself; his mother and sisters were never to know that Dante Gabriel had attempted suicide. Meanwhile Christina had to live through a night and a day of racking fear and uncertainty before on Monday afternoon William could at last send her a reassuring note which was confirmed by news brought by their good friend Madox Brown. 'I know not (having heard of one fearful alternative) what to hope:' she wrote in her reply to William, 'but with my whole heart I commit our extremity to Almighty God.'[3] Not knowing the true facts, and believing that Dante Gabriel had been struck down by some form of seizure, she had good reason to fear that he might recover his life only to lose his sanity.

Dante Gabriel did not die nor did he become insane. A long convalescence resulted in partial recovery though he was never fully to regain either his health or his spirits. He spent several weeks in Scotland and then went to Kelmscott, the manor-house near Lechlade which he and William Morris shared as co-tenants. Here he had the company of Janey Morris with whom he was now deeply in love. Christina saw him for the first time since his illness when on September 4th he broke his journey from Scotland to Gloucestershire in order to spend a few hours in London with his family, a visit which he described as the first happy time he had enjoyed for many months. Christina herself was at last on the road to recovery although for the next year or so there were to be many alarms and set-backs before she could safely regard herself as restored to even tolerably good health. In July she had been sent away for change of air, first to Hampstead and then to Glottenham in Sussex near to the home of Barbara Bodichon who was as kind and welcoming now as she had been long ago to Lizzie. Christina was none the less suffering from the depression and boredom typical of convalescence. 'As to my shaky self these last two days or so I have been feeling a little less well but on the whole I am perhaps better,'[4] she wrote not very optimistically to William.

The letters which she sent William from Sussex are full of affection and concern for 'my brother of brothers'. In one she tells him that she is looking forward to the time when 'I may keep house with you, as in old days, in much harmony',[5] in another she signs herself 'truly (as well I may be) your affectionate sister'.[6] During all this troubled time William had been a tower of strength to his family but now, worn out by the double strain of his sister's long illness and his brother's mental collapse and also, it should be added, by the difficult task of dealing with Dante Gabriel's tangled finances, he himself was on the verge of a breakdown. His lack of spirits and obvious depression were a source of great anxiety to his mother and sisters. In a letter to Christina, Frances Rossetti recorded with relief that he was 'somewhat less dull and sleeping better'[7] but later wrote of him as having 'much need for anything that can turn his mind from anxious thoughts'.[8] Throughout all the troubles which beset her family this remarkable old lady never appears to have broken down or to have lost her admirable calm.

Illness had inevitably involved extra expense. As a means of making money Christina toyed with the idea of looking out some old poems not previously considered worthy of publication and printing them under a pseudonym. With his habitual common sense William scotched this notion by pointing out that second-rate poetry published under an unknown name was not likely to prove a saleable commodity. Very few new poems date from this period, almost certainly because during her long illness Christina had been too unwell to concentrate on the effort to write. Now, however, in October 1872 a series of poems on the birth of Venus sent to her by the ever-faithful Cayley called forth in reply a charming sonnet in mannered Elizabethan style entitled *Venus's Looking-Glass*. With this Christina chose to couple a very different sonnet, much more personal in tone, to which she gave the title *Love Lies Bleeding*:

> Love, that is dead and buried, yesterday
> Out of his grave rose up before my face;
> No recognition in his look, no trace
> Of memory in his eyes dust-dimmed and grey;
> While I, remembering, found no word to say,
> But felt my quickened heart leap in its place;
> Caught afterglow thrown back from long-set days,
> Caught echoes of all music past away.
> Was this indeed to meet?—I mind me yet
> In youth we met when hope and love were quick,
> We parted with hope dead but love alive:

> I mind me how we parted then heart-sick,
> Remembering, loving, hopeless, weak to strive:—
> Was this to meet? Not so, we have not met.

When the sonnets came to be published Christina wisely dropped the idea of linking them together. The only possible connection between them in her mind would seem to be some thought of Cayley; but though the first sonnet was certainly inspired by his own poems the second appears to have little relevance to his attitude of unaltered and unalterable devotion towards her.

Though none of Christina's religious poems definitely date from this period, if it were permissible—which it is not—to date poetry solely by its subject-matter two or three of the poems listed by William as written before 1875 or 1876 would fit well enough with this time of illness and sorrow. On the evidence of subject-matter alone Mrs Packer believes that the poem *Love is strong as Death* 'reflects the experience of this gloomy period when her only recourse was prayer'.[9] Partial quotation can distort or even destroy the meaning of a poem; and nowhere is this more true than in Christina's religious poetry where the second or final verse often gives the answer to the agonised questioning of earlier verses. So frequently, however, is the question quoted without the answer that Christina's religious poetry is commonly though erroneously supposed to be despairing and gloomy in outlook. Thus Mrs Packer quotes the first verse of *Love is strong as Death*:

> I have not sought Thee, I have not found Thee,
>   I have not thirsted for Thee:
> And now cold billows of death surround me,
> Buffeting billows of death astound me,—
>   Wilt Thou look upon, wilt Thou see
>   Thy perishing me?

She omits to give the second verse, in which despair changes to hope, danger to security. The antithesis is made particularly telling by the repetition of words and rhymes, almost of punctuation. Now it is Christ who speaks:

'Yea, I have sought thee, yea, I have found thee,
   Yea, I have thirsted for thee,
Yea, long ago with love's hands I have bound thee:
Now the Everlasting Arms surround thee,—
   Through death's darkness I look and see
   And clasp thee to Me.'

This last verse may not be such good poetry as the first one but it is none the less an integral and essential part of the poem. No poem ending thus can possibly be described as a cry of gloom or near-despair.

Dante Gabriel remained at Kelmscott till Christmas when he made one of the family party in Euston Square. Eighteen-seventy-three promised to be a less catastrophic year for the Rossettis than its predecessor had been. Dante Gabriel was back at work on his painting, the big picture of the moment being *Proserpine*, perhaps the best known of all his likenesses of Janey Morris. Thanks in part to his own industry, in part to William's devoted efforts, his debts had been paid and he was once again solvent. As for Christina she was restored to tolerable health and spirits and her appearance had improved, though she was never to regain her lost beauty. Her recovery was confirmed and crowned by a mid-summer visit to Kelmscott where for three weeks she and her mother had their fill of country delights. 'My funny old mummy trots about enjoying herself immensely,' Dante Gabriel wrote to Fanny Cornforth, 'and Christina seems really to benefit from the change more than I could possibly have hoped.'[10] Fanny herself, the 'dear elephant', never came to Kelmscott; neither there nor in London was she ever allowed to come in contact with Dante Gabriel's mother and sisters. How much Christina guessed it is impossible to say. An undated letter written to Dante Gabriel in 1874 or 1875 may be no more than a wry coincidence; it is nevertheless tempting to read into it a demure hint that she knew of Fanny's existence, knew too of her lack of means and her unending demands for money:

Let me renew my thanks for the poor dear 'Elephant' book, whose pathetic ending is truly painful and goes to one's heart. Delicious is the prosperous elephant ladling out rice to mendicants: I wish all Elephants were prosperous.[11]

Janey was away, and Fanny forbidden to show her face at Kelmscott, but a model Dante Gabriel must have if he were to continue to work at his painting. His choice fell on Alexa Wilding, who presented him with quite a different type of social problem. In London models came and went by the hour, but in the country they were of course obliged to stay in the house, respectable ones ranking in the social scale more or less with governesses. 'About the model,' Dante Gabriel wrote to his mother apropos the proposed visit, 'it would be Miss Wilding, who is a *really* good creature, fit company for any one, only not gifted or amusing. Thus she might bore you at meals and so on (for one cannot put her in a cupboard)...'[12]

In point of fact Christina and her mother got on very well with Alexa Wilding. A more interesting guest was Theodore Watts, afterwards Watts-Dunton, critic, novelist, and almost professional befriender of poets in distress. (Later he was to take a very firm grip on Swinburne.) Gabriel's pace on a country walk was too fast for Christina; instead, she would stroll slowly along the river bank with Watts or wander with him in the orchard admiring the many-coloured lichens and mosses growing on the trunks of the old apple trees. Sometimes when they were sitting indoors Frances Rossetti would read aloud. Years later Watts remembered how the listeners could hear 'through the open casement of the quaint old house, the blackbirds from the home field trying in vain to rival the music of that half-Italian, half-English voice'.[13] He admired Christina's voice as much as he admired her mother's, commenting especially on her 'clear-cut method of syllabification', a characteristic noted by many other friends, in particular by the poet William Sharp, better known under his pseudonym of Fiona Macleod.

One person was missing who might have been expected to form an integral part of the Kelmscott party. That person was Janey Morris. In theory Dante Gabriel shared the house with the Morrises; in practice he and Janey spent weeks and months there together whilst William Morris busied himself with the affairs of his textile and furniture firm, or went on long expeditions to Italy or Iceland. Of Christina's reaction to this situation we know tantalisingly little. She could not have been unaware of the position since her brother made no secret of his infatuation with Janey. Though a certain ambiguity hangs over their relationship, as over his pre-marital relationship with Lizzie, the pair certainly behaved in a manner which gave their friends reason to believe that they were lovers in the full sense of the word.

Nevertheless Christina accepted Janey as she had never accepted Lizzie, though the two women seldom came into direct contact with one another. Janey would write to Christina asking for particulars of a hospital at Eastbourne which might prove suitable for one of Morris's Icelandic protégés. If Christina was writing to Dante Gabriel as a matter of course she would send friendly if formal messages to 'dear Mrs Morris' and comment on any news there might be of Janey—'I also might gasp a moment at the vision of beautiful Mrs Morris with her family boating on river Thames for a week'.[14] Christina was one of those rare people who can honestly hate the sin while loving the sinner; she was far more tolerant of immorality than of unbelief. Moral issues apart, a love-affair can be ignored where a marriage must be acknowledged; moreover, the practical situation had changed greatly since Lizzie's day. In 1854 Dante Gabriel had been a young man with his way to make in the world, now he was an established success both as poet and painter. His love for Janey might affect his private happiness but it could not blight his career. A liaison with the wife of one of his best friends was not pretty to contemplate; but if William Morris did not openly object it was not for the Rossetti family to cause gossip and scandal by protesting on their own account. They may even have believed, as some people have since believed, that the affair was an innocent one. Paradoxically, the fact that the situation was so clear and obvious made it the easier to turn a blind eye. Because Janey and Dante Gabriel made no attempt at concealment it was possible to suppose that there was nothing to conceal.

During their happy stay at Kelmscott Christina and her mother received news of William's engagement to Lucy Madox Brown. 'You have brought a fresh spring of happiness and interest into our family,' Christina wrote to William. 'Her sweetness, amiability, and talent, make her a grace and honour to us'.[15] To Lucy herself she sent a warm letter of welcome. 'I should like to be a dozen years younger, and worthier every way of becoming your sister; but, such as I am, be sure of my loving welcome to you as my dear sister and friend.'[16] The engagement particularly delighted Christina because she believed that the lethargy and depression which had hung over William ever since Dante Gabriel's collapse would be dispelled by the sunshine of this new happiness. Shortly after the Rossettis returned to London Scott came to dine with them in Euston Square. 'We touched upon William,' Scott told Alice Boyd, 'and they . . . but especially Christina, confided in me how very much alarmed they had been for William ever since Gabriel's illness, and that they were truly glad of the Lucy advent, as they would [be] of anything else that might break the spell that seemed to hold him. For weeks they said he never uttered a word to any of them, and now he talked [of] "When Lucy is here".'[17]

The excitement following William's engagement had hardly had time to die down before another member of the family announced that she too was about to take an important step in life. Earlier in the summer of 1873 Maria had been ill first with erysipelas, then with the first symptoms of the cancer which was to kill her. She may have had some premonition of coming death, or she may merely have thought that the changes which must follow on William's marriage made this a suitable time in which to make her own move; in any case, she now announced her intention of joining the Anglican sisterhood of All Saints.

Dante Gabriel was much perturbed by Maria's decision. 'I hear today from Maria about her very serious step,' he wrote to William on September 6th, 'and with an intimation of her renewed illness, which seems to make such a step still more serious.'[18] The cold and discomfort of convent life appalled him as he made clear in a later letter:

I have really felt very seriously anxious about Maria since what you tell me of no fires in this blessed place. I simply could not exist on such terms—it would be a noviciate for another world; and I view the matter as most serious for her.[19]

He was also distressed by the gap Maria's absence would make in the family circle. 'She will indeed be a great loss,' he wrote to his mother on September 13th, 'being much the healthiest in mind and cheeriest of us all, except yourself. William comes next, and Christina and I are no-where.'[20]

Christina was only too well aware of what Maria's loss would mean, yet she saw her sister's decision as being a right and a reasonable one. As a young woman she had seen something of the pioneer Anglican sisterhood in Albany Street and later she had, of course, become an Associate of the Order Maria now joined, and had worked at their House of Charity. From the early days of *Maude* she had written much poetry about nuns. Nearly all of these poems are cries of thwarted love—one of the best of them, *Sœur Louise de la Misericorde*, is put into the mouth of Louis XIV's mistress Louise de la Vallière—but nevertheless she had real understanding and sympathy for those who practised what is techni-cally called the Religious Life, although she herself had never felt drawn in that direction. Maria on the contrary had a genuine vocation, and found great happiness and a sense of fulfilment in what she habitually described as 'this blessed life'. She was by temperament the more religious of the two sisters. 'Of all the people I have known,' said William, 'Maria was the most naturally and ardently devotional—certainly more so than Christina, as a matter of innate tendency.'[21]

With Maria gone and William about to marry it seemed as if the family group was on the verge of breaking up. William, however, was determined that this should not happen; instead of setting up house on his own, or suggesting that his mother and sister should do so, he planned to bring his bride back to the family home in Euston Square. Christina was very doubtful of the wisdom of his plan. She knew that her physical disabilities made her a difficult inmate of any household, and she feared to put too great a strain on Lucy's tolerance. On this issue brother and sister had one of their rare quarrels. On November 5th she wrote to William apologising for an outburst of temper and arguing that it would be wise not to attempt to live together but to set up two separate establish-ments:

> I am truly sorry for my ebullition of temper this morning (and for a hundred other faults), and not the less so if it makes what follows seem merely a second and more serious instance.
>
> My sleeping in the library cannot but have made evident to you

Maria Rossetti as an Anglican nun, by Lucy Madox Brown

Lucy Madox Rossetti and her daughter, by Ford Madox Brown

how improper a person I am to occupy any room next a dining-room. My cough (which surprised Lucy, as I found afterwards, the other day at dinner) . . . makes it unseemly for me to be continually and unavoidably within earshot of Lucy and her guests. *You* I do not mention, so completely have you accommodated yourself to the trying circumstances of my health: but, when a 'love paramount' reigns amongst us, even you may find such toleration an impossibility. I must tell you that not merely am I labouring under a serious relapse into heart-complaint and consequent throat-enlargement (for which I am again under Sir William Jenner's care), but even that what appeared the source of my first illness has formed again, and may for aught I can warrant once more have serious issues.

She went on to point out that her mother and she might set up house with the two aunts, 'thus securing to us no despicable amount of cheerful companionship, and of ready aid in sickness'. She knew that the problem had been causing much anxiety both to William and to her mother:

Dear William, I should not wonder if you had been feeling this obvious difficulty very uncomfortably, yet out of filial and brotherly goodness had not chosen to start it: if so, I cannot rejoice enough that my perceptions have woke up to some purpose. . . . Of course Mamma is in grief and anxiety; her tender heart receives all stabs from every side.

For herself she declared that she could see no solution short of separation, and she ended with the revealing sentence, 'If you wonder at my writing instead of speaking, please remember my nerves and other weak points.'[22]

William had his way; but Christina was proved right in her judgement. The combined household did not work harmoniously. Fond as they had previously been of one another Christina and Lucy proved incompatible elements when living together under one roof. Lucy, who was nearly twenty years the younger of the two, may have felt that the generation gap was too wide to bridge, and she may also have resented her husband's unquestioning devotion to his mother and sister and his absorption in their affairs. The real clash, however, was between Christina's tenaciously held religious views and Lucy's agnosticism. To the younger woman, brought up in the free-thinking atmosphere of the Madox Brown household, Christina's constant preoccupation with the minutiae of religious belief and practice was both irritating and incomprehensible. For her part, in theory Christina believed that it was a mistake to try to convert anybody except by prayer and love. 'If we are half heart-broken by a friend's doubts, let us beg faith for our friend and for ourself,' she was to write; 'only still more urgently let us beg love. For love is more potent to breed faith than faith to breed love.'[23] In practice, however, as her letters both to William and to Lucy prove, she was only too apt to give cause for irritation by frequent and tactless references to religion. This tendency, together with the fact that she made not the least attempt to conceal her own opinions or to modify her rigid rule of life in order to avoid giving offence to Lucy, made it impossible for the sisters-in-law to understand or to tolerate one another so long as they were obliged to live together at close quarters.

Short holidays away from home did something to relieve the tension. Christina and her mother spent much time in Bloomsbury Square with the two aunts, Charlotte and Elizabeth Polidori, and in May 1874 they took these aunts on a holiday to Eastbourne. In the summer of 1875 and again in 1876 they stayed at the All Saints Mission House in Clifton where Maria was now working. At Clifton Christina had the chance to meet Dora Greenwell whose acquaintance she had first made during her Newcastle visit. In her writing of poetry, her absorption in religion, and her continual ill health Dora Greenwell might have been described as Christina writ small.

In November 1875, immediately after Maria's final profession as a nun, Christina and her mother spent some time at Aldwick Lodge, a house near the sea at Bognor which Dante Gabriel had taken as a temporary refuge from the domestic and financial troubles which threatened to overwhelm him at Tudor House. For fellow guests they had Theodore Watts and the younger George Hake, the son of Dante Gabriel's doctor. During their stay at Aldwick Lodge a gale blew down a great elm in the garden. Dante Gabriel, who was once more in a highly neurotic and unbalanced state, persisted in regarding this as an evil omen; but Christina, who maintained a healthy disbelief in superstition in spite of her interest in ghosts and the occult, smiled incredulously at his forebodings.

Speaking Likenesses, a fairy-story illustrated by Arthur Hughes, and *Annus Domini*, a book of prayers for each day of the year, appeared in 1874; and the following year Macmillan published the first collected edition of Christina's poems. Lucy gave birth to a daughter in September 1875, so that the Rossetti home was now uncomfortably crowded. Many authors would have found it difficult to work in such surroundings; but Christina could write anywhere, even on occasion using the corner of her wash-stand for a desk. She was also amusing herself by drawing designs for wallpapers. One, later to be known as 'my fruitless apple-tree', pleased Dante Gabriel so much that he sent it to Morris, suggesting that it might be suitable for reproduction by his firm. Morris, however, was not impressed, writing kindly enough to Christina but, as she told Dante Gabriel, 'setting up a standard of such complicated artistic perfection as (I fear) no alteration of mine can ever by any possibility attain'. She quoted ruefully from one of her own poems, 'In due season I found no apples there.'[24]

Meanwhile, the position in Euston Square was growing more and more difficult; and in the late summer of 1876 a parting was agreed upon. Maria's illness had declared itself; and in August she had been sent to the convalescent hospital at Eastbourne run by the All Saints sisters in the hope that sea air might prove of some benefit. There Christina and her mother joined her, well aware that the illness was a serious and probably a fatal one. Mother and daughter had already taken Number Thirty Torrington Square, a house which they planned to share with the two aunts, Eliza to be a permanent inmate and Charlotte to come and go as suited her convenience. From Eastbourne Christina wrote Lucy a humble and loving letter:

I hope, when two roofs shelter us and when faults which I regret are no longer your daily trial, that we may regain some of that liking which we had as friends, and which I should wish to be only the more tender and warm now that we are sisters. Don't please, despair of my doing better.[25]

Christina and her mother removed themselves in September 1876. In one of the many drowsy, faded ebb-tide squares of central London, Christina had found the house which was to be her home till death.

Chapter Ten

A Time for Grief

For Christina and her mother life in their new home began in grief. Their daily round centred on visits to Maria, who clearly had only a short time to live. Another source of wearing anxiety was Dante Gabriel's condition both physical and mental. With his mother and sisters, however, he was almost invariably gentle and considerate, making a real effort to control his black humours. 'Gabriel paid her [Maria] a very loving visit on Friday,' Christina wrote to William on October 9th, 'sitting with her between one and two hours I think, quite composed, tender and conversable. We left together, he bringing me home in his fly; when he came in, saw Mamma, and liked our dining-room.'[1]

Maria died on November 24th. There was no bitterness in Christina's grief for this dearly-loved sister, who had herself forbidden any gloomy display of mourning. Christina was thus to describe her funeral:

And at a moment which was sad only for us who lost her, all turned out in harmony with her holy hope and joy. Flowers covered her, loving mourners followed her, hymns were sung at her grave, the November day brightened, and the sun (I vividly remember) made a miniature rainbow in my eyelashes.[2]

Christina's first thought had been for the strain which the funeral might impose on Dante Gabriel. She begged him only to attend the service in the Convent chapel and not to go on to the cemetery. 'The latter is of course distressingly public, and the Sisters' habits render a funeral exceptionally noticeable,' she wrote to William. 'I dread the cemetery for him with all his peculiar feelings.'[3]

Ready as always with sympathy and comfort, Charles Cayley sent Christina a translation he had made from Petrarch which perhaps held

for her some meaning not to be discerned by the ordinary reader. It is
a fair sample of Cayley's always obscure verse:

> Ah, me! That comely face with earth is blent
> Which faith amongst us oft
> In Heaven and in the Weal above conveyed.
> To Paradise the viewless form is lent,
> That veil now being doft
> From which her blooming years received a shade
> To be yet re-arrayed
> Therewith and nevermore to be made bare
> When we shall mild and fair
> Behold her, as eternal beauty far
> Exceeds those that of mortal nature are![4]

Christina herself commemorated her sister in a better poem. 'Moon' had
been her favourite nickname for Maria:

> My love whose heart is tender said to me
>   'A moon lacks light except her sun befriend her.
> Let us keep tryst in heaven, dear Friend,' said she,
>   My love whose heart is tender.
>
>   From such a loftiness no words could bend her:
> Yet still she spoke of 'us' and spoke as 'we',
>   Her hope substantial, while my hope grew slender.
>
> Now keeps she tryst beyond earth's utmost sea,
>   Wholly at rest, tho' storms should toss and rend her;
> And still she keeps my heart and keeps its key,
>   My love whose heart is tender.

Some critics have believed that Maria was a major influence upon Christina's development. The existing evidence is too slight to make it possible
either to prove or disprove this theory. Very few letters survive—and
indeed, since the two were seldom apart, very few can have been written

except in the early days at Frome. A beloved elder sister, in whose company so much of her time was spent, must inevitably have had some effect upon Christina. Maria, who combined an excellent brain with an extremely narrow outlook, may well have fostered and encouraged her sister's scrupulosity. Christina actually expressed admiration for 'the courageous reverence with which one to whom a friend was exhibiting prints from the book of Job, avowed herself afraid to look at a representation which went counter to the Second Commandment, and looked not at it.'[5] The reference is to Maria, whose attitude towards Blake's genius appears to be less akin to reverence than to the most narrow bigotry. Clearly Maria's influence can only have strengthened Christina in her obsession with small failings and her over-anxious preoccupation with the letter of the law.

Maria had been content and even happy to die. The tragedy for Christina lay not in her sister's death but in her brother's life of progressive deterioration. In the following year, 1877, much of her time and thought was given to Dante Gabriel. For his part, he was always ready in the midst of his own troubles to interest himself in her writing and to give her help and advice. 'You shall see one or two pieces more;' she wrote to him on New Year's Day, 'but the one I sent you is a favourite of my own, and I doubt if you will unearth one to eclipse it: moreover, if I remember the mood in which I wrote it, it is something of a genuine "lyric cry", and such I will back against all skilled labour.' Clearly the old friendly argument between them still persisted, he urging her to work hard at her poetry, she maintaining that she could write well only in moments of inspiration. Famous author though she now was, she was still shy as a schoolgirl where her poetry was concerned—'I will either hand you my infinitesimal budget of pieces tomorrow, or I will send it you afterwards: but please respect my *thin skin* and do not start the subject in public.'[6] A letter dated March 6th begins 'I have thickened my skin and toughened the glass of my house sufficient to hear some fraternal stone-throwing.'[7] Shy she might be but she could stand up to criticism. 'Now my little piece satisfies myself'[8] she wrote to Dante Gabriel in reply to various objections he had raised against the poem *Mirrors of Life and Death*, and in another letter she wrote apropos the same poem, 'My mouse and my mole I incline to cling to on grounds that seem to me of some weight.'[9] Cling to them she did; and the mouse and the mole duly appeared in print.

In May and June, following an operation for hydrocele which would not have been serious had he not persisted in postponing it, Dante Gabriel was so ill that his life was believed to be in danger. Even when he had recovered some measure of physical health his mental depression was such that by August the doctors declared bluntly that he must leave London or die. A house was found at Hunter's Forestall, near Herne Bay; and there Dante Gabriel went on August 17th. With him were Treffry Dunn, 'art assistant' and general factotum, and a trained nurse Mrs Mitchell, whose chief duty was to make sure that the patient did not exceed the prescribed dose of chloral. Christina and her mother arrived a few days later, hoping that their presence might help to cheer Dante Gabriel and rouse him from gloom.

At first the change did him some good. Though he was still unwell and painfully depressed Christina noted thankfully that his room was no longer kept in semi-darkness and that 'he does not now sit in that attitude of dreadful dejection with drooping head'.[10] In an effort to keep him amused she and her mother read to him, played chess with him, and, most important of all as a means of raising his spirits, sat to him for several portrait-drawings. His greatest fear had been that his illness would interfere with his power to work; but, though his hand was tremulous, during the stay at Hunter's Forestall he completed two crayon portraits of Christina, one of his mother, and one of the two together, all of them, but especially the double portrait, worthy to rank among his best drawings.

Frances Rossetti was a constant comfort and support, 'the down pillow of the company'. Friends came and went, including Ford Madox Brown, 'the good, active friend he has ever been', Theodore Watts, who persuaded Christina to get up early one morning to watch the first sunrise she had ever seen, and the North Country artist Frederick Shields, to whom she took an immediate liking, describing him as 'most unselfish and friendly'. The friendship thus begun was to be an important element in Christina's later life. The bond between them was twofold—love and admiration for Dante Gabriel and an implicit Christian faith. 'He does not treat sacred themes merely as an artist,' Christina said of Shields.

'They are part of his life in a way that I have never known them to be of any other artist, and that is one cause of his marvellous power.'[11] Posterity, however, has not been greatly impressed by the paintings of this now forgotten artist. His best works are his early drawings and book illustrations which were justly praised by Ruskin. In later life he turned to what might be called didactic painting (at one time he seriously considered abandoning art and turning instead to preaching). His last and most important work was to decorate the Chapel of the Ascension in Bayswater Road, covering the entire wall-space with a series of religious pictures; and those who can remember that building before it was destroyed by a bomb probably do not regret overmuch the disappearance of these sermons in paint.

As a character Shields was an oddity—and oddities were very much to Christina's taste. He abhorred noise; barrel-organs were anathema to him, and even the singing of blackbirds in his garden could drive him to the verge of hysteria. At the age of forty he married an extremely pretty, totally uneducated girl of sixteen whom he left at the church door, afterwards parking her in a school for young ladies. The son of a small tradesman, Shields had struggled hard and faced much privation before he had succeeded in establishing himself as an artist, and even at the height of his career, when he was receiving profitable commissions from such patrons as the Duke of Westminster, he remained convinced that he was penniless and that his lot in life was a peculiarly hard one. 'I knew Shields for forty years,' said his friend Charles Rowley, 'and never knew him without an agony of some kind.' Christina herself poked gentle fun at this determined misery. 'Poor Shields, I hope his tour was less dismal than your narrative suggests' she wrote to Dante Gabriel on August 9th 1880: '*why* it should be so extra-dismal I do not exactly see; but one certainly may walk the world as one's own wet blanket, and perhaps such is our friend's well-known tourist costume.'[12] None the less she liked and admired Shields, helping him, for instance, with the iconography of a design for 'the noble army of martyrs' and entering into a long correspondence as to the meaning of the name 'Azazel', ending with an appeal to Charles Cayley, whose learning exploded her fanciful derivation—'Mr Cayley, (who asks to be remembered to you) has come to the rescue, and has gone far to test my Hebrew!'[13]

Unlike some Victorian women authors Christina could write openly about the problems of unmarried mothers and illegitimate children, but she could also on occasion display an almost incredible prudery. Shields was hardly the man to encourage lewd pictures or any form of indecency in art, yet even he unwittingly succeeded in shocking her as she makes plain in an undated letter written probably in 1880 or 1882:

> I must beg your patience and favourable construction for this letter for it may appear to you that I ought not to write it. Even if so, you are one to make allowance for a conscientious mistake. I think last night in admiring Miss Thomson's work I might better have said less, unless I could have managed to convey more. I do admire the grace and beauty of the designs, but I do not think that to call a figure a 'fairy' settles the right and wrong of such figures. You (as far as I know) are no dealer in such wares. Therefore I think it possible you will agree with me in thinking that *all* do well to forbear such deline-ations, and that most of all women artists should lead the way. I ought not now—I fear—to be having to say awkwardly what should not have been so totally ignored in my tone last night, but last night's blunder must not make me the slave of false shame this morning.[14]

The offending nudes were drawings of child-fairies intended to be reproduced as Christmas cards. Reading this letter it is easy to understand how a young woman like Lucy Rossetti would have been irritated by the narrow limits which her religious views imposed upon Christina's taste and judgement, by her anxious scrupulosity and by her inconvenient determination to testify in season and out of season to what she believed to be right.

Hunter's Forestall was a pleasant enough place in summer; but when the weather changed Dante Gabriel began to hanker after London. Christina too was depressed by the autumnal dreariness of her surround-ings, which she described in a poem entitled *An Autumn Garden*:

> In my Autumn garden I was fain
>   To mourn among my scattered roses;
>   Alas for that last rosebud which uncloses

> To Autumn's languid sun and rain
> When all the world is on the wane!
>   Which has not felt the sweet constraint of June,
>   Nor heard the nightingale in tune.

Though she could sympathise with his wish to return home she was horrified by the thought of Dante Gabriel living alone at Tudor House. 'My chief fear is for the future,' she wrote to Lucy on October 26th, 'for the moment when Mrs Mitchell will no longer have doses under her control and pressure of insomnolence has to be coped with by no one beside my poor dear brother himself. God help us all.'[15] So strongly did they feel his need for cheering company and for someone to supervise his consumption of chloral that Christina and Mrs Rossetti suggested that they should leave Torrington Square and move into Tudor House. At first Dante Gabriel seemed pleased with this idea but soon he began to see its disadvantages. the chief among them being of course Fanny Cornforth. His relationship with her was essential to his way of life. Reluctantly it was agreed that the scheme was not a practical one; and in November Dante Gabriel returned alone to Tudor House while Christina and Frances Rossetti rejoined Aunt Eliza in Torrington Square.

For the next few years Christina's life followed its usual quiet round, varied only by the yearly holiday at the seaside or in the country, Walton-on-the-Naze, Eastbourne, Seaford, Sevenoaks. Anxiety for Dante Gabriel hung over her like a dark cloud. He remained almost completely shut up in his own house and garden, seldom venturing out except for an occasional visit to Torrington Square, usually after dark. Like a child, in his extremity he turned instinctively to his mother, his dear 'Teaksicunculum'. 'Nothing could have brought so much pleasure to my solitary room as your entrance,'[16] he wrote when she was obliged to postpone a visit to Tudor House. He set special store by the family gathering at Christmas, allowing himself to become seriously agitated if anything threatened to prevent this reunion—'if we were apart this Christmas, I should view it as a bad omen for the coming year.'[17]

Dante Gabriel never lost his interest in Christina's writing or his concern for her success. Either in 1880 or 1881—the dates on letters are contradictory—he helped her to avoid what might have been an awkward predicament. An unremarkable but blameless composer called Aguilar had already set *Goblin Market* to music; now she was approached with a similar suggestion from a very different quarter. 'My sister has received a request from Lord Henry Somerset to consent to his publishing a considerable concerted piece from her poetry,' Dante Gabriel wrote to Watts. 'Is not this the gentleman who was connected with others in a judicial matter you spoke of to me?'[18] Christina was probably familiar with Lord Henry's sentimental ballads, which were very popular in Victorian drawing-rooms, but she was not to know that he was separated from his wife and involved in homosexual scandal. In the existing climate of opinion she would have committed a *gaffe* of the first order had she allowed him to set her poems to music.

Dante Gabriel warned her not to agree to Lord Henry's request. Remembering that in the eighteen-eighties women of Christina's class and upbringing were supposed to be ignorant of the fact that homosexuality existed it would be interesting to know just how explicit that warning may have been, the more so because Lord Henry now wrote to her asserting his innocence. A letter to Dante Gabriel shows how heavily the matter was weighing on her mind:

——has written in answer. He does not say a word about the setting; but asserts himself 'an innocent man' (promising he 'will not affect to misunderstand' my letter) and appears what in one case I consider justly hurt and in the other resentful. I am very much pained, and think I shall write once more—*finally*—not of course to reconsider the question of the music, but to make myself less uncomfortable in case (however blindly) I have been unjust. No explanations or details or assertion will be needed, and under no possible circumstances can harm ensue. Do not laugh; I am weighed upon by the responsibility of all one does and does not do; besides, I think our dearest Mother inclines in the same direction practically as I do in this affair.[19]

Christina's letter did not put an end to the matter for Lord Henry continued to protest his innocence. Once again she wrote explaining her point of view to Dante Gabriel:

I have made up my mind what to do. —— wrote again enclosing strong evidence on his side. Two documents there were: one I think any candid person would admit carried great weight, the other goes far with me, but I do not feel a right to let them out of my hands or even to show them except to our Mother who is at least as favourably impressed as I am. The practical point to which this tends is that I am going to send —— back his letters and papers, so that he may feel sure they neither in my lifetime nor afterwards pass into other keeping. . . . Poor fellow, whatever his case may be he is infinitely to be pitied.[20]

Remembering the taboo on homosexuality and the existence of the law of libel it is understandable that Christina should have left a blank rather than write Lord Henry's name even in a private letter to her brother but it is surprising to find her leaving a similar blank in another letter which could have no possible reference to criminal behaviour. It is difficult to say with certainty to whom this letter refers, but in all probability the man in question is Dante Gabriel's kind and generous patron, F. R. Leyland, who had started life as an office-boy:

. . . I believe you considered I ignored —— last Sunday. No, I did not do that because I bowed to him when leaving the room, but with your habitual acuteness you detected the underlying feeling which checked sociability. I had long thought of that acquaintance as one to be avoided rather than courted.[21]

William shared something of Christina's antipathy to Leyland, but he was altogether more generous in his judgement. 'Mr Leyland, the wealthy Liverpool shipowner, was not so attractive to me,' he wrote; 'he was, however, a man of judgement and refinement, and had a keen affection for my brother.'[22]

In 1881 came the news of James Collinson's death. Christina had never quite forgotten her first love. She inserted a sonnet by him into *Time Flies* under the date January 24th, and she wrote to a Mr Haden, editor of an anthology of religious verse who had asked for permission to print some of her poems, suggesting that he should also consider 'a blank verse poem of some length on the "sorrowful mysteries" of Our Lord's life written by James Collinson, an artist not long deceased, and published in a now rare magazine entitled *The Germ*'.[23]

During these years Christina published two short books in prose. *Seek and Find* is a devotional commentary on the Benedicite, the canticle which begins 'O all ye Works of the Lord, bless ye the Lord'. The book contains one or two interesting passages, including the very practical remark, 'Not to fathom the origin of evil but to depart from evil is man's understanding.' More debatable is the comment 'a work is less noble than its maker; he who makes a good thing is himself better than it', a curious point of view to be adopted by someone who had lived all her life among artists and who knew very well how a fine work of art can often be produced by a person of extremely faulty character. Christina's faith may have been rigid, but it was not obscurantist; her explanation of the days of Creation as 'lapses of time by us immeasurable' would have been considered slightly 'advanced' in 1879, the date of the publication of *Seek and Find*.

Commenting on the verses 'Oh ye Whales and all that move in the waters, bless ye the Lord,' she adds to great Leviathan the tiny sea-anemones, shrimps, crabs and the like which she delighted to study on her seaside holidays: 'A myriad of inferior creatures wriggle in wet mud and burrow in wet sand or take their station between high and low watermark.' So, five years later, in a letter to Lucy, then on holiday at Ventnor, she enquired about 'marine trophies'—'Do any of his[William's] children inherit his and my taste for such guests?' she asked. 'To this day I think I could plod indefinitely along shingle with my eyes pretty well glued to the ground.'[24] Cayley had shown real perception when he gave her the gift of a sea-mouse; such small, strange creatures were to her a source of intense joy. She saw the sea itself as a symbol of sadness and division, looking forward to a heaven where 'There shall be no more blight nor need, Nor barrier of the sea.' Her interest was not in the vast depths of ocean but in its more accessible edges. The barren magnificence of sea and mountains had little appeal for her; she preferred sandy beaches and fertile meadows, rejoicing in 'the inexhaustible cheerfulness of all green things'.

Called to be Saints, a book on the minor festivals of the Church, published in 1881, contains a passage which suggests that however contented Christina may have appeared outwardly, she knew moments of inward rebellion against the limitations and sameness of her life in a dull London house with only three old ladies for company:

> When it seems (as sometimes through revulsion of feeling and urgency of Satan it may seem) that our yoke is uneasy and our burden unbearable because our life is pared down and subdued and repressed to an intolerable level; and so in one moment every instinct of our whole self revolts against our lot, and we loathe this day of quietness and of sitting still, and writhe under a sudden sense of all we have irrevocably foregone, of the right hand or foot or eye cast from us, of the haltingness and maimedness of our entrance (if enter we do at last) into life—then the Seraphim of Isaiah's vision making music in our memory revive hope in our hearts.
>
> No lack there, nothing subdued there; no bridle, no curb, no self-sacrifice; outburst of sympathy, fulness of joy, pleasure for evermore.

There is pathos in this vision of a splendidly free and exuberant Heaven if we remember how full of bridle and curb and self-sacrifice was Christina's life upon earth.

Incongruously enough, *Called to be Saints* was the book which Christina presented to Swinburne, always an enthusiastic admirer of her poetry. In 1882 he sent her a copy of his own poem *Tristram*: and Christina could find nothing suitable to send him in return. 'This is the fourth book he has sent me, and I not one hitherto to him,' she lamented to William, 'so for lack of aught else I am actually offering him a *Called to be Saints*, merely however drawing his attention to the verses.'[25] Swinburne accepted this present in the spirit in which it had been sent, giving great pleasure to Christina by his praise of her verses for the festivals of Saint Barnabas, Holy Innocents and Saint Philip and Saint James.

More important than either of these slight prose works was the book of poems which Christina published in 1881 entitled *A Pageant and Other Poems*. Friends and relations were enthusiastic. 'I think her *Pageant* most lovely,' Dante Gabriel wrote to his mother, 'as does Watts also, and we are both deeply impressed by the beauty of the *Monna*

Innominata series'[26]—a sequence also praised by Scott, who judged the book as a whole to be 'rich in beautiful thoughts but sometimes a little puzzling in the execution'.[27] Swinburne's reaction was said to amount to 'a dancing and screaming ecstasy'.[28] Modern readers, however, may find the book slightly disappointing after the more obvious beauties of the two earlier volumes. Christina seems to have lost, or perhaps deliberately forgone, her gift of song; there is nothing here so enchantingly melodious as 'When I am dead, my dearest' or *A Birthday*, or *Birds of Paradise*. The poem which gives the book its title is not an inspiriting one. To Dante Gabriel Christina described *The Months: A Pageant* as 'among the best and most wholesome things I have produced'.[29] Wholesome these verses well may be, but like most wholesome things they have an insipid taste. This pageant was intended to be performed by children, a purpose for which it is admirably suited. The Rossettis made a family joke of the lines with which October ushers in November—

> Here comes my youngest sister, looking dim,
> And grim
> With dismal ways.

declaring that they might have been spoken by Dante Gabriel about their own younger sister.

As well as the lovely *Monna Innominata* sequence, almost certainly written some twelve or fifteen years earlier, the book contains a second sonnet-sequence entitled *Later Life*. The sub-title, 'A Double Sonnet of Sonnets', suggests that Christina saw these fourteen poems as an integral whole joined together by a more important link than the chance that they were all written in later life. Such a connection, however, is hard to find. The sequence contains the beautiful sonnet, 'Star Sirius and the Pole Star dwell afar', also two sonnets on the subject of Eve, mother of all mankind, a favourite topic with Christina. This provided her with a chance to air her views on the position of women:

> Let woman fear to teach and bear to learn,
> Remembering the first woman's first mistake.
> Eve had for pupil the inquiring snake

In a poem of much later date she was even more outspoken about what she believed to be the proper relationship between man and woman:

> Woman was made for man's delight;
> Charm, O woman, be not afraid!
> His shadow by day, his moon by night,
> Woman was made.

She would have agreed with Miss Yonge's view that the role of a good wife is that of 'helpmeet'. On occasion, however, Christina could show surprising sympathy with the Suffragists, and in a letter to Augusta Webster, in her day a well-known poetess, she put forward some startlingly advanced views:

> ... if female rights are sure to be overborne for lack of female voting influence, then I confess I feel disposed to shoot ahead of my instructresses, and to assert that female *Members of Parliament* are only right and reasonable. Also I take exceptions at the exclusion of married women from the suffrage,—for who so apt as mothers—all previous arguments allowed for the moment—to protect the interests of themselves and of their offspring?[30]

In January 1881 Dante Gabriel fell into one of his worst fits of depression; and his physical health began to deteriorate fast. Christina and her mother stayed with him for a short time in April, a visit which brought him some temporary happiness and comfort. 'I have enjoyed nothing so much for years as your and Christina's short stay here,'[31] he wrote to Frances Rossetti. From now onwards she and Christina did their best to pay him a visit at least once a week. For daily company he had living with him Hall Caine, a young man with literary ambitions who was later to make a great name for himself as a popular novelist. This anxious and dreary period was made slightly more cheerful to Christina by frequent visits from her new friend Frederick Shields and from the ever-faithful Cayley.

In September Dante Gabriel set off for the Lake District to try whether he might benefit from a change of air and surroundings. With him went

Hall Caine and Fanny Cornforth. Three weeks in the Vale of Saint John left him worse rather than better; the solitude of the mountains produced in him what Doughty describes as 'a renewed desolation of spirit beyond all consolation or cure',[32] and he was glad to return to the more familiar solitude of Tudor House. From there he scribbled a note to Fanny begging her to discontinue her frequent visits at least for the present: 'Such difficulties are now arising with my family that it will be impossible for me to see you here till I write again.'[33] This has been read as proof that his family were deliberately depriving the sick man of the company of a woman who, whatever her faults, had brought much warmth and cheerfulness into his life. The fact is that Dante Gabriel had always been at pains to keep Fanny away from his mother and sister who, now that he was in so critical a condition, were liable to call in upon him without previous notice. An encounter between them and Fanny was more than the sick man could bear to contemplate, hence his request to her to keep away 'till I write again', which, of course, he was never to do.

A sense of guilt oppressed Dante Gabriel. He was haunted by memories of long ago when, as William puts it, 'his desultory habits of work, or lack of filial deference, used to annoy our father, and elicit some severe expressions from him'.[34] He now declared that he would like to make confession to a priest. William could make nothing of his brother's memories of the past or of his present penitence, but when he confided in Christina he found that she understood both very well:

> Thinking about what you said of poor dear Gabriel's distress, I seem to recover a shadowy recollection of the incident, and, if I am right, Mamma used her influence successfully to get the words unsaid. . . . No wonder that in weakness and suffering such a reminiscence haunts weary days and sleepless hours of double darkness. How exceedingly I wish Mr. Burrows* or one like him had access within the nearly-closed precincts: you must laugh at me if you will, but I really think a noble spiritual influence might do what no common sense, foresight of ruin, affection of friends, could secure. And Mr. Burrows I know he respects.[35]

*Incumbent of Christ Church, Albany Street, and an old family friend.

To Dante Gabriel himself she wrote one of her rare self-revealing and openly loving letters:

> I write because I cannot but write, for you are continually in my thoughts, and always in my heart, much more in our Mother's who sends you her love and dear blessing.
>
> I want to assure you that, however harassed by memory or by anxiety you may be, I have (more or less) heretofore gone through the same ordeal. I have borne myself till I became unbearable by myself, and then I have found help in confession and absolution and spiritual counsel, and relief inexpressible. Twice in my life I tried to suffice myself with measures short of this, but nothing would do; the first time was of course in my youth before my general confession, the second time was when circumstances had led me (rightly or wrongly) to break off the practice. But now for years past I have resumed the habit, and I hope not to continue it profitlessly.
>
> > ' 'Tis like frail man to love and walk on high,
> >   But to be lowly is to be like God,'
>
> is a couplet (Isaac Williams) I thoroughly assent to.
>
> I ease my own heart by telling you all this and I hope I do not weary yours. Don't think of me merely as the younger sister whose glaring faults are known to you, but as a devoted friend also.[36]

This letter hints at some unknown, unidentifiable crisis in Christina's inner life, and gives yet another indication of the difficulties confronting anyone who tries to penetrate below the surface of so reticent and private a character.

William believed that his brother's troubles were for the most part imaginary and capable of being cured by a determined effort of will. Christina was wiser, realising that Dante Gabriel could make no such effort and that an illness is none the less real because it has its origin in the mind of the sufferer. Gently she begged William to try to be a little more patient, a little more understanding:

> Don't you think neither you nor I can quite appreciate all he is undergoing at present, what between wrecked health at least in some measure,

nerves which appear to falsify facts, and most anxious money-matters? It is trying to have to do with him at times, but what must it be TO BE himself?[37]

On December 11th Dante Gabriel suffered a paralytic attack, and in the New Year was once again ordered by the doctors to leave London. The architect John Seddon offered him the use of Westcliff, a large bungalow at Birchington-on-Sea; and there Dante Gabriel went on February 4th, with a professional nurse in attendance, also Hall Caine and Caine's twelve-year-old sister, Lily. Dante Gabriel had hoped that his mother and Christina would also accompany him, but the doctor forbade Mrs Rossetti, aged eighty-five and slightly ailing, to leave home in the cold wintry weather, and not till the end of February would he allow her to travel as far as Birchington. This delay was a bitter disappointment to Dante Gabriel. Unlike his friends and relations he was very well aware of the dangerous and precarious nature of his condition. 'My state is faint and feeble to a degree,' he wrote to Christina; 'full of pains, and unable to walk* to any purpose. But, as you must find this out some time, why not now?'[38]

Once arrived at Birchington Christina realised that her brother was indeed very seriously ill. On March 4th she wrote William a far from optimistic letter in which she described Dante Gabriel's sad state of mind and body and the evils he was bringing on himself by what she aptly called his 'inert imprudence'. He had brought painting equipment with him to the bungalow and one or two canvases—Christina noted the finished *Proserpine* and a *Jeanne d'Arc*—but he was incapable of doing any work. Instead he read 'amusing books', *The Tale of Two Cities*, Miss Braddon's *Dead Men's Shoes*, Wilkie Collins's thriller *The Moonstone*, or if reading to himself proved too great an effort Christina would read aloud to him. Sometimes he would find pleasure in talking over with her their shared memories of a distant, happy past. She noted that although his body was wasting away his mind was perfectly clear and he no longer suffered from any form of delusion.

The care of her brother left Christina with no time for her own writing. She had recently been asked to contribute to a series of biographies of

*Doughty believes this to be a misreading for 'work'.

famous women, the subjects proposed to her being Elizabeth Fry, Mary Lamb, Adelaide Ann Proctor, or Lady Augusta Stanley. Since she was unable to undertake any such book herself, she suggested that the editor of the series should apply instead either to Letitia Bell Scott or to William's old love, Henrietta Rintoul.

To William himself she wrote frequently, giving him ominous and explicit accounts of his brother's condition, telling him, for instance, that the nurse considered Dante Gabriel to have retrograded seriously since his arrival at Westcliff, believing 'there are grounds to fear that some terrible mischief lurks in his constitution'. 'This is sad indeed,' she commented, 'but the not saying it is vain.' Unlike Christina, William still refused to face the realities of the situation, clinging to his belief in the imaginary nature of Dante Gabriel's ailments. 'Pray do not doubt the *reality* of poor dear Gabriel's illness;' Christina begged in this same letter, 'do not let any theory or opinion influence you to entertain such a doubt.'[39] The urgency of her letters suggests that she herself knew Dante Gabriel's illness to be a fatal one. However, as late as March 24th she could report that the local doctor 'considers the case very serious but *not* irremediable', urging that Dante Gabriel should be encouraged to exert himself and take up some form of occupation. 'And I think he suggested amusement,' Christina wrote, adding the comment, 'This last of course is no easy item.'[40]

In any previous crisis William had always been ready to drop his own concerns and rush to the help of his family. Now, however, he made no attempt to come to Birchington, although he must have known that his presence there would not only give great pleasure to his brother but would also bring incalculable relief to his much-pressed sister. Though Hall Caine was constantly at hand and other friends, Watts and Shields amongst them, came down for short periods, she was the person on whom the double burden of anxiety and responsibility rested most heavily. Not only was she kept busy in an effort to provide Dante Gabriel with the 'amusement' which the doctor considered so desirable, but she also had the care of her mother on her shoulders. As always in moments of stress, Frances Rossetti remained commendably calm; nevertheless, Christina was well aware of the strain imposed on this frail old woman of over eighty, and she was alert for any sign of damage to health or spirits. Presumably Christina was also responsible for the housekeeping for a party of six to eight persons, not counting the servants. 'Could you believe that down here I feel over-full of occupation!!'[41] she wrote to William. For a delicate semi-invalid the physical strain was severe; but above all she felt herself to be over-pressed emotionally, yearning for what she described as 'leisure of feeling'.[42]

Not till March 28th did Willam propose coming to Birchington and then only for a night or two. 'Seeing what we do see here, we cannot but rejoice at the prospect of your flying visit,' Christina wrote, adding the news that the doctor had showed 'the gravest apprehension as to mental (he always uses the word *nerves*) despondency, and plainly said that an eye must be kept on G.'[43] William duly came and went, returning to London on April 3rd. Two days later Christina wrote telling him plainly that kidney disease had declared itself and that the doctors considered the case hopeless. On April 6th, William, Theodore Watts, and the specialist Marshall were all summoned to Birchington by telegram, Dante Gabriel having taken a sudden turn for the worse. He had known for a long time that he was dying although those around him had never admitted that fact. 'Then you really think I am dying?' he now asked Hall Caine. 'At last you think so, but *I* was right from the first.'

On Saturday April 8th, Easter Eve, Frederick Shields arrived at Westcliff. That night Christina sat up with the sick man, beginning at midnight, and watching through the small hours which are so often the hours of death. When morning came she admitted to being too exhausted to go to church, even though she must miss her Easter communion. With her mother and William and the little group of friends she was at Dante Gabriel's bedside when he died at half-past nine that Easter Sunday evening.

Dante Gabriel was buried not in the family grave at Highgate but in Birchington churchyard. After the funeral was over four or five of the mourners returned to place on the grave a particularly fine wreath sent by his friend and patron, Lady Mount-Temple. This done, Christina handed to her mother a few sprays of woodspurge which she had picked from the garden at Westcliff. Frances Rossetti knelt down, and beside the handsome wreath she placed the little bunch of the tiny green flowers which Dante Gabriel had made memorable in one of his best-known poems:

> The wind flapped loose, the wind was still
> Shaken out dead from tree and hill;
> I had walked on at the wind's will,—
> I sat now, for the wind was still.
>
> Between my knees my forehead was,—
> My lips, drawn in, said not Alas!
> My hair was over in the grass,
> My naked ears heard the day pass.
>
> My eyes, wide open, had the run
> Of some ten weeds to fix upon;
> Among these few, out of the sun,
> The woodspurge flowered, three cups in one.
>
> From perfect grief there need not be
> Wisdom or even memory;
> One thing then learnt remains to me,—
> The woodspurge has a cup of three.

Chapter Eleven

Devoted Daughter

The last twelve years of Christina's life were uneventful ones punctuated only by the deaths of friends and relatives. The period was unproductive of new writing; she published two devotional books but though she continued to write poems she produced no volume of poetry except *Verses* (1893), a collection of the various poems scattered throughout the prose religious books which she had previously published with the S.P.C.K. Because they can be dated more or less accurately her early religious poems have already been discussed as they occurred in the course of her life-history; but perhaps this is as good a place as any to give brief consideration to her religious poetry as a whole.

As a whole it must be treated; it cannot be considered chronologically because of the highly inconvenient way in which William chose to arrange the religious poems. When he came to edit Christina's collected works he printed the 'secular' poems in some sort of chronological order but the religious ones he grouped together under subject-headings chosen by himself, 'Songs for Strangers and Pilgrims', 'Some Feasts and Fasts', 'New Jerusalem' and the like. He gave dates for each poem; but apart from some early poems, the majority of these dates are vague and tentative. 'Before 1893' is a typical and frequent entry, one which tells us no more than the obvious fact that the poem was written some time before its date of publication. Christina's manuscript note-books stop short at 1866 so that the work of rearranging these poems in chronological order demands long and detailed research. A new edition of the *Collected Works* is in preparation in America. For the present, however, the general reader cannot read the religious poems in any sort of reasonable sequence.

William's scheme of arrangement has another disadvantage. When Christina herself arranged the order of poems in the various volumes published in her lifetime she took great care to do this in such a way as to provide variety of tone and subject. William's method of placing the poems under headings means that poems similar in mood and subject-matter are grouped together, the inevitable effect being one of monotony and sameness. To read Christina's religious poetry in the form in which it is most readily available demands an effort of concentration and will-power severe enough to discourage the average reader.

These poems are in fact seldom read today although Christina is still frequently described as a religious poet. For a hundred readers of the love poetry or of *Goblin Market* there is probably only one who has any acquaintance with the specifically religious poems apart from the few to be found in hymn-books or anthologies. In her own day this was not so, least of all on the other side of the Atlantic. Christina herself had no great liking for American writing: 'I do not feel drawn to transatlantic liter-ature' she confessed, though she had read enough to know that she preferred John Greenleaf Whittier to James Russell Lowell.[1] Her own poems, however, found many American admirers, some of whom sent her charming gifts such as 'a very pretty present . . . of American foliage, in autumnal tints, mounted on paper',[2] or called upon her when they were visiting Europe. It was her religious poetry that especially appealed to Americans. 'We scarcely take to Rossetti's poetry,' Emerson wrote to Scott. 'It does not come home to us; but we like Christina's religious pieces.'[3]

Religious poetry as such is of course less popular than it was a hundred years ago, but as the case of Gerard Manley Hopkins clearly shows, it is still widely read for its literary merit—if it has any. Modern readers, however, are apt to find Christina's religious outlook over-precise and circumscribed. Her central theme is of course the love of God. By that word she does not mean the first principle of the universe, a Words-worthian 'motion and a spirit that impels all thinking things'; she means the Christian God as expressed in the person of Jesus Christ. The same might of course be said of the Roman Catholic Hopkins; but his range is wider and less limited. (Incidentally, in his youth Hopkins greatly ad-mired Christina's poetry.) Children often enjoy the rhythm and language of a love-poem, but they are not in complete and satisfying sympathy with the author because they have not yet been in love. So non-Christians enjoy and appreciate the literary quality of Christina's religious poetry, but they find difficulty in responding to it emotionally. Christians and non-Christians alike can appreciate and assent to Emily Brontë's great confession of faith 'No coward soul is mine'; but over the door to Christina's religious poetry might be written the words 'For Christians Only'.

Not, be it noted, for Anglo-Catholics, or even for Anglicans only. Christina's poetry is surprisingly free of any sectarian element; it might have just as easily been written by a Roman Catholic or a Methodist. In this she differs from that other poet of the Oxford Movement, John Keble, whose work she did not admire, though she took the trouble to illustrate her own copy of *The Christian Year* with naïve little marginal drawings. (Oddly enough, she liked and admired the work of a lesser Tractarian versifier, Isaac Williams.) Yet her Anglo-Catholicism was a basic influence on her poetry, an essential element in her individual genius. This point is well put by Humphry House in his essay on Pre-Raphaelite poetry:

> There seemed to be an irreparable cleavage between the facts of modern society and the depths it was recognised poetry ought to touch. . . . They saw that mediaeval modes of apprehending reality were productive of great and satisfying works of art, as the modern modes of mixed science and sentimentality were not. They attempted by exploring the possibilities of allegory and symbolism to restore a harmony they thought modern life had lost. . . . We have to consider the status of symbols, allegories and emblems, the kind of significance they were supposed to have, and the means by which they were supposed to have any significance at all.

The Pre-Raphaelites as a whole never reached any satisfactory conclusion on this subject because 'the sense of identity between symbol and thing symbolised was little understood'. Only one of them had any clear perception of that identity, only one of them achieved the aim which they had set before themselves:

> Christina solved the problem within her own compass almost to perfection. . . . She seems to have assimilated in her youth something

of the essential quality of the mediaeval method and to have adapted it without strain or affectation to contemporary feelings; in her religious poems she avoids the problem of modern or mediaeval dress and keepings by emphasising neither; but still her persons and situations have a clarity and sharpness which belong with the Pre-Raphaelite aims. . . . Because Christina was a devout Anglo-Catholic she was able to use Catholic symbolism with complete internal conviction; there is no uncertainty about her levels.[4]

Christina's religious poetry is curiously intense:

> My heart is yearning:
> Behold my yearning heart,
>   And lean low to satisfy
>   Its lonely beseeching cry,
> For Thou its fulness art. . . .
>
> My heart is yearning,
> Yearning and thrilling thro'
>   For Thy Love mine own of old,
>   For Thy Love unknown, untold,
> Ever old, ever new.

Or again:

> My faith burns low, my love burns low,
>   Only my heart's desire cries out in me;
> By the deep thunder of its want and woe
>   Cries out to Thee.
>
> Lord, Thou art Life though I be dead,
>   Love's fire Thou art, however cold I be;
> Nor heaven have I, nor place to lay my head,
>   Nor home, but Thee.

Clearly the passion for which she could find no satisfaction in her thwarted experience of *eros* spilled over into her expression of *agape*; but to explain her intense love of God simply in terms of repressed sex is too cheap and easy an answer. Love is none the less genuine because it is 'sublimated', to use the cant term. For centuries the masters of the religious life have known that there is a definite connection between chastity and mystical experience; all that the psychologists have done is to find new terms in which to express an old truth.

In spite of the passionate nature of her love of God Christina was in fact no mystic if that word be taken in what William Temple described as 'the proper sense of the word mystical as signifying a direct apprehension of God by the human mind'.[5] Once again comes the unavoidable comparison with Emily Brontë. Christina was a Christian without being a mystic; Emily was a mystic but not necessarily a Christian one. Nowhere in Christina's poetry is there any description of a moment of direct apprehension such as Emily gives in the poem generally known as *The Prisoner*:

> There dawns the Invisible; the Unseen its truth reveals;
> My outward sense is gone, my inward essence feels;
> Its wings are almost free—its home, its harbour found,
> Measuring the gulf, it stoops, and dares the final bound.

Christina longed and prayed for just such an experience:

> Two things, Lord, I require,
> Love's name and flame
> To wrap my soul in fire.

She admitted, however, that this fire had not descended on her:

> We are of those who tremble at Thy word;
> Who faltering walk in darkness toward our close
> Of mortal life, by terrors curbed and spurred:
>   We are of those.

> We journeyed to that land which no man knows
> Who any more can make his voice be heard
> Above the clamour of our wants and woes.

Not ours the hearts Thy loftiest love hath stirred,
Not such as we Thy lily and Thy rose:—
Yet, Hope of those who hope with hope deferred,
    We are of those.

Christina had a great liking for the roundel form in which this poem is written and used it frequently in her religious verse although the formal scheme with its repetition of rhyme and phrase seems ill adapted to such themes.

Yet it is in a roundel that Christina best expresses that near-identification of *eros* with *agape* which is the hallmark of her religious poetry. This roundel has been rightly placed by William in the religious section but it would not appear out-of-place among the secular poems:

Love understands the mystery, whereof
    We can but spell a surface history:
Love knows, remembers: let us trust in Love:
    Love understands the mystery.

Love weighs the event, the long pre-history,
Measures the depth beneath, the height above,
    The mystery, with the ante-mystery.

To love and to be grieved befits a dove
    Silently telling her bead-history;
Trust all to Love, be patient and approve:
    Love understands the mystery.

Now that Dante Gabriel and Maria were dead and William married to the rather uncongenial Lucy, Christina's life centred entirely on her mother, with the two elderly aunts as shadowy figures in the background. Her letters become more and more concerned with the trivialities of daily life, less and less with outside events, and hardly at all with her own writing.

Sorrow followed on sorrow. Early one cold morning in January 1883

Christina was sent for to be told that William's baby son Michael was dying. The agnostic William and Lucy had with good logic refused to have their children baptised, a refusal which was a great grief to Christina. Sitting beside the dying baby she begged to be allowed to baptise him herself. To their great credit the parents gave consent, believing that baptism could neither help nor hinder the child, and knowing how much it would distress his aunt to see him die unbaptised. In a set of charming verses Christina commemorated Michael, thus become her special child:

> The youngest bud of five,
> The least lamb of the fold,
> Bud not to blossom, yet to thrive
>   Away from cold:
> Lamb which we shall not see
> Leap at its pretty pranks,
> Our lamb at rest and full of glee
>   On heavenly banks.

Later that same year Christina suffered a far more painful loss. In February 1883 Charles Cayley wrote to her asking her to be his literary executor. His letter has not survived, but its contents are made clear by Christina's reply:

My dear old Friend,
    I will not dwell too much on the sad possibility you hint to me, but rather will put forward—as I sincerely can—the apparently at least equal possibility that I may become the leader and not the follower along that path. Nor will I care what are the steps so long as the goal is good. Nor will I despair of the good goal for either of us. Meanwhile I hope you have shaken off the neuralgia, of which I also well know the pain, and that many happy hours with the Leif-childs* and other valued intimates remain in store for you.
    But, all else assumed as inevitable, I should value though I should

*The families of two brothers, one a sculptor, one with 'literary ambitions', friends of Cayley and of the Rossettis.

not need a memorial. And three of the translations would be very dear: watching over them, I might in a measure nurse your name and fame. Yet, if you think any of your family could feel hurt, do not do it: very likely there was a moment when—and no wonder—those who loved you best thought very severely of me, and indeed I deserved severity at my own hands,—I never seemed to get much at yours. And some trifle that you had been fond of and perhaps had used would be precious to me.

Now let us suppose the reverse position, and let me explain my own plans. If my dearest Mother outlives me, everything I have (a mere trifle in all) goes to her: perhaps you may recollect my telling you that even now I am not so much as independent, so little indeed have I. Beyond this immediate vista,—William made me a home for so many years that (especially now that he has a young family) I am inclined to rate the money-portion of my debt to him at (say) £100 a year for twenty years: here at once is £2000! and far enough am I from possessing such a sum. Not that William puts forward any such view, but *I* entertain it all by myself. So, to sum up, you see I am an indefinite distance off from having much at my pure disposal. If I live long enough, that is if I survive certain members of my family, I believe I shall be amply provided for: but this is no contingency to count upon. I dare say you will trace, though I certainly have not stated, what sort of train of thought set me upon saying all this. . . .[6]

Clearly Christina would have wished to leave some money to Cayley had she not been tied by what she considered to be a debt of honour to William. Equally clearly, Cayley had hinted in his letter at the probability of his early death; nevertheless, Christina continued to believe and hope that she would be the one to go first, as well she might, her health being so precarious. But she was wrong. On December 5th 1883, Christina's fifty-third birthday, Charles Cayley was found dead in his bed. On hearing the news she set off for the Excise Office to tell William. She did not break down, but her face was something her brother was never to forget.

'You were, I know, the friend he valued most'[7] wrote Cayley's sister Sophie, who might well have been one of those who, in earlier days, had 'thought very severely' of Christina. In his will Cayley bequeathed to 'my dear and kind friend Christina Rossetti . . . the remainder of such books as have been published for me by Messrs. Longmans & Co,' a bequest which gave Christina great pleasure but no financial profit since the books in question were valueless. Still more dear to her was a second bequest—'And the said Christina Rossetti is also to have my best writing-desk, and any packet that may be lying therein addressed to her, and she shall be entitled to reclaim or order to be destroyed any letters of hers which may be found among my papers or effects.'[8]

As Cayley had supposed, Christina asked that her letters be destroyed, and she herself doubtless destroyed any packet addressed to her which she may have found inside her desk. According to Sophie Cayley the desk also contained a letter from Christina herself and a ring. That ring possibly appears again in Christina's story.

William definitely connected the poem *One Sea-side Grave* not with Dante Gabriel but with Charles Cayley, who was buried at Hastings:

> Unmindful of the roses,
>   Unmindful of the thorn,
> A reaper tired reposes
>   Among his gathered corn;
>   So might I, till the morn!
>
> Cold as the cold Decembers,
>   Past as the days that set,
> While only one remembers
>   And all the rest forget,—
>   But one remembers yet.

The poem is dated April 1884. In January of that year Christina had made a special journey to Hastings to visit Cayley's grave, a fact which makes William's attribution all the more probable. However, in her thesis on Christina's unpublished poetry Mrs Hatton quotes a poem from one of the manuscript notebooks, dated February 8th 1853 and headed *From the Antique*.

I wish that I were dying
Deep drowning without pain,
I wish that I were lying
Beneath the wind and rain,
Never to rise again.

Forgetful of the roses,
Forgetful of the thorn
So sleeping, as reposes
A child until the dawn,
So sleeping without morn.

Cold as the cold Decembers,
Past as the days that set;
While only one remembers
And all the rest forget,
But one remembers yet.

This poem seems itself to be derived from another one dated December 10th 1852 in a different metre but with the same title. Mrs Packer will have it that because this first version was written thirty years before Cayley's death the published poem can have no connection with him. This is not necessarily true. In the 1853 version only the third verse has much merit. It is possible that this one good verse out of a bad poem sang itself in Christina's memory, as such verses will, and that she came to see how well it fitted Charles Cayley, dead in one of those cold Decembers and unlikely to be remembered by anyone except herself, who could never forget him. She scrapped the first verse, re-cast the weak second verse to fit better with her new subject, and left the third untouched, thus producing a poem which William rightly connected with Cayley though its origins went back to 1853.

Two other poems written about this time fit well with Christina's muted love for Charles Cayley. The first is headed *Parted*:

Had Fortune parted us,
Fortune is blind;

Had Anger parted us,
　Anger unkind—
But since God parts us
　Let us part humbly,
Bearing our burden
　Bravely and dumbly.

And since there is but one
　Heaven, not another
Let us not close that door
　Against each other.
God's Love is higher than mine,
　Christ's tenfold proved,
Yet even I would die
　For thee, Beloved.

The second verse calls to mind a phrase from Christina's letter to Cayley, 'Nor will I despair of the good goal for either of us.' The second poem, written in 1884, and from its dating apparently connected with Cayley, is much less frequently quoted than either *One Sea-side Grave* or *Parted*. It is headed *Who shall say?*:

I toiled on, but thou
　Wast weary of the way,
And so we parted: now
　Who shall say
Which is happier—I or thou?

I am weary now
　On the solitary way:
But art thou rested, thou?
　Who shall say
Which of us is calmer now?

Still my heart's love, thou,
　In thy secret way,

Art still remembered now:
Who shall say—
Still rememberest thou?

Christina had genuinely loved Charles Cayley, and she continued to love him until the day of her death. But the love which she felt for this untidy, tongue-tied scholar was not Browning's 'lyric Love, half angel and half bird and all a wonder and a wild desire', the love which she herself had sung in poem after poem. Her love for Cayley more closely resembled the deep, appreciative, tolerant love which a devoted wife feels for her husband, recognising and perhaps wryly amused by his imperfections and idiosyncrasies. A passage in *Time Flies* may be indicative of Christina's feeling towards Cayley after his death:

> ... we also love our own beloved without on the whole wanting them to be different. They are themselves, and this suffices. We are quite ready to like something superior, but it contents our hearts to love them. And when once death has stepped in, dividing as it were soul from spirit, the friend that is as one's own soul from oneself, then half those banished peculiarities put on pathos. We remain actually fond of the blameless oddities, the plain face abides as the one face we prefer.[9]

Cayley was gone; but other friends remained to cheer Christina with their affection. Their visits did something to relieve the monotony of life in the Torrington Square house, that place of shadows and silence— 'Entering it you felt the presence of very old age, a silence that draped and muffled the house.'[10] Letitia Scott was a frequent visitor, but William Bell Scott came only in the winter months, since he now spent all his summers at Penkill. In April 1885, whilst he was still in London, he suffered a severe heart attack which left him a permanent invalid. As soon as he was fit to travel Alice Boyd carried him off to Penkill, where she devoted herself to the business of nursing him. Christina was never to see him again.

At Penkill Scott occupied his time in making an etching of Dante Gabriel's portrait of what Christina described as Alice's 'comely face', sending proofs of the etching to his friends for Christmas presents. On

receiving this etching Christina sent a letter of warm thanks which, says
Vera Walker, 'showed a very real affection for Scott and for A.B. (Alice
Boyd) and a deep concern for his health'. With the letter she included
a verse:

> Hail, noble face of noble friend:—
> Hail, honoured master-hand and dear!
> On you may Christmas gifts descend
> And blessings of the coming year
> So soon to overtake us here
> Unknown yet well-known: I portend
> Love starts the course, love seals the end.[11]

Neither the verse nor its superscription, 'Grateful C.G.R. to A.B. and
W.B.S.', reads as if Christina were addressing the man whom she had
deeply loved and the woman who had robbed her of his love.

The oddest and most unexpected of Christina's friendships was her
friendship with Swinburne. She had first met him at Tudor House, when
she had been charmed and touched by his attention to her mother.
Frances Rossetti was always to keep a warm spot in her heart for Swinburne, which may be the reason why Christina, influenced as she was
by her mother's opinions, accepted him as a friend in spite of his drunken-
ness and also his atheism, which in her eyes was a far greater stumbling
block. (She may well have been completely ignorant of his sexual aber-
rations.) And if Christina's liking for Swinburne was connected with her
feeling for her mother he in his turn recognised in the Rossetti family
something which reminded him of his own mother and sisters and the
High Church atmosphere of the home to which, although he had rebelled
against it, he still looked back with nostalgic affection.

The real link between the two poets was, however, each one's admiration for the other's work. Christina might paste little slips of paper over
the 'anti-God' passages in *Atalanta in Calydon*, but she admired the poem
as a whole and greatly valued the copy given her by the author. As
for Swinburne himself, he might declaim against 'the pale Galilean', but
he could and did praise Christina's religious poetry extravagantly. In a
Ballad of Appeal to Christina Rossetti in which he begged her to produce

more 'Sweet water from the well of song', he wrote of her poems 'Prayer's perfect heart spoke here'—not that Swinburne was an authority on the subject of prayer. In 1883 he asked if he might be allowed to dedicate to her his new book *A Century of Roundels*. Surprisingly, she consented, and on reading the dedicatory roundel wrote, 'my name might well blush into red ink at the honour done to it':[12]

> Songs light as these may sound, though deep and strong
> The heart spake through them, scarce should hope to please
> Ears tuned to strains of loftier thoughts than throng
>   Songs light as these.
>
> Yet grace may set their sometime doubt at ease,
> Nor need their too rash reverence fear to wrong
> The shrine it serves at and the hope it sees.
>
> For childlike loves and laughter thence prolong
> Notes that bid enter, fearless as the breeze,
> Even to the shrine of holiest-hearted song,
>   Songs light as these.

Though the roundels themselves were innocuous, Swinburne's poetry was so inextricably connected in the public mind with atheism of the most blatant sort that it seems astonishing that Christina should have allowed her name to be associated in this manner with any of his writings.

In 1883 and 1884 Christina and her mother spent their annual holiday at Birchington so that Frances Rossetti might enjoy what Christina described as 'the heart's-ease of being near Gabriel's grave'.[13] Memorials to Dante Gabriel were the subjects of innumerable letters to William, to Madox Brown, and to Shields. Madox Brown was to design the tombstone, Shields the two memorial windows in Birchington Church, one of them to be given by Frances Rossetti herself. This window was the subject of many and exasperating delays, which kept Christina and her mother waiting week after week in Birchington until in October 1883 Christina could write to Shields 'At last I enjoy the pleasure of telling you that we have seen the beautiful worth-waiting-for window, and that it exceeds my mother's hopes.'[14] The sentence is typical. Seldom in any of these letters does Christina express her own views, never does she admit to differing from her mother even in the smallest detail; she simply submerges her point of view in that of the older woman.

There was to be no holiday in 1885. Frances Rossetti was beginning to fail although she was still well enough to enjoy the company of her family and friends. The young Irish poet Katharine Tynan Hinkson, who visited the house in Torrington Square several times in the winter of 1884–5, has left a description of what she saw on the first of these visits. Frances Rossetti, still bright-eyed and alert, was sitting in a big chair by the fire:

> She had still the remains of the noble beauty which is in her son's portraits of her, and struck me as looking a really great old woman. I remember the gesture with which she turned to her daughter, laying a fine old hand on hers. 'My affectionate Christina,' she said.

Christina herself somewhat disappointed her admirer, who, like so many young enthusiasts, had expected a famous poet to be the embodiment of romantic melancholy:

> . . . she was so much more brisk and cheerful than I expected. I must have said something of the sort to her, for she said: 'I was a very melancholy girl; but now I am a very cheerful old woman.'

After Frances Rossetti had gone to her room to rest Christina talked more freely to Katharine, showing her various relics of Dante Gabriel and the sketches by him which hung on the walls, in particular a pencil drawing of Lizzie:

> 'Poor little Lizzie,' Miss Rossetti called her. She also told me that when she and Mrs. Morris appeared at an evening party, both being brides, no one could say which was the more beautiful, the fair or the dark beauty. 'Lizzie was so graceful,' she said.

Afterwards the two talked of books, Christina singling out Alice Meynell's poetry for special praise. She insisted on lending her own copy of *Cran-*

ford to Katharine, who had never read the book—'I remember how she sat running over the chapters and laughing here and there at bits she well knew and loved.'[15]

In 1885 Christina published *Time Flies*, described as 'a reading diary' and consisting of short passages of poetry or prose, one for every day of the year. It is interesting because it contains various of Christina's own poems and many of her personal recollections, as well as reminiscences of Maria, including the much-quoted one recorded under July 4th.

> Meanwhile I well remember how one no longer present with us, but to whom I cease not to look up, shrank from entering the Mummy Room at the British Museum under a vivid realisation of how the general resurrection might occur even as one stood among those solemn corpses turned into a sight for sightseers.

Every writer knows the predicament which she describes in the entry for January 27th:

> Suppose our duty for the moment is to write: why do we not write?
> —Because we cannot summon up anything original, or striking, or picturesque, or eloquent, or brilliant.
> But is a subject set before us?—It is.
> Is it true?—It is.
> Do we understand it?—Up to a certain point we do.
> Is it worthy of meditation?—Yes, and prayerfully.
> Is it worthy of exposition?—Yes, indeed.
> Why not then begin?

This is hardly the frame of mind in which an author composes a masterpiece. Christina wrote poetry only if and when she felt inspired to do so; this passage must therefore refer to those religious books in prose, which were to her a duty rather than a pleasure. When Dante Gabriel objected to the waste of time and talent on work which could add nothing to her reputation but rather detract from it she replied that she would be glad 'to throw my grain of dust into the religious scale'.[16] That grain of dust sometimes cost her a heavy effort.

Lucy's health had now become a source of great anxiety to the whole family. In February she fell seriously ill with pneumonia, forerunner of the tuberculosis which was to kill her. From now on she was obliged to spend more and more time abroad or at the seaside while William remained tied to London by his work at the Excise Office. Because Lucy and their children were then at Ventnor he spent the Christmas Day of 1885 with his mother and sister, and as Christina put it, 'dropped back into your old place in your old family'.[17] After Christmas dinner was over he gave them special pleasure by reading aloud from an article he was writing about Dante Gabriel. His presence made Frances Rossetti's last Christmas a particularly happy one, as Christina was afterwards to remember with thankfulness. She looked to his visits as the best means of dispelling the inevitable cloud of depression which at times hung heavily over that quiet household where three old women sat waiting for death. 'When you can reappear you may help to scoop us all out of "the dumps", our actual habitat,' she wrote to him on January 29th 1885, then, quoting from her own poem, she added, ' "Does the road wind uphill all the way?—Yes, to the very end"—But, Oh! if we *all* meet on the summit what will these weary steps matter?'[18]

For many years Christina had written a set of verses to be presented to her mother on St Valentine's Day, a gift which Frances Rossetti always received with delighted surprise, making polite pretence that it was an unexpected one. On February 14th 1886 Christina gave her mother the last of this long series of valentines. That winter was a particularly long and bitter one:

> Winter's latest snowflake is the snowdrop flower,
>   Yellow crocus kindles the first flame of the Spring,
> At the time appointed, at that day and hour,
>   When life reawakens and hope in everything.
>
> Such a tender snowflake in the wintry weather,
>   Such a feeble flamelet for chilled St Valentine,—
> But blest be any weather which finds us still together,
>   My pleasure and my treasure, O blessed Mother mine.

The cold weather had added to the hardship which working-class people were already enduring because of widespread unemployment; and the subsequent poverty and distress was severe enough to give rise to serious rioting in London and in one or two other cities. The miseries of the poor weighed on Christina's heart as she made clear in a letter to Lucy dated February 16th:

It is just as well that you escaped the alarm of the riots, which were serious enough as they were, and alarmed one lest they should become yet more so. But, however one may deplore lawlessness, it is heart-sickening to think of the terrible want of work and want of all things at our very doors,—we so comfortable. Emigration is the only adequate remedy which presents itself to my imagination: and that, of course, may leave the mother country to die of inanition a stage further on: yet no one can call upon people to starve to-day lest England should prove powerless to hold her own to-morrow.[19]

This letter is interesting as being one of the very few in which Christina touches on social or political issues; as she herself wrote to Lucy, her views on such matters were 'not very intricate'. To William who was then with his family at Ventnor she sent a more light-hearted letter enclosing in it a riddle for his children illustrated by scribbled drawings of a donkey's head.

A few days after Christina wrote these letters Frances Rossetti had a bad fall from which she was never to recover. She lingered for some weeks in considerable pain and discomfort, dying on April 8th a few days after her eighty-sixth birthday. That evening Christina made a final entry in the family diary: 'I, Christina G. Rossetti, happy and unhappy daughter of so dear a saint, write the last words.'[20]

Chapter Twelve

'Sleeping at last'

Christina was too sensible a person and too good a Christian to make a tragedy of the death of an old woman of eighty-six. But her scheme of things had centred on her mother; and now that centre had gone. She did not think to rebuild her life round her writing although she was only fifty-five and might have had many years of work still before her. 'All that remained to her was religious resignation for a sorrowful interval and a looking forward to the end,' William wrote; 'the care of two invalided aunts occupied her hours and sapped her strength.'[1]

A semi-invalid herself, Christina was now left in charge of two elderly invalids. Nurses and domestic staff, in those days so easily available, were there to do the physical work: but she was the responsible person who must be always at hand, dealing with the organisation of the household and keeping the old ladies happy and amused, duties which left her with little time and less energy for writing. Her many illnesses had sapped her store of strength; she must carefully husband what little remained to her if she were to be strong enough to do the work that lay immediately to hand. It is not surprising that *The Face of the Deep*, the only book written after her mother's death, took her seven years to complete.

Once again Christina appears in the incongruous role of a Miss Yonge heroine. The waste of time and talent which seems to us so unfortunate, to say the least, would have been accepted by Miss Yonge without question and as a matter of course. For her the claims of the old were paramount; in book after book, *Heartsease*, for example, or *The Young Stepmother*, a young woman abandons other and to the modern mind more important claims upon her time and attention in order to devote herself to the care of an elderly relative. Christina in fact had little option; no one else was available to look after Aunt Charlotte and Aunt Eliza. It is not strange that she should have taken upon herself so obvious a duty; the strangeness lies in the fact that neither William nor anyone else thought to lament the inevitable slackening in her literary output.

In all the world the person who now mattered most to Christina was 'my dear delightful William'. 'A great slice of my heart travels about with him now',[2] she wrote to Lucy on January 25th 1887. With Lucy and the children so frequently away William's life was a lonely one; and Christina grieved to think of him solitary in his empty house—'I cannot call it home'. In her letters she would sometimes refer to the religion which meant so little to him but all the world to her—'It seems unnatural to love you so much and yet never say one word about matters which colour my life.' She even begged her agnostic brother for his prayers:

Perhaps you do so already,—but if not, and if you would not think it wrong, I wish you would sometimes pray for me that I may not, after having (in a sense) preached to others, be myself a castaway. Of course you and yours are very much in my prayers.[3]

To Lucy she wrote long and frequent letters full of talk of the children and of domestic affairs, but with no mention of books or pictures or intellectual matters in general. Before her marriage Lucy had intended to become a professional artist but finding that the cares of a family made this impossible she turned from art to literature and in 1890 published a Life of Mary Wollstonecraft Shelley, a fitting complement to William's studies of Shelley himself. Perhaps the relationship between the sisters-in-law would have been an easier one had Christina thought to treat Lucy not invariably as a wife and mother but occasionally as a fellow-author.

Because they were so frequently away from London Christina could not see as much as she might have wished of her surviving nephew Arthur and her three nieces, Olive, Helen and Mary. She took Olive as her companion on a holiday at Brighton in the summer of 1886, she taught Italian to Arthur and Olive by means of letter-writing, and she was careful to keep in touch with all four children, sending them presents of suitable books. To Olive she gave Maria's book, *The Shadow of Dante*, glad that it should be appreciated by a younger generation:

I am very glad you like *The Shadow of Dante*. It is indeed a work written from a fund of knowledge far wider and deeper than could be compressed into its pages, eloquent and elegant, the fruit of a fine mind, and a noble soul. And to me, tho' not to you, it is graced with the endearing charm of resembling its beloved author by being full of goodness and with no insignificant touch of greatness. I do not think that it is sisterly partiality which thus draws her portrait.[4]

Sometimes Christina would recommend to Olive books that she herself had been reading, among them Miss Yonge's historical story, *Unknown to History*:

I fancy it might interest you as it did me. Queen Elizabeth seems to me a masterly portrait and the plot of the novel—the imaginary plot, I mean—is by no means without interest and ingenuity.[5]

In other letters she occasionally mentions Miss Yonge, but she gives no clear indication as to whether or not she had ever read the long family chronicles whose heroines are so strangely accurate a reflection of the pattern she had imposed on her own life and character.

Lucy was obliged to spend the winter of 1886–7 on the Riviera where William was able to join her for a short holiday. On February 5th Christina wrote him a letter expressive of the detachment which was now her dominant mood:

It sounds earthly-paradise-like, your sketch of San Remo: but even there it would behove me to feel, 'Arise ye and depart, for this is not your rest'. I am glad you have more happy and endeared ties than I have,—I am glad, as so it is: otherwise I should be afraid of wishing it for you any more than for myself, and for myself I do not wish it.[6]

Christina herself was recovering from a bad bout of debilitating illness. The doctors had ordered her to Torquay, the place where she now spent such holidays as she was obliged to take for the sake of her health, but though she enjoyed the change and the freedom from care she was glad when the time came to return home—'I feel that here is my proper place.'[7] Her recent illness had left lasting effects both physical and mental. 'I may claim to have made a ten years' stride both as to looks and feelings in these last weeks,' she told William, adding the characteristic comment, 'If so, not by any means to be regretted.'[8] On her first visit to Torrington Square after Frances Rossetti's death Katharine Tynan Hinkson was struck by this change in Christina—'I noticed that the brisk cheerfulness which had disappointed me on my last visit had departed. She was allowing herself to grow old.'[9]

Frederick Shields was a fairly frequent visitor, and so too was a new friend, Mackenzie Bell, who was later to write her biography. Although they could no longer see each other, her playfully affectionate relationship with William Bell Scott remained unchanged. On his seventy-sixth birthday, September 12th 1887, she sent him the present of a jesting poem:

> A roundel seems to fit a round of days,
> Be they the days of upright man or scoundrel.
> Allow me to construct one in your praise,
>   A roundel.

> (This flower of wit turns out a weed like groundsel:
> Yet deign to welcome it, as loftiest bays
> Grown on the shore of Girvan's ocean groundswell.)

> Accept the love that underlies the lays;
> Condone the barbarous rhymes that will not sound well
> In building up, all poets to amaze,
>   A roundel.

To this she added a note—'W.B.S. spurns the birthday tribute of C.G.R., *tableau* visible to the "fine frenzied eye".'[10]

Since they had been separated for so long Scott's death in November 1890 could not affect her very closely. In January of that same year Aunt Charlotte had died, aged ninety-two. She left her money to Christina, who now for the first time in her life found herself reasonably well-off. The chief use she made of this new-found wealth was to give much of it away. It gave her great pleasure to know that William would one day inherit a comfortable sum as sole beneficiary under her own will, and still more pleasure to be able to help with the heavy expenses of Lucy's long illness. Less deserving characters also benefited. She had always been an easy prey to begging-letter writers, even in the days when a shilling was all that she could send in answer to their demands. Now not only did she send larger sums to such beggars, but she insisted on taking on herself the support of a distant relation and protégé of Aunt Charlotte's one Luigi Polidori, 'sending him,' according to the justly annoyed William, 'no doubt a good deal more money than she ought to have allowed him to wring out of her.'[11]

Her reaction to these appeals is illustrative of yet another tension within her two-sided character. In 1882 she had been asked to sign a petition for the grant of a Civil List pension to Leigh Hunt's daughter. Her reply clearly reveals the battle in her mind between natural generosity and conscientious scruple:

I am sorry not to sign. But without pretending to be very deeply versed in Leigh Hunt as regards either personality or literature, my impression of him is not of one on whose merits a claim upon the nation can be soundly based. Meanwhile I am happy to think that the omission of my name may make no difference.

Suppose, however, that this Civil List pension proves unattainable, it is perhaps not impossible that a private fund might be raised among friends on Mrs Cheltman's behalf: if so, and if quite small contributions would not be rejected, I would ask you kindly to afford me the opportunity of offering a guinea—as much as I can afford. For I heartily wish well to the distressed lady, whose need constitutes a claim on all fellow-Christians.[12]

Christina was now left alone with Aunt Eliza, a witless old woman whose mind had failed. The dreary days were lightened by a new friendship with a young and intelligent woman named Lisa Wilson, who had first called simply to pay her respects to the famous poet, and then, emboldened by Christina's kindness, had sought advice about her own writing. Lisa presented a little book of her own verses to Christina who inserted into it a poem headed 'To my Fior-di-Lisa', the Italian version of *Fleur-de-lys* and her pet name for this new friend:

The Rose is Love's own flower, and Love's no less
    The Lily's tenderness.
Then half their dignity must Roses yield
    To Lilies of the field?
Nay, diverse notes make up true harmony;
    All-fashioned loves agree:
Love wears the Lily's whiteness, and Love glows
    In the deep-hearted Rose.

Christina would take immense pains to help young authors who, like Lisa Wilson, asked for her criticism and advice, but she could also be extremely astringent. If Ford Madox Ford (Hueffer) is to be believed—and it is not always safe to do so for he was one of the most accomplished literary liars—'she was, upon occasion, perfectly able to keep her own end up and rather more than up'. Ford describes one such occasion:

A young poet of an ingenuous and seraphic appearance once went to see her. He wanted to offer homage, and he had the top of a thin volume peeping out of his jacket pocket. He belonged to a school that in those days was called *fin-de-siècle*, his verse was rather aggressively decadent, and he was in a small way well known. I suppose she considered that his coming was in the nature of an aggression, and almost, before one had realised that conversation had begun, she was talking about modern verse—deploring its tendencies, deriding its powers of expression, and attacking it in a gentle voice with words keen, sharp and precise, like a scalpel. It was an uncomfortable twenty minutes, and the young poet went away with his volume still in his pocket.[13]

Other admirers who were personally unknown to her wrote begging for autographs or asking permission to set some of her poems to music; she was particularly amused by one such letter which began 'Distinguished Lady'. Some of these unknown admirers developed into 'pen friends'. One of them, Miss Newsham, was a bedridden invalid who had first written to say how much she had been helped and comforted by reading some of Christina's poems; another, Miss May, was apparently going through troubles similar to Christina's own. 'Be sure of my sympathy to you both in your sore trial:' Christina wrote to her; 'I assure you you have not confided your trouble to one who cannot enter into it. I hope peaceful friendship may one day be permitted; more than that I will not look for in this life—but in the next!'[14]

Although Christina could still enjoy visits from old and new friends she no longer had the strength nor the will to go visiting on her own account. 'No, after such a rare and ambitious proceeding as lunching at your house last week I have exhausted my spirit of enterprise,' she wrote to Lucy on March 20th 1892, declining a further invitation. Lest Lucy should take her refusal as an indication of ill health she went on to quote the opinion of the doctor then in charge of her:

Mr Stewart is keeping guard over me at present, and the other day suggested that he does not see why (like others of us) I should not live to be eighty. Time will show, and I only wish what God wills; but I do not run up like quicksilver at the announcement.[15]

Mr Stewart's judgement was soon proved wrong. Two months later, almost to the day, Christina wrote to tell William that 'it seems that something brooding in my health has reached a point demanding sharp treatment'.[16] She had developed cancer of the left breast and shoulder. A formidable operation brought some temporary relief but could do little to check the progress of the disease.

Christina had become somewhat of a celebrity, and her illness was news not only for her friends but for the general public. With rare wisdom she, the most shy and retiring of people, decided that any attempt at secrecy would be a mistake and that the only honest and sensible course was to give a direct question a direct and truthful answer. In a letter to William, written in a very shaky hand, she made her point of view plain:

I see quite clearly that we cannot avoid answering direct questions. I would rather appear in a hundred paragraphs than incur evasions. So please you and yours answer everyone whatever they ask. I shall gratefully remember the affection that endeavoured to keep my secret, and which, at my request, abandoned secrecy.[17]

Convalescence at Brighton was made pleasant to Christina by what she described to Lucy as 'the invaluable loan of William; he transforms our enforced expedition into quite a holiday'.[18] Back again in London she beguiled the time by reading books about Dante—'all too late I am being sucked into the Dantesque vortex'.[19] The recently published *Autobiographical Notes* by William Bell Scott had given great offence to Dante Gabriel's friends and relations. Christina refused to read the book, a decision prompted as much by respect for her friend's memory as for her brother's.

One great pleasure was the publication of her own book, *The Face of the Deep*, which proved to be an immediate success. This devotional commentary on the Apocalypse is chiefly interesting for the many poems scattered throughout its pages. They include some of her finest religious poetry; and the general impression they make is one of deep happiness:

> Long and dark the nights, dim and short the days,
> Mounting weary heights on our weary ways,
>   Thee our God we praise.
> Scaling heavenly heights by unearthly ways,
> Thee our God we praise all our nights and days,
>   Thee our God we praise.

So she writes at the beginning of the book; by the end she has scaled those heights and won the heaven of her desire:

> Hark! the Alleluias of the great salvation
>   Still beginning: never ending, still begin,
> The thunder of an endless adoration:
> Open ye the gates, that the righteous nation
>   Which have kept the truth may enter in.

> Roll ye back, ye pearls, on your twelvefold station:
>   No more deaths to die, no more fights to win!
> Lift your heads, ye gates, that the righteous nation,
> Led by the Great Captain of their sole salvation,
>   Having kept the truth may enter in.

Aunt Eliza died in May of the following year, 1893, leaving Christina alone in the big, gloomy house, with only the servants and her cat Muff for company. Fortunately her maid, Harriet Read, was an efficient and kindly woman who could act as nurse when necessary. Though her heart was giving trouble and though she knew that the cancer had returned Christina was not unhappy. She could still get to church and in warm weather she could sit in the square garden enjoying the sun and the greenery. She had told her niece Olive how it grieved her to see the trees lopped—'Each branch is a loss to me; I am so fond of trees and foliage.'[20] Though she could no longer write anything new she could employ herself happily in copying out poems for the volume of her religious verse to be published by the S.P.C.K. Her chief concern, however, was not for herself, but for William and his family, and above all for the decline in his wife's health.

Though nothing could now save Lucy she was still advised to avoid the English winter, and in October 1893 she settled with her three daughters at Pallanza on Lake Maggiore. Left alone in their house in St Edmund's Terrace, William suggested that Christina should leave Torrington Square and join him there for the winter. This, however, she could not do because the steep stairs would put too great a strain on her heart. She was toying with the idea of buying a London 'cottage', but in her heart she knew that to move house would be but lost labour —'I of all people need not lay remote plans for the future.'[21] William's mention of an intended exhibition brought to mind a grief of long ago— 'I shall be really pleased if our poor Lizzie's name and fame can be brought forward and will gladly lend my St Agnes which is such a beauty.'[22] Christina had never forgotten her lovely and unhappy sister-in-law; on the wall of her room hung a constant reminder in the shape of Dante Gabriel's beautiful drawing of Lizzie asleep in an arm-chair.

The news from Italy gave rise to 'grave apprehension'. Lucy was clearly no better but on the contrary growing worse. Since William could not leave London Christina made the desperate suggestion that she herself might go out to Pallanza accompanied by a nurse. When this plan was not surprisingly vetoed she wrote again to William begging him not to let expense stand in the way if he could possibly go to Pallanza himself. 'Of course, if I could have managed my own journey thither, I could be your banker as well or better.'[23] Meanwhile Lucy moved from Pallanza to San Remo. On March 10th William received a telegram so alarming that he started for Italy immediately. Once again Christina offered financial help, suggesting that she should pay the expense of sending Lucy's English doctor out to San Remo. William however replied that they were perfectly satisfied with the local Italian doctor. All that Christina could do was to write loving letters to William sending him scraps of news that she thought might interest him, telling him, for instance, that her *Pageant* was to be performed for charity and that she had much enjoyed a visit from Charles Cayley's niece, Mary. She thanked the three girls for the present of a box of flowers and sent in return a dried sprig of heartsease—'I wish I could send you its sentiment as well as itself.'[24]

Lucy died on April 12th. By her will she left everything she owned not to William but to her four children, a reasonable enough arrangement when it is remembered that on Christina's death, which could not be far distant, William would inherit a comfortable sum of money. Unfortunately, however, the house in St Edmund's Terrace had been Lucy's property so that William now found himself a guest in his own home. Christina's annoyance over this unhappy situation shows clearly enough through the tactfully worded sentences of a letter dated April 18th. Even in death it seemed that Lucy could still provoke her sister-in-law:

> I will not venture to say that I regret anything in Lucy's will, and I will not suppose it possible that any trouble can arise about the house. If for any reason you should wish entirely to recast your plans, I remind you that mine are wholly unsettled, and that, if any combination with me would help towards an arrangement, it seems probable that I should be available—available, that is, if life lasts so long. But, if not, I have the comfort of knowing that your income would be increased.[25]

Life was not to last so long. On July 24th William noted that Christina was in considerable pain and that her state appeared critical. In August she took permanently to her bed which was moved into the drawing-room. Here she had around her all the things she most valued, her collection of ferns, her small library of books, most of them old ones which had belonged to her mother, her favourite pictures, portraits of both her brothers and of her uncle John Polidori, Dante Gabriel's portrait of Frances Rossetti, his 1860 drawing of Christina herself, the drawing of Lizzie, and photographs of some of his other pictures. Full in view from her bed hung Shields's drawing of *The Good Shepherd,* a picture in which she particularly delighted. All these last years Shields had been a frequent visitor; and now that she was too ill to see her friends she wrote him a letter of farewell which, by an inconvenient scruple, Mackenzie Bell considered to be 'of too sacred a character' to print.

The drawing-room was the prettiest and most cheerful room in the house, but it had the disadvantage of fronting on the square so that all sounds were easily audible. William had been warned by the doctors that Christina was subject to hysterical attacks so that he may not have been surprised when one of the neighbours wrote to complain of 'the distressing screams that sound clear from her drawing-room to mine'.[26] Only once did he himself see any sign of hysteria in Christina; on every other occasion she appeared calm and collected and though her pain continually increased she never complained, and seldom even mentioned her illness. (To Mackenzie Bell, however, she made a pathetic request— 'Will you now promise me to put up one short prayer for me; I have to suffer so *very* much!')[27] Up to the end of October she remained 'perfectly conversable', reciting verses, enjoying the letters which were read aloud to her including one from Alice Boyd, talking over childhood memories with William and correcting him on points of detail which he had forgotten but she vividly remembered.

At the beginning of November he noted a change. The hysterical screaming ceased; she grew noticeably weaker and less capable of sustained attention. Her mind was troubled by dark thoughts: 'Religious ideas seem to me predominant herein'[28] William commented, grieved and surprised that religion did not bring to Christina the comfort and peace which Maria had known when dying. He could not understand why a devout Christian who had longed so fervently for Heaven should in the face of death appear troubled and dismayed, and he was puzzled by this final contradiction in Christina's contradictory life and character.

William did not realise that Christina's experience, though unusual, was not unique. Saints are rarities. Not many people have seen a saint die, but those who have done so know that such a death is not always an easy one. Some holy people die peacefully, but others suffer extraordinary desolation and distress of spirit. A more simple-minded generation might have described this as a last desperate assault by the devil; but whatever may be the explanation the fact remains that it is often the saint rather than the sinner who must pray 'suffer us not in our last hour for any pains of death to fall from thee'.

Christina was disturbed by the memory of trifling faults committed long ago, a frequent trouble with very sick or dying people. On November 9th William found her very weak and unable to speak distinctly, but sufficiently clear-headed to follow and understand several letters which he read aloud to her. 'She then said that she wished to obtain my forgiveness for two old matters. One (I did not understand the details very clearly) was that several years ago after I had recommended her not to see people, she went to lunch with or received Cayley at lunch—"I was so fond of him." The second relates to early childhood; that she had promised to give me a box of paints but never did so (!)'[29] Thus almost on her death-bed, did she admit her long-enduring affection for Charles Cayley.

She lingered on over Christmas, in no great pain now, and though wandering a little in her mind, sometimes capable of intelligent speech and conversation. One day she startled William by mentioning Sir Walter Scott's *Lord of the Isles*, criticising the poem in an apposite, even pungent manner. To Harriet Read she remarked that her illness had humbled her—'I was so proud before'—a strange saying probably connected in some way with the dark terror which oppressed her spirit. When William visited her on December 27th she could not or would not speak to him. For hour after hour she lay still and quiet, only her lips moving as if in prayer. On December 28th she was clearly near to death; but when William kissed her goodbye he did not realise that it was for the last time. Only Harriet Read was in the room when at daybreak next morning, she gave one sigh and died.

Christina left a brief note headed 'Memoranda for my Executor'. Among other instructions she directed that 'the three rings on my wedding finger are to be put into a Church offertory'.[30] One she described as her mother's wedding-ring, of the other two she said nothing. It is tempting to suppose that one of those two was the ring which Cayley had placed inside the desk he left to her in his will, a wedding ring given to her as it were after his own death. Among her papers she also left some manuscript verses, the last poem she was ever to write:

> Sleeping at last, the trouble and tumult over,
> Sleeping at last, the struggle and horror past,
> Cold and white, out of sight of friend and of lover,
>   Sleeping at last.
>
> No more a tired heart downcast or overcast,
> No more pangs that wring or shifting fears that hover,
> Sleeping at last in a dreamless sleep locked fast.
>
> Fast asleep. Singing birds in their leafy cover
> Cannot wake her, nor shake her the gusty blast.
> Under the purple thyme and the purple clover
>   Sleeping at last.

Notes and References

Manuscript Material

The principal sources of unpublished material on which I have drawn are the papers once belonging to W. M. Rossetti's daughter, Mrs Helen Angeli, and now in the possession of the University of British Columbia, Vancouver, and the papers in the possession of Mrs Lucy O'Conor. These are referred to as B.C. and O'Conor respectively. As the photostats of the B.C. papers lacked any catalogue marking wherever possible I have given the date as a means of identification.

Published Work

Dante Gabriel Rossetti, His Family Letters was published with a Memoir by W. M. Rossetti in 1895. W. M. Rossetti also edited *Family Letters of Christina Rossetti* published in 1908. He also wrote a Memoir of Christina Rossetti which is printed as a Foreword to his edition of her *Collected Poems*, published in 1904. These three are referred to as Memoir (D.G.R.), Family Letters (C.R.) and *Collected Poems* respectively.

The edition of Dante Gabriel Rossetti's letters edited by O. Doughty and J. Wahl in 1965 is referred to as D and W.

Time Flies, by Christina Rossetti is a collection of readings for every day in the year. As this book went into several editions for convenience's sake I have given the day of the year for reference rather than the page number.

Chapter One

1 *The Fortnightly Review*, Vol. LXXXI Old Series 1904, p. 393.
2 Ibid., p. 405.
3 *Time Flies*, January 2.
4 Ibid., February 5.
5 Sharp, William in *Atlantic Monthly*, Vol. LXXV 1895, p. 738.
6 *The Athenaeum*, January 5 1895, p. 16.
7 Waller, R. D. *The Rossetti Family*, Manchester, 1932, p. 75.
8 Memoir (D.G.R.), p. 64.
9 Ashmolean. Undated letter.
10 O'Conor.
11 B.C.
12 Gosse, Edmund *Critical Kit-Kats*, London 1896, pp. 104–11.
13 Memoir (D.G.R.), p. 31.
14 Waller, R. D., op. cit., p. 132.

Chapter Two

1 Packer, Lona Mosk 'Swinburne and Christina Rossetti', *University of Toronto Quarterly*, October 1963: C.R. to A.C.S., November 19th 1884.
2 Rossetti, W. M., *Reminiscences*, Vol. I, London 1906, p. 42.
3 *Collected Poems*, p. lxvi.
4 Ibid., p. lv.
5 Ibid., p. lxviii.
6 Ibid., p. l.
7 Ibid., p. l.
8 Bell, Mackenzie, *Christina Rossetti*, London 1898, pp. 20–1.
9 *Maude* Prefatory Note, ed. Crump, R. W., Hamden, Connecticut 1976.
10 *Time Flies*, January 3.
11 Doughty, Oswald and Wahl, J. R. eds., *Letters of Dante Gabriel Rossetti*, Vol. I, Oxford 1965, p. 31.
12 Packer, Lona Mosk *Christina Rossetti*, Cambridge 1963, p. 23.

13 Hatton, G., Thesis on C.R. unpublished poems, p. lxvii
14 Packer, L. M., op. cit., p. 23.
15 Gaunt, William *The Pre-Raphaelite Tragedy*, London 1942, p. 43.

Chapter Three

 1 Grylls, Rosalie Glynn *Portrait of Rossetti*, London 1964, p. 25.
 2 Hunt, Holman *Pre-Raphaelitism*, Vol. I, London 1905, p. 129.
 3 Ibid., p. 129.
 4 Rossetti, W. M. *Reminiscences*, p. 72.
 5 Sandars, M. *Christina Rossetti*, London 1930, p. 72.
 6 Stuart, D. M. *Christina Rossetti*, London 1930, p. 72.
 7 Sharp, William in *Atlantic Monthly*, Vol. LXXV, p. 738.
 8 Rossetti, W. M. *Reminiscences*, p. 72.
 9 Hunt, Holman, op. cit., p. 154.
10 *Collected Poems*, p. lxi.
11 Rossetti, W. M. (ed.) *Family Letters of Christina Rossetti*, London
   1908, pp. 3–4.
12 Ibid., p. 1.
13 For this and following quotations for Christina Rossetti's letters from
   Mansfield see Family Letters (C.R.), pp. 5–9.
14 Bell, Mackenzie, op. cit., p. 23.
15 *Collected Poems*, p. lvi.
16 Family Letters (C.R.), p. 10.
17 Princeton Papers, January 18th 1850.
18 D and W, p. 56.
19 Ibid., p. 54.
20 Ibid., p. 88.
21 Doughty, Oswald *A Victorian Romantic* London, 1949, p. 89.
22 Princeton Papers, April 28th 1849.
23 Doughty, Oswald, op. cit., p. 101.
24 Family Letters (C.R.), p. 13.
25 Ibid., p. 15.
26 Rossetti, W. M. *Reminiscences*, p. 73.

Chapter Four

1 Scott, William Bell *Autobiographical Notes*, Vol. I, London 1892, pp. 247–8.
2 Rossetti, W. M. *Reminiscences*, p. 59.
3 Scott, William Bell *Autobiographical Notes*, Vol. I, p. 245.
4 Packer, L. M., op. cit., p. 60.
5 Bowra, M. *The Romantic Imagination*, Oxford 1950, p. 261.
6 Packer, L. M., op. cit., p. 154.
7 Rothenstein, W. *Men and Memories*, London 1932, p. 138.
8 Memoir (D.G.R.), p. xii.
9 *Collected Poems*, p. lii.
10 *Fortnightly Review*, Vol. LXXXI Old Series 1904, p. 396.
11 Packer, op. cit., p. 50.
12 Grylls, op. cit., p. 122.
13 Doughty, op. cit., p. 120.
14 Rossetti, W. M. *Rossetti Papers*, p. 78.
15 D and W, Vol. I, p. 108.
16 Rossetti, W. M. *Reminiscences*, p. 99.
17 Ibid., p. 260.
18 Ibid., p. 89.
19 Family Letters (C.R.), p. 55.
20 Family Letters (C.R.), p. 54.
21 D and W, Vol. III, p. 1380.
22 Woolf, Virginia *The Common Reader*, London 1932, second series, p. 243.
23 Hunt, Holman, op. cit., p. 347.
24 B.C. September 18th 1853.
25 B.C. December 3rd 1853.
26 B.C. September 19th 1853.
27 D and W, Vol. I, p. 148.
28 Bodleian Stephens Papers, e. 76.
29 Princeton Papers, September 24th 1849.
30 B.C. dates as given.

Chapter Five

1 Woolf, Virginia *The Common Reader* second series, p. 242.
2 Stuart, D. S., op. cit., p. 177.
3 *The Romantic Imagination*, p. 269.
4 D and W, p. 222.
5 Ibid., p. 183.
6 Ibid., p. 183.
7 Memoir (D.G.R.), p. 177.
8 Packer, L. M., op. cit., p. 99.
9 D and W, p. 269.
10 Doughty, Oswald *A Victorian Romantic*, p. 192.
11 D and W, p. 363.
12 Rossetti, W. M. *Reminiscences*, p. 260.
13 D and W, p. 182.
14 Rossetti, W. M. *Reminiscences*, p. 261.
15 B.C. date as given.
16 *Time Flies*, Aug. 22.
17 Family Letters (C.R.), p. 24.
18 *Collected Poems*, p. lv.
19 Rossetti, W. M. *Reminiscences* , p. 264.
20 *Collected Poems*, p. 473.
21 *Wallington Papers*, undated.
22 Rossetti, W. M. *Ruskin, Rossetti and Pre-Raphaelitism*, London 1899, p. 38.
23 Rossetti, W. M. *Reminiscences*, p. 174.
24 Packer, op. cit., pp. 361–2.
25 Rossetti, W. M. *Reminiscences*, p. 174.
26 Packer, L. M., op. cit., p. 78.

Chapter Six

1 *Collected Poems*, p. 485.
2 Packer, op. cit., p. 153.

3 Ibid., p. 154.
4 *Collected Poems*, p. 483.
5 D and W, p. 389
6 Ibid., p. 391.
7 Ibid., p. 391.
8 Ibid., p. 390.
9 B.C., undated.
10 *Collected Poems*, p. li.
11 *The Rossetti-Macmillan Letters*, Cambridge 1963, p. 6.
12 *The Common Reader*, second series, p. 242.
13 *Fortnightly Review*, Vol. LXXXI Old Series, p. 403.
14 Bowra, M. *The Romantic Imagination*, p. 247.
15 Packer, op. cit., p. 141.
16 Ibid., p. 150.
17 Duffy, M. *The Erotic World of Faery*, London 1974, p. 273.
18 Ibid., p. 271.
19 Ibid., p. 271.
20 *Collected Poems*, p. 479.
21 Packer, op. cit., p. 94.
22 Ibid., p. 95.
23 British Library, Ashley Mss, 1451.

Chapter Seven

1 Rossetti, W. M. *Rossetti Papers*, p. 50.
2 Ibid., pp. 68–9.
3 Ibid., p. 82.
4 Ibid., p. 83.
5 Ibid., p. 77.
6 Ibid., p. 69.
7 Ibid., p. 74.
8 Ibid., p. 77.
9 Ibid., p. 88.
10 Packer, op. cit., p. 183.
11 Ibid., p. 232.

12 Rossetti, W. M. *Reminiscences*, p. 312.
13 Family Letters (C.R.), p. 124.
14 Rossetti, W. M. *Rossetti Papers*, p. 83.
15 Packer, L. M. ed. *Rossetti-Macmillan Letters*, p. 56.
16 Family Letters (C.R.) p. 29.
17 Stuart, D. M., op. cit., p. 66.
18 B.C., December 24th 1869.
19 B.C., no date.
20 Rossetti, W. M. *Reminiscences*, p. 312.
21 Dorothy Middleton *Victorian Lady Traveller*, London 1965, p. 20.
22 *The Romantic Imagination*, p. 254.
23 Ibid., p. 270.

Chapter Eight

 1 B.C., August 28th 1881.
 2 Packer, L. M. ed. *Rossetti-Macmillan Letters*, p. 72.
 3 D and W, p. 826.
 4 Burne-Jones, G. *Memorials of Edward Burne-Jones*, Vol. I, London 1904, p. 293.
 5 B.C., 'Friday afternoon, 14th'.
 6 Bell, Mackenzie, op. cit., p. 51.
 7 B.C., undated.
 8 Rossetti, W. M. *Rossetti Papers*, p. 202.
 9 Mackenzie Bell, op. cit., p. 38.
10 B.C., July 7th 1870.
11 B.C., August 31st 1870.
12 Family Letters (C.R.), p. 33 (B.C.).
13 Bornand, O. ed. *Diary of W. M. Rossetti 1870–1873*, Oxford 1977.
14 Family Letters (C.R.), p. 35.
15 D and W, p. 1022.
16 Bornand, op. cit., p. 127.
17 B.C., undated.
18 D and W, p. 1035.
19 Bornand, op. cit., p. 198.

Chapter Nine

1 Bornand, op. cit., p. 195.
2 Ibid., p. 205.
3 Family Letters (C.R.) p. 36.
4 B.C., August 31st 1872.
5 Ibid.
6 B.C., September 5th 1872.
7 B.C., June 23rd 1872.
8 B.C., July 5th 1872.
9 Packer, op. cit., p. 287.
10 D and W, p. 1186.
11 Troxell, J. C. *Three Rossettis*, Harvard 1937, p. 161.
12 D and W, p. 1174.
13 *Athenaeum*, January 5th 1895.
14 Family Letters (C.R.) p. 88.
15 Ibid., p. 40.
16 Ibid., p. 39.
17 Weintraub, S. *Four Rossettis*, New York 1976, p. 218.
18 D and W, p. 1213.
19 Ibid., p. 1234.
20 Ibid., p. 1213.
21 Rossetti, W. M. *Reminiscences*, p. 427.
22 Family Letters (C.R.), p. 42.
23 *Time Flies*, December 20th.
24 Family Letters (C.R.), p. 45.
25 Family Letters (C.R.), p. 58.

Chapter Ten

1 Family Letters (C.R.), p. 61.
2 *Time Flies*, November 7th.
3 B.C., Sunday afternoon (November 26th).
4 B.C. Inscribed in Christina's handwriting, 'In memory of dear Maria translated from Petrarch by Charles Bagot Cayley'.

5 *Time Flies*, April 15th.

6 Family Letters (C.R.), p. 65.

7 British Library, Ashley Mss. 1386.

8 Family Letters (C.R.), p. 66.

9 British Library, Ashley Mss. 1386.

10 Family Letters (C.R.), p. 69.

11 Bell, Mackenzie, op. cit., p. 152.

12 Family Letters (C.R.), p. 89.

13 Mills, Ernestine *The Life and Letters of Frederick Shields*, London 1912, p. 270.

14 Ibid., p. 247.

15 B.C., date as given.

16 D and W, p. 1830.

17 Ibid., p. 1538.

18 Ibid., p. 1883.

19 B.C., September 6th 1880.

20 B.C., September ? 1880.

21 B.C., Christmas Day 1881.

22 Rossetti, W. M. *Reminiscences* p. 341.

23 Bodleian don. d. 120. f. 169.

24 B.C., January 1886.

25 Family Letters (C.R.) p. 120.

26 D and W, p. 1919.

27 B.C., August 28th 1881.

28 D and W, p. 1920.

29 Family Letters (C.R.), p. 98.

30 Bell, Mackenzie, op. cit., p. 112.

31 D and W, p. 1866.

32 Doughty, Oswald *A Victorian Romantic* p. 645.

33 D and W, p. 1942.

34 Memoir (D.G.R.), p. 378

35 Family Letters (C.R.), p. 102.

36 Ibid., p. 103.

37 Ibid., p. 106.

38 D and W, p. 1950.

39 Family Letters (C.R.), pp. 111–12.

40 Ibid., p. 114.
41 Family Letters (C.R.), p. 110.
42 B.C., March 17th 1882.
43 Family Letters (C.R.), p. 115.

Chapter Eleven

1 Bodleian. Ms autograph C19 ii.
2 Bornand ed. *The Diary of W. M. Rossetti*, p. 203.
3 Packer, op. cit., p. 333.
4 House, H. *All in Due Time*, London 1955, p. 151.
5 Temple, *Readings in Saint John's Gospel*, London 1939, Introduction p. xx.
6 Family Letters (C.R.) p. 124.
7 Ibid., p. 139.
8 Ibid., p. 140.
9 *Time Flies*, September 4th.
10 *The Bookman*, Vol. I, 1895, p. 28.
11 Walker, *Thesis on W. B. Scott*, p. 218.
12 Packer, L. M. 'Swinburne and Christina Rossetti' in *University of Toronto Quarterly*, October 1963, p. 39.
13 Family Letters (C.R.), p. 135.
14 Mills, *Frederick Shields*, p. 283.
15 *The Bookman*, Vol. I, 1895, pp. 28–9.
16 Family Letters (C.R.), p. 92.
17 B.C., December 20th 1886.
18 B.C., date as given.
19 Family Letters (C.R.), p. 152.
20 Ibid., p. 232.

Chapter Twelve

1 Rossetti, W. M. *Reminiscences*, p. 526.
2 Family Letters (C.R.), p. 159.

3 Ibid., p. 165.

4 O'Conor.

5 O'Conor.

6 Family Letters (C.R.), p. 159.

7 Ibid., p. 164.

8 Ibid., p. 163.

9 *The Bookman*, Vol. I, 1895, p. 29.

10 B.C., undated.

11 Family Letters (C.R.), p. 179.

12 British Library, Ashley Mss. 1386.

13 *Fortnightly*, Vol. LXXXI Old Series, 1904, p. 396.

14 Bodleian Mss. autograph C. 19 ii.

15 B.C. date as given.

16 Family Letters (C.R.), p. 185.

17 B.C., June 5th 1892.

18 Family Letters (C.R.), p. 187.

19 Ibid., p. 188.

20 O'Conor.

21 B.C., October 16th 1893.

22 B.C., November 10th 1893.

23 Family Letters (C.R.), p. 201.

24 Ibid., p. 203.

25 Ibid., p. 204.

26 Packer, op. cit., p. 399.

27 Bell, Mackenzie, op. cit., p. 167.

28 Family Letters (C.R.), p. 221.

29 Rossetti, W. M. *Reminiscences*, p. 538.

30 B.C., undated.

Select Bibliography

L. M. Packer's biography contains an admirable bibliography up to the year 1963. The *Reference Guide* compiled by R. W. Crump and published in 1976 lists every book, pamphlet or article dealing with Christina Rossetti and appearing before that date. The serious student already has two excellent and exhaustive bibliographies ready to hand. This 'Select Bibliography' is therefore merely a list of the books and pamphlets which I personally found most useful.

BELL, MACKENZIE. *Christina Rossetti.* Hurst and Blackett, 1898

BORNAND, ODETTE. *Diary of W. M. Rossetti, 1870–1873.* Oxford, 1977

BOWRA, C. M. *The Romantic Imagination,* Oxford, 1950

CRUMP, R. W. *Christina Rossetti, a Reference Guide.* Boston, Mass., 1976

DOUGHTY, OSWALD. *A Victorian Romantic, Dante Gabriel Rossetti.* Muller, 1949

DOUGHTY, O. and WAHL, J. *Letters of Dante Gabriel Rossetti.* Oxford, 1965

DUFFY, MAUREEN. *The Erotic World of Faery.* Panther, 1974

GAUNT, WILLIAM. *The Pre-Raphaelite Tragedy.* Cape, 1942

GRYLLS, ROSALIE GLYNN. *Portrait of Rossetti.* Macdonald, 1964

HOLMAN HUNT, W. *Pre-Raphaelitism and the Pre-Raphaelite Brotherhood.* Macmillan, 1905

HOUSE, HUMPHRY. *All in Due Time.* Hart-Davis, 1955

MILLS, ERNESTINE. *Life and Letters of Frederick Shields.* Longman Green, 1912

PACKER, LONA MOSK. *Christina Rossetti.* Cambridge, 1963

PACKER, L. M. *The Rossetti-Macmillan Letters.* University of California, 1963

ROSSETTI, W. M. *Dante Gabriel Rossetti, his Family Letters with a Memoir.* Ellis and Elvey, 1895

ROSSETTI, W. M. *Pre-Raphaelite Diaries and Letters*. Hurst and Blackett, 1900

ROSSETTI, W. M. *Rossetti Papers*. Sands, 1903

ROSSETTI, W. M. *Some Reminiscences*. Brown Langham, 1906

ROSSETTI, W. M. *Family Letters of Christina Rossetti*. Brown Langham, 1908

SANDARS, MARY F. *Christina Rossetti*. Hutchinson, 1930

SCOTT, WILLIAM BELL. *Autobiographical Notes*. Osgood McIlvaine, 1892

STUART, D. M. *Christina Rossetti*. Macmillan, 1930

TREVELYAN, RALEIGH. *A Pre-Raphaelite Circle*. Hamish Hamilton, 1975

TROXELL, JANET. *Three Rossettis, unpublished Letters*. Harvard, 1937

WALLER, R. D. *The Rossetti Family 1824–1854*. Manchester, 1932

WEINTRAUB, S. *Four Rossettis*. Weybright and Talley, New York, 1976

WOOLF, VIRGINIA. *The Common Reader*. Hogarth Press, 1932

Pamphlets

FREDEMAN, W. E. Letters of Pictor Ignotus, William Bell Scott's correspondence with Alice Boyd. Manchester, 1967

– Prelude to the Last Decade, Dante Gabriel Rossetti in the summer of 1872. Manchester, 1971

– Pre-Raphaelitism, a Biblio-critical Study. Harvard, 1965

Unpublished Theses

HATTON, GWYNNETH. The Unpublished Poems of Christina Rossetti. Oxford

SMITH, VERA. William Bell Scott. Durham University

Index

The works of Christina and Dante Gabriel Rossetti,
are indexed under these two main entries

Acland, Dr (later Sir) Henry, 68
Aldwick Lodge, Bognor, 156
Alfieri, Vittorio, 14
Alice in Wonderland (Carroll), 110
All Saints, Anglican sisterhood of, Maria
   joins, 153–4, 156, 157
Allingham, William, 69, 83
Alps, 122
Ancient Mariner, The (Coleridge), 111
Andermatt, 122
Anglo-Catholicism, 30–3, 72, 78, 180,
   181
Arabian Nights, The, 20, 21
Arpa Evangelica (G. Rossetti), 81
Atalanta in Calydon (Swinburne), 190
Athenaeum, 98
Atlantic Monthly, 35n
Austen, Jane, 21
Avranches, 101

Ballad of Appeal to Christina Rossetti
   (Swinburne), 190
Barile, Enrica, 124
Basle, 122
Bateman, Isabel, 129
Bath, Lady, 72
Beerbohm, Max, 19
Bell, Mackenzie, 56, 76n, 199, 206;
   quoted, 34
Bennett, W. J. E., 72
Bergamo, 123
Bilchett, Godfrey, 35
Birchington-on-Sea: Dante Gabriel's last
   days at, 174–6; memorial windows,
   191
Bodichon, Barbara, 68, 147

Bonaparte, Joseph, 14
Bowra, Sir Maurice, quoted, 61, 81, 102,
   130, 131
Boyd, Alice, 153: lifelong love affair
   with W. B. Scott, 61, 106, 125–6,
   134, 189–90; friendship with Christina,
   138, 140, 142, 190, 206
Brett, John, subject of *No thank you,
   John*, 69–70
Brighton, 47, 65, 203
Brontë, Branwell, 62
Brontë, Emily, compared with Christina,
   62, 180, 182
Brown, Ford Madox, 83, 138, 147;
   accepts Dante Gabriel as pupil, 45;
   his classes attended by Christina, 71,
   73; on Cayley, 91; 'good active
   friend' to Dante Gabriel, 162; designs
   his tombstone, 191
Brown (later Rossetti, q.v.), Lucy
   Madox, 142
Browning, Elizabeth Barrett, 132
Browning, Robert, 88, 108, 138–9,
   189
Buchanan, Robert, 146
Burden, Jane – *see* Morris, Jane
Burne-Jones, Edward, 64
Burne-Jones, Georgina, 138
Burrows, Rev. H. W., 172
Byron, Lord, 14

Caine, Hall, as Dante Gabriel's
   companion, 171, 172, 174, 175, 176
Caine, Lily, 174
Cameron, Julia, 139
Carroll, Lewis, 88, 138

Cayley, Charles Bagot, 109, 163, 168; as pupil of Gabriel, 29, 91; first meeting with Rossettis, 91; appearance and character, 91–2; friendship with Christina, 92–3, 120–2, 126–30, 140, 141, 148–9, 171; Christina's poems associated with, 121, 132–4, 186–9; delayed proposal, 121–2, 126, 129: gift of 'sea mouse', 127, 168; as a poet, 128–9, 148, 159–60; asks Christina to be his literary executor, 184–5; death, 185; bequests to Christina, 186, 208; her love for, 187–9, 207
Cayley, Sophie, 185, 186
Century of Roundels, A (Swinburne), dedicated to Christina, 191
Charity Boy's Debut, The (Collinson), 46
Cheltman, Mrs (Leigh Hunt's daughter), 200
Chiavenna, 123
Child Jesus, The (Collinson), 46, 54
Christ in the House of His Parents (Millais), 54
Christian Year, The (Keble), 32, 180
Clayton, John, 88
Clifton, All Saints Mission House at, 156
Clough, Arthur Hugh, 53
Collins, Charles Allston, 87
Collinson, Charles, 51, 52
Collinson, James, 43, 63, 109; and Pre-Raphaelite Brotherhood, 44, 46, 49–50, 52, 54, 57, 74; and Roman Catholic Church, 46, 47, 52, 55; introduction to Rossettis, 46–7; engagement to Christina, 47–8, 49, 59, 65; her attitude to him, 47–8, 56, 61, 65; his unsuccessful portrait of Christina, 48, 81; holiday with William, 50; engagement broken off, 55–7; death. 167
Collinson, Mrs, 50
Collinson, Mary, 50–1, 52
Como, 122
Confessions of an English Opium-Eater, The (De Quincey), 110

Cornforth, Fanny, relationship with Dante Gabriel, 42, 150–1, 165, 172
Cornhill, The, 98, 99
Coutances, 101
Crabbe, George, 41
Cranford (Gaskell), 192
Crashaw, Richard, 23
Critic, The, 69

Dalrymple, Mrs, 139
Dante Alighieri, 21, 42, 129, 203
Darleston Hall (Staffs), 72
De Quincey, Thomas, 110
Deverell, Walter, 68
Divine Comedy (Dante), 21, 91
Dixon, Thomas, 89
Dodsworth, Rev. William, 30, 31, 55
Don Giovanni (Mozart), 105
Doughty, Oswald, 172, 174n
Duffy, Maureen, on eroticism of *Goblin Market,* 105, 106
Dunn, Treffry, 162

Eastbourne, 156, 157, 165
Ecclesiological Society, 31
Ellis, F. S., 136, 142
Emerson, Ralph Waldo, 179
Erotic World of Faery, The (Duffy), 105
Excursion, The (Wordsworth), 23

Fairchild Family, The (Sherwood), 21
Fleshly School of Poetry, The (Buchanan), 146
Folkestone, 140, 141
Ford, Ford Madox (Hueffer), 13, 63, 102, 201
Fox, Vanessa, 135n
Fredeman, Professor W. E., 65
Frome, Rossetti family's year in, 72–5
Fry, Elizabeth, 175

Gaskell, Mrs, 99
Gaunt, William, 42
Germ, The, 52–4, 69, 98, 168
Gilchrist, Alexander, 139
Gilchrist, Ann, 89, 138, 139
Gilchrist, Grace, 139

Gladstone, William Ewart, 55, 56, 94
Gladstone, Mrs, 94
Glottenham (Sussex), 147
Good Shepherd, The (Shields), 206
Gorham Judgment (1847), 55, 56
Gosse, Edmund, 24, 88
Greenwell, Dora, 89, 90, 156
Grisi, Giulia, 19
Grylls, Rosalie Glynn, quoted, 44, 65

Hake, Dr George, 146
Hake, George jr, 156
Hallam, Arthur, 69
Hare, Dr Charles J., 34, 35, 36
Hastings: Dante Gabriel at, 81, 82;
    Christina recuperates at, 83, 87; her
    1864–5 winter at, 114, 122; Cayley
    buried at, 186
Hatton, Gwynneth, 186; quoted, 41
Heartsease (Yonge), 196
Heimann, Mrs, 101
Herbert, George, 23, 80
Hinkson, Katharine Tynan, 192, 199
'Hodge Podge' (family magazine), 23
Holmer Green, grandparents' home at,
    23–6, 79
Holst, Gustav, 13
Hopkins, Gerard Manley, 179
House, Humphry, quoted, 180–1
House of Charity, Highgate, 94, 96, 154
Howitt, Mary and William, 89
Hughes, Arthur, 142, 157
Hunt, Leigh, daughter of, 200
Hunt, William Holman, 52, 74, 84n;
    shares studio with Dante Gabriel, 45,
    59; and formation of Pre-Raphaelite
    Brotherhood, 45–6; opinion of
    Collinson, 46; on Christina as Dante
    Gabriel's Mary Virgin, 48; shares
    studio with Collinson, 52n;
    Christina as model for, 71
Hunter's Forestall (Kent), Dante
    Gabriel at, 162, 164

Idylls of the King (Tennyson), 116
Ingelow, Jean, 88

Jarvis, Swynfen, 72
Jenner, Sir William, 35, 140, 142,
    155
Jerrold, Douglas, 69
Jersey, 101
Jesse, Mrs, 69

Keats, John, 21, 79
Keble, John, 30, 31, 32, 56, 180
Kelmscott: Dante Gabriel at, 147, 150–1;
    Christina at, 150–2
Kingsley, Charles, 50
Kohl, James A., 35

Lamb, Mary, 175
Latham, Dr Peter, 35
Lecco, 123
Leifchild families, 184
Lewes, G. H., 69
Lewis, 'Monk', 21
Leyland, F. R., 167
Light of the World, The (Hunt), 71
Locock, Dr (later Sir) James, 34, 35, 36
London:
    Arlington Street (No. 28), 72; move
        to, 71
    Bloomsbury Square, 156
    Charlotte (now Hallam) Street, 58;
        childhood in, 17–24, 26; move from
        71
    Chatham Place, Blackfriars, Dante
        Gabriel at, 72, 101
    Christ Church Albany Street, 30, 31,
        46, 55, 172n
    Euston Square (No. 56), 146, 150,
        153; move to, 138; difficulties of
        shared household, 154–6, 157–8
    Hampstead, 88, 141, 147
    Regent's Park, 19
    Torrington Square (No. 30):
        Christina's last home at, 157–8, 165,
        196, 204–7; visitors to, 189, 192,
        199, 200
    Tudor House, Cheyne Walk, 190;
        Dante Gabriel at, 102, 156, 165,
        171–2

London —*cont.*
　Upper Albany Street (No. 45), 82;
　　move to, 73; move from, 138
　Zoological Gardens, 19
Longleat, 72
Lord of the Isles (Scott), 207
Lowell, James Russell, 179
Lucerne, 122

MacCracken, Francis, 85n
Macdonald, Alice (later Mrs John
　Lockwood Kipling), 120
Macgregor, Sir Patrick, 15
Macmillan, Alexander, 99, 100; as
　Christina's publisher, 101, 111, 114,
　125, 136, 157
Macmillan's Magazine, 99, 100, 120
Manet, Edouard, 122
Manning, Henry, Cardinal, 30, 55, 56
Mansfield (Notts), 51
Maturin, Charles, 21, 41
May, Miss, 201–2
Melmoth the Wanderer (Maturin), 41
Metastasio, Pietro, 21
Meynell, Alice, 192
Milan, 123
Millais, John Everett, 45, 54, 74
Mitchell, Mrs (nurse), 162, 165
Morris (formerly Burden), Jane, 42,
　192; Dante Gabriel meets, 84; in love
　with, 147, 150, 151–2; his picture of,
　150
Morris, William, 84, 136, 152;
　nicknamed 'Prudent', 110; at
　Kelmscott, 147; not impressed by
　Christina's wallpaper design, 157
Mount-Temple, William Cowper-
　Temple, Lord, 88
Mount-Temple, Lady, 88, 176
Mozart, 105
Murat, Joachim, 14

Naples, 14
Newcastle-upon-Tyne, Bell Scott home
　at, 58, 59, 76n, 89
Newman, John Henry, Cardinal, 30, 56

Newsham, Miss, 201
Nightingale, Florence, 25, 82
Northanger Abbey (Austen), 21
Notes and Queries, 35

Olympe (Manet), 122
Orme, Mrs, 69
Orme, Miss, 70, 71
Orvieto, 14
Oxford, 84
Oxford Movement, 30, 31–2, 56, 180

Packer, Mrs L. M., 34, 36, 42, 47, 76n,
　187; her theory of romance between
　Christina and W. Bell Scott, 58,
　59–66, 106, 109, 134; quoted, 92, 96,
　105, 106, 109, 119, 121, 149
Pallanza, 204
Paris, 101, 122
Parkes, Bessie (later Mrs Belloc), 67, 68
Patmore, Coventry, 52, 54, 88
Paule, Rev. T. W., 22
Pavia, 123
Penkill Castle (Ayrshire), 62, 125–6,
　134, 138, 189
Phillpotts, Henry, Bishop of Exeter, 55
Pierce, 'Mrs' (great-aunt), 26
Pisa, 45
Playboy, 105
Pleasley Hill (near Mansfield), Collinson
　home at, 50–1
Polidori, Anna Maria (grandmother),
　15, 23–4, 25, 73
Polidori, Charlotte (aunt), 25, 72, 156;
　aid to Dante Gabriel and Lizzie, 68,
　82; shares Christina's home, 157, 183,
　194, 196; death, 199
Polidori, Eliza Harriet (aunt), 25, 88,
　146, 156, 157; store-keeper at Scutari,
　25, 87; shares Christina's home, 157,
　165, 183, 194, 196; Christina's care of,
　196, 200; death, 204
Polidori, Gaetano (grandfather), 15,
　23–4, 26–7; private printing-press,
　27, 39–40; death, 73
Polidori, Henrietta (cousin), 25, 114

Polidori (later Polydore), Henry (uncle), 25
Polidori, John (uncle), 14, 35
Polidori, Luigi, 200
Polidori, Margaret (aunt), 25, 138
Polidori, Philip (uncle), 25, 26
Potter, Cipriani, 18
Pre-Raphaelite Brotherhood (P.R.B.). 50, 66, 89; formation of, 44–6; magazine of (*The Germ*), 52–4; attacks on, 54; Collinson resigns from, 57, 74; break-up, 74–5; poetry of, 180
Pre-Raphaelite Circle, A (Trevelyan), 125
Princesse du Palais de Porcelaine (Whistler), 122
Prinsep, Val, 139
Prisoner, The (Brontë), 182
Proctor, Adelaide Ann, 175
Pusey, Edward Bouverie, 30, 56

Rachel, 19
Radcliffe, Mrs, 21
Raleigh, Walter, quoted, 13
Read, Harriet, 204, 207
Renunciation of Saint Elizabeth, The (Collinson), 50, 55, 57
Rintoul, Henrietta, 69, 175; abortive love affair with William, 85–6
Rintoul, Robert, 69, 85
Roehampton, Dante Gabriel at, 146
Romantic Movement, 31, 42–3
Rossetti, Arthur (nephew), 197
Rossetti, Christina Georgina: ancestry, 14–16; birth, 16; quick temper, 16–17, 28; warm-heartedness, 17, 28; appearance, 17, 48–9, 141; childhood, 17–27; early verses and stories, 20–1; favourite reading, 21, 41; devotion to mother, 22, 137–8; early education, 22–3; country holidays at grandparents' home, 23–6; first experience of death and corruption, 25; earliest surviving poems, 26–7; conflict of character, 27, 34, 36, 81; changed character at sixteen, 28, 33–6; delicate health, 29, 33–6, 50, 83, 88, 114, 122, 140–2; as 'escaped governess', 29; influence of Anglo-Catholicism, 30–3, 46, 78, 180; repression and reticence, 33; physical change, 33–6; possible breakdown, 34–6; self-portraiture in early 'short-story', 37–9; over-scrupulosity, 38, 164; technique of early poems, 40–1; preoccupation with change, death and decay, 41–2; first love in Collinson, 43, 46, 47–8, 56, 61, 65, 81; as model for Pre-Raphaelites, 48–9, 53, 125; new breakdown in health, 50; stay with Collinson family, 50–2; her shyness, 51, 69, 74, 139; contributes to *The Germ*, 53, 54; breaks off engagement to Collinson, 55–7, 60; physical collapse, 57; supposed romance with W. Bell Scott, 59–66, 96, 106, 109, 134; theme of guilt underlying her love poetry, 61, 64–6; literary and artistic contacts, 69–71, 88–9, 138–9; wry humour, 70; assists mother in day-school, 71, 73, 75; year at Frome, 72–5; over-politeness, 74; return to London, 75; poems of the eighteen-fifties, 76–81; on love as bringer of grief, 76, 77; and desirability of death, 76, 77–80; contradictory view of life after death, 78–80; religious poetry, 78–81, 111–12, 117–19, 149–50, 178–83, 203; coldness between herself and Dante Gabriel over Lizzie, 82–3, 98; sympathy with William's love for Henrietta, 86; abortive scheme to go to Scutari, 88; brief spell as governess, 88; Newcastle holiday with Scotts, 89; new friends, 89, 90–1, 124, 138, 200–1; friendship with Cayley, 92–3, 120–2, 126–30, 140, 141, 148–9, 171; work with Anglican sisterhood, 94, 154; concern with 'fallen women', 94–7, 164; attempts at publication, 98–100; first poems

Rossetti, Christina Georgina—*cont.*
accepted, 99–100; first holiday
abroad, 101; success of first book
(*Goblin Market*), 101–3, 114;
technical skill, 102; mistaken diagnosis
of tuberculosis, 114, 122; winter at
Hastings, 114–15; prepares second
volume, 115–20; poems associated
with Cayley, 121, 132–4, 186–9; visits
Italy, 122–3; publication of second
volume, 124–5; refuses Cayley, 126–7,
129–30; sublimation of sex in love of
God, 130–1, 181–2; Italian poems,
133–4; short-lived change of
publisher, 136, 142; short stories,
136–7; prose not her *forte*, 136–7,
193; humdrum life as spinster
daughter and sister, 137–8, 165, 183,
189; declining health, 140–2, 144–5,
146; Graves's disease, 141; ruined
looks, 141; publication of children's
verse, 142–4; serious collapse, 144–5,
146; convalescence, 147, 150; at
Kelmscott, 150–2; her voice, 151;
tension of shared household, 154–6,
157; holidays away from home, 156,
165, 191; first collected edition of
poems, 157; death of sister Maria,
159–60; sees her first sunrise, 162;
friendship with Shields, 162–4, 171,
175, 199, 206; occasional prudery,
164; and Collinson's death, 167;
publishes two short prose works,
168–9; inward rebellion against dull
life, 169; advanced views on role of
women, 171; and Dante Gabriel's last
days and death, 171, 173–6; not a
mystic, 182; near-identification of
eros with *agape*, 181, 183; and Cayley's
death, 185–7; her love for him,
187–9, 207; visits from friends, 189,
192, 199, 202; on miseries of poor,
195; deaths of mother and aunts, 195,
199, 204; as Yonge heroine, 196;
interest in nephew and nieces, 197–8;
bad bout of illness, 198–9; response
to begging letters and petitions, 200;
attitude to young authors and
admirers, 101–2; cancer, 202, 204;
publication of last book, 203; last
days, 205–8; hysterical attacks, 206;
'dark thoughts', 206–7; death, 207;
last poem, 208
WRITINGS:
'A pair of brothers brotherly', 73
'A roundel seems to fit a round of
   days', 199
'A Venus seems my Mouse', 128
After Death, 108
Afterthought, An, 107
'All the world is making love', 87
Apple Gathering, An, 100, 101
Autumn Garden, An, 164
Better Resurrection, A, 111–12
Bird and Beast, 107
Birds of Paradise, 119
Birthday, A, 100
Bourne, The, 120
By Way of Remembrance, 135
Called to be Saints, 168–9
'Come back to me, who wait and
   watch for you', 133
Commonplace, 136–7, 142
Cousin Kate, 94–5
'Dervise, The' (uncompleted), 20
Death's Chill Between, 42
Dreamland, 53
Echo from Willow-wood, An, 135,
   136
End, The, 53
Eve, 107
Face of the Deep, The, 196, 203
'Folio Q', 99
From the Antique, 186–7
'Go from me, summer friends, and
   tarry not', 96
Goblin Market, 99, 101, 102–13, 117
'Goodbye in fear, goodbye in sorrow'
   144
'Hail, noble face of noble friend', 190
'Hark! the Alleluias of the great
   salvation', 203

Heart Knoweth Its Own Bitterness, The, 130–1

Heart's Chill Between, 42

'Her hair is like the golden corn', 66

Horses of the Sea, The, 143

Hour and the Ghost, The, 108

'I heard the songs of Paradise', 80

'I listen to the holy antheming', 38

'I tell my secret? No, indeed, not I', 93

'I will accept thy will to do and be', 80–1

Imalee, 41

In an Artist's Studio, 84, 97

'In the bleak mid-winter', 13

In the Round Tower of Jhansi, 108

Iniquity of the Fathers upon the Children, The (formerly *Under the Rose*), 61, 95

Is and Was, 51

Isidora, 41

'It is not for her even brow', 76

Later Life, 170

'Long and dark the nights, dim and short the days', 203

Love is strong as Death, 149–50

Love Lies Bleeding, 148–9

'Love understands the mystery, whereof', 183

Martyr, The, 41

Maude, 37–9

Mirrors of Life and Death, 161

Monna Innominata, 132–3, 170

Months, The: A Pageant, 170

'My baby has a mottled fist', 143

My Dream, 109–11, 115

'My faith burns low, my love burns low', 181

'My heart is yearning', 181

'My love whose heart is tender said to me', 160

Nightmare, A, 108

No thank you, John, 69–70

Noble Sisters, 108

'Now if I could guess her secret', 93

'O celestial mansion', 78

'Oh roses for the flush of youth', 54

'Oh what comes over the sea', 126

'Oh what is that country', 120

Old and New Year Ditties, 112–13

One Sea-side Grave, 186

Pageant and Other Poems, A, 169–71

Parted, 187–8

'Parting after parting', 89–90

Pause, A, 76–7

Pause for Thought, A, 54

Per Preferenza, 134–5

Prince's Progress, The, 115–17, 124–5

'Remember me when I am gone away', 53, 107

'Retribution' (uncompleted), 21

Rosseggiar dell' Oriente, Il, 133–5

Seek and Find, 168

Sing-Song, 142–4

Sister Maude, 108

Sleep at Sea, 111

'Sleeping at last, the trouble and tumult over', 208

Soeur Louise de la Misericorde, 154

Tasso and Leonora, 41

Testimony, A, 54

'The blindest buzzard that I know', 121

'The P.R.B. is in its decadence', 75

'The Rose is Love's own flower, and, Love's no less', 201

'The wind shall lull us yet', 77–8

'The youngest bud of five', 184

Three Nuns, 39

Time Flies, 87, 90, 167, 187, 193

'To come from the sweet South to the North', 123

'To-day's your natal day', 27

Today and Tomorrow, 87–8

Twice, 117–19

Two Thoughts of Death, 78–9

'Underneath the growing grass', 78

Up-hill, 99–100

'Vanity of vanities, the Preacher saith', 38

Venus's Looking-Glass, 148

Rossetti, Christina Georgina—*cont.*
　'We are of those who tremble at Thy
　　word', 182–3
　'We Englishwomen, trim, correct',
　124
　What?, 77
　'When I am dead, my dearest', 64–5
　Who shall say?, 188
　Wife to Husband, 97–8
　Will those Hands ne'er be clean?, 41
　'Winter's latest snowflake is the
　　snowdrop flower', 194
　'Your brother has a falcon', 143
Rossetti, Dante Gabriel (brother), 19,
　42, 48, 70, 111, 120, 132, 139, 170,
　204; appearance, 16, 116;
　irresponsibility, 16, 116; early
　artistic ambition, 20; at day school,
　22; holidays with grandparents, 24;
　artistic training, 29, 43, 44–5; brief
　attraction to Tractarianism, 30, 31;
　psychological imbalance, 35, 146–7,
　156, 159, 171; not impressed by
　Christina's early poems, 40; ability to
　separate sex from love, 42; and Pre-
　Raphaelite Brotherhood, 44–7, 52–4;
　urges Christina to accept Collinson,
　47; his portraits of Christina, 48–9,
　53, 54; and *The Germ*, 52, 53, 54;
　praise of Bell Scott's *Year of the
　World*, 58; Christina's letters to, 61,
　67, 115–16, 124, 150, 157, 161, 163,
　166–7, 173; relationship with
　Elizabeth (Lizzie) Siddal, 66–8, 72,
　82–4, 85, 98; liking for nicknames,
　67, 110; unable to afford marriage,
　68, 82; grief at breaking-up of home
　circle, 74; paints Oxford Union hall,
　84; meets Jane Burden (later Morris),
　84; marriage to Lizzie, 85; pre-
　occupation with prostitution, 94;
　efforts to get Christina's work
　published, 98–9; and Lizzie's death,
　101–2; pleasure in Christina's success,
　102, 114, 115, 161, 165–7; illustrates
　Goblin Market, 106; well-meant but

bad advice, 114, 115–16, 136;
illustrates *The Prince's Progress*, 124–5;
shocked by effect of Graves's
disease on her, 141; depression and
delusions, 146–7; attempted suicide,
146; partial recovery, 147, 150; love
for Jane Morris, 147, 150, 151–2; at
Kelmscott, 147, 150–1; resumes
painting, 150, 151; relationship with
Fanny Cornforth, 150–1, 165, 172;
concern at Maria's joining Anglican
sisterhood, 153–4; at Aldwick Lodge,
156; renewed depression, 159, 162,
171; progressive deterioration, 161–2,
171–6; at Hunter's Forestall, 162,
164; return to London and virtual
seclusion, 165, 172; sense of guilt,
172–3; at Birchington, 174–6; death
and burial, 176; memorials to, 191
　WORKS:
Blessed Damozel, The, 54, 58
Church Porch, The, 31
Ecce Ancilla Domini, 53, 54, 85n
Found, 94
Girlhood of Mary Virgin, The, 48
Jeanne d'Arc, 174
Jenny, 94
My Sister's Sleep, 53, 58
Proserpine, 150, 174
'Roderick and Rosalba. a Tale of the
　Round Table', 21
'Willow-wood' sonnet, 135
'Wind flapped loose', 177
Rossetti, Frances (mother), 21, 25, 35,
　47, 101, 140, 141, 190; ancestry and
　marriage, 14–16; domestic life, 18–20,
　29; children's attitude to, 27; and their
　early education, 22–3; return to
　teaching, 29; Anglo-Catholicism, 30;
　as model for Dante Gabriel's Saint
　Anne, 48; nickname, 67; opens day-
　school, 71; move to Frome, 72; death
　of parents, 73, 75; return to London,
　75; attitude to Elizabeth Siddal, 82,
　83; in Italy, 122; close relationship
　with Christina, 137–8, 183, 192; and

Dante Gabriel's troubles and illnesses, 148, 162, 171, 174, 175; at Kelmscott, 150, 151; difficulties of shared household, 155, 156, 157–8; new London home, 157, 159, 165; at Dante Gabriel's death, 175, 176; holidays at Birchington, 191; gives memorial window, 191; failing health, 192; her last Christmas, 194; Christina's last valentine to, 194; death, 195

Rossetti, Gabriele (father), 35; ancestry and marriage, 14–16; domestic life, 17, 18–20; as Professor of Italian, King's College, 17; musical gifts, 20; Dante cult, 21; children's attitude to, 21–2, 30, 172; permanent invalidism and poverty, 29, 30, 71, 73; W. B. Scott's introduction to, 59; move to Frome, 72; return to London, 75; death, 81

Rossetti, Helen (niece), 197

Rossetti, Lucy (formerly Madox Brown), 164; engagement to William, 152–3; Christina's letters to, 152, 157, 165, 168, 195, 197, 202, 203; difficulties of sharing household, 154–6, 157; agnosticism, 156, 184; birth of daughter, 157; death of son, 184; ill-health, 194, 198, 200; as author, 197; declining health and death, 204–5

Rossetti, Maria (sister), 26, 72, 82, 127, 142, 193; birth, 16; appearance and character, 16, 22; jealousy of Christina, 17, 26; most in sympathy with father, 22; home education, 22; as governess, 29; *Rivulet* allegory, 40; changed attitude to Christina, 48; unrequited love for Ruskin and Collins, 87; at Folkestone, 140, 141; her *The Shadow of Dante*, 144, 197–8; illness, 153, 159; joins Anglican sisterhood, 153–4, 156; death, 159–60; possible influence on Christina, 160–1

Rossetti, Mary (niece), 197

Rossetti, Michael (nephew), 184

Rossetti, Olive (niece), 197–8, 204

Rossetti, William Michael (brother), 15, 28, 46, 59, 69, 72, 96, 132, 133, 185; character, 16, 62–3; memoir and recollections quoted, 17, 24, 25, 30, 32, 33, 34, 38, 48, 49, 51, 63, 88, 89, 90, 91, 92, 94, 101, 121, 129, 167, 196, 207; on Dante, 21; attitude to parents, 22; at day school, 22; holidays with grandparents, 24, 25; clerk in Excise Office, 29, 194; agnosticism, 30, 184, 197; on Christina's religion, 32, 33; on her health, 34, 36, 65, 140, 141, 142, 144; on autobiographical nature of *Maude*, 37; on Christina's 'scrupulosity', 38; acid comment on Collinson, 48; visits Collinson's mother and sister, 50; Christina's letters to, 50, 51, 52, 54, 57, 73, 74, 86, 88, 127, 139, 141, 147, 152, 154–5, 159, 169, 172, 173, 175, 176, 194, 195, 197, 198, 199, 202, 204, 205; and *The Germ*, 52, 53; discovers that Scott is married, 59, 64, 65; omission of facts from Memoir, 63; in love with Henrietta Rintoul, 69; on Christina's studied politeness, 74; makes home for family, 75; end of love affair with Henrietta, 85–7; on Cayley, 91, 92, 129; on Christina's *Wife to Husband*, 97; visits France, 101; visits Italy, 122–3; offers to share home with Christina and Cayley, 127; verge of breakdown, 148, 153; engagement and marriage to Lucy Madox Brown, 152–3; difficulties of combined household, 154–6; puzzled by Dante Gabriel's sense of guilt, 172, 173; doubts reality of Dante Gabriel's illness, 173, 175; at his death, 176; as editor of Christina's collected works, 178–9, 183, 186, 187; death of baby son, 184; wife's ill-health, 194, 197, 200, 204–5; at mother's last Christmas, 194; importance in Christina's last years,

Rossetti, William Michael—*cont.*
  194, 197, 203, 206–7; death of wife,
  205
Rossetti Family, The (Waller), 19
Rothenstein, Sir William, quoted, 62–3
Rouen, 101
Rowley, Charles, 163
Royal Academy, 1850 exhibition, 54
Ruskin, John, 163; aid to Elizabeth
  Siddal, 82; Maria's love for, 87;
  unhelpful over Christina's poems,
  98–9, 102
Ryder, George, 55

Sacred Harp, The, 22
Saint's Tragedy, The (Kingsley), 50
Saint Lô, 101
San Remo, Lucy Rossetti's death at,
  205
Sandars, Mary, 47
Sandford and Merton (Day), 21
Scott, Letitia, 89, 94, 175, 189; *ménàge-à-
  trois* with husband and Alice Boyd,
  125–6
Scott, Sir Walter, 21, 42, 207
Scott, William Bell, 89, 90, 136, 153,
  179; first meeting with Christina,
  58–9; beginning of friendship with
  Rossetti family, 59; supposed
  romance with Christina, 59–66, 96,
  106, 109, 134; love affair with Alice
  Boyd, 61, 106, 125–6, 134, 189–90;
  praise for Christina's *Monna
  Innominata* and *Pageant*, 132, 170;
  permanent invalid, 189; Christina's
  birthday poem to, 199; death, 199;
  Autobiographical Notes, 203
Seaford, 165
Seddon, John, 174
Sevenoaks, 165
Sharp, William, 16, 35n, 151
Shields, Frederick: friendship with
  Christina, 162–4, 171, 175, 199, 206;
  oddity, 163; at Dante Gabriel's death,
  176; designs memorial windows, 191;
  Christina writes farewell letter to, 206

Siddal, Elizabeth (Lizzie), 62, 192, 204;
  relationship with Dante Gabriel, 42,
  66–8, 72, 82–4, 85, 98; Rossetti
  family's attitude to, 67–8, 82–3, 98;
  increasing ill-health, 82, 84, 98;
  marriage to Dante Gabriel, 85;
  stillbirth, 98; death, 101
Somerset, Lord Henry, 166–7
Sonnets from the Portuguese (E. B.
  Browning), 132
Spectator, The, 69
Spencer, Herbert, 69
Stanley, Lady Augusta, 175
Stephens, Frederick George, 46, 52,
  74
Stone Breaker, The (Brett), 69
Stuart, D. M., 47, 76, 127
Swinburne, Algernon Charles, 88, 136,
  138, 151; Christina's letter to, 29;
  praise of Christina's 'Passing away'
  poem, 113; exchange of poems, 169;
  praise of Christina's *Pageant*, 170;
  Christina's friendship with, 190–1

Tebbs, Mrs Vertue, 139
Temple, William, 182
Tennyson, Alfred Lord, 116, 139
Tennyson, Frederick, 69
Thynne, Lord Charles, 29
Torquay, 198
Tractarianism, 30–3, 46
Trevelyan, Sir (Walter) Calverley, 89
Trevelyan, Pauline, 89, 90–1
Trevelyan, Raleigh, 125
Tristram of Lyonesse (Swinburne), 169
Two Gentlemen of Verona, 84n
Two Guardians, The (Yonge), 129

Unknown to History (Yonge), 198

Vampire, The (Polidori), 14
Vasto, 14
Vaughan, Henry, 23
Verona, 123
Victorian Studies, 65
Vita Nuova (Dante), 21

Walker, Mrs Vera, 60, 190
Waller, R. D., quoted, 19
Wallington (Northumberland), 89, 105
Walton-on-the-Naze, 165
Watson, Dr (later Sir) Thomas, 35
Watts, G. F., 139
Watts (later Watts-Dunton), Theodore,
  17, 156, 162, 166, 176; at Kelmscott,
  151; praises *Pageant*, 169; at Dante
  Gabriel's death, 176
Webb, Benjamin, 31
Webster, Augusta, 171
Whistler, J. M., 122, 138
Whittier, John Greenleaf, 179
Wilberforce, Henry, 55

Wilberforce, Robert, 55
Wilding, Alexa, 151
Williams, Isaac, 173, 180
Wilson, Lisa, 200–1
Woolf, Virginia, quoted, 70, 76, 102
Woolner, Thomas, 46, 53, 74
Wuthering Heights (Brontë,) 61, 62

Yarborough, Earl of, 26
Year of the World, The (Scott), 58
Yonge, Charlotte M., 24, 56, 129, 171;
  and Anglo-Catholicism, 32–3; her
  typical heroines, 196, 198
Young Stepmother, The (Yonge), 196